Test Automation using HP Unified Functional Testing (UFT)11.5

Navneesh Garg

- Step by step guide

- Learn automation on a web based application

- Real life examples

- Interview Questions on Automation

HP UFT Step By Step Guide

ISBN - 978-0-9922935-0-5

Publisher: AdactIn Group Pty Ltd.

Contents

෴

About the Author

Navneesh Garg

Navneesh Garg is a recognized test automation architect and corporate trainer, specializing in test automation, performance testing, security testing and test management. Certified in HP QTP, HP Quality Center, HP LoadRunner, and IBM Rational Functional Tester and as a Certified Ethical Hacker, he has proven success in managing a wide array of testing and automation projects, leading test teams, designing automation frameworks and providing technical training. As a tool specialist, he has worked on a variety of functional automation tools including Selenium, TestComplete, TestPartner, SilkTest, Watir, RFT, HP QTP/UFT and on varied technologies including Web, Java, Dot-net, SAP, Peoplesoft, and Seibel.

He is an entrepreneur and founder of several successful IT companies, which encompass the AdactIn Group, CresTech Software, and Planios Technologies.

As an experienced corporate trainer, he has trained professionals in HP QTP/UFT and other test tools across a wide range of global clients such as Macquarie Bank, Corporate Express, Max New York Life, Accenture, NSW Road and Maritime Services, Australian Dept of Education, HCL Technologies, Sapient, Fidelity Group, Adobe Systems, and many more. He has training experience in diverse geographies such as Australia, India, Hong Kong and USA.

He has worked with Mercury (now HP) and led the design of instructor led courses for QuickTest Professional tool and HP Quality Center, as a subject matter expert. He holds Bachelors in Computer Science from NSIT, Delhi University, India.

As a technical test delivery head for his company, he has led and managed functional automation testing and performance testing teams across a wide range of domains, using commercial tools and open source tools. In addition, he has also designed several advanced automation frameworks using these tools.

∾

Preface

My motivation for writing this book stems from my hands-on experience in the IT and testing domain and the experience I have gained as an automation consultant working in numerous complex automation projects. It disheartens me when I come across automation and frameworks being implemented without much forethought. Even basic automation guidelines and principles are not followed. This leads to maintenance nightmares and automation failure causing stakeholders to lose their trust in test automation.

The key objective of this book is to impart a deeper understanding of the **internals of automation so that IT teams see value in automation.** .

Scope of Topics

HP recently launched the upgraded QuickTest Professional (QTP) version, 11.5 which is combination of traditional HP QTP with HP Service Test (formerly a separate tool to test web services and APIs). This newly upgraded and packaged version is now called HP UFT (Unified Functional Testing). Besides new features, UFT still has all the original QTP 11.0 features. We will be using the word UFT or QTP interchangeably throughout the book. **HP Service Test features are out of scope** of this book.

For scope of this book, we will primarily discuss **GUI based Tests,** which are similar to QuickTest Tests in previous versions of QTP. API tests, Business Process Test, and Business Process Flow are not intended to be covered in this book.

Any references made to HP QTP in this book, refer to features of QuickTest Professional version 11.0

My intent in this book is to discuss the key features of UFT and cover all crucial aspects of the tool which help to **create effective automation frameworks**.

Key Audience

The target audience for this book are manual functional testers who want to **learn UFT quickly** and who want to create effective automation frameworks that generate positive ROI's to stakeholders.

Salient Features for this Book

Test Automation using HP Unified Functional Testing (UFT) is the **first HP UFT book released globally** to cater to the latest version of the QuickTest Professional.

This book has been designed with the objectives of **simplicity and ease of understanding**.

A major highlight of this book is a custom **developed web based application used throughout the book**. As a corporate trainer, every time I imparted QTP/UFT training using the standard desktop based flight reservation application (that comes by default with HP QTP/UFT), I saw a need amongst participants to use more realistic real world application that was preferably web based. They wanted a feature and test scenario rich application for their automation learning needs. For this book we have developed a web-based application, which has enhanced test scenarios that will make your learning experience as close as possible to the real world applications.

This book follows a **unique training based approach** instead of a **regular text book approach**. Using a step by step approach, it guides the student through the exercises using pictorial snapshots.

Another differentiator is that I have tried to include **many practical examples and issues** which most of the automation testers encounter in day-to-day automation. These experiences will give you an insight into what challenges you could face with automation in the real world. Practical examples cover how to use most of the features within HP UFT.

It also covers aspects of **Integration of HP UFT with HP ALM** (Quality Center) platform. It explains how we can connect from UFT to HP ALM, store our scripts in ALM, execute our scripts from ALM, and view test results.

The book also covers the most **common interview questions** on automation.

Sample Application and Source Used in Book

The sample application used in the book can be accessed at the below URL

www.adactin.com/HotelApp/

The Source code used in the book can be found at below link

www.adactin.com/store/

Feedback and Queries

For any feedback or queries you can contact the author at www.adactin.com/contact.html or email navneesh.garg@adactin.com

Order this book

For bulk orders, contact us at *orders@adactin.com*

You can also place your order online at *adactin.com/store/*

Acknowledgements

I would like to thank my family (my parents, my wife Sapna, my wonderful kids Shaurya and Adaa) for their continued support. Without them this book would not have been possible.

Special thanks to S. Constâncio Colaço and Philip Smith for their reviews and feedback, which immensely helped as I worked on this book.

I would also like to thank my colleagues and clients for the inspiration, knowledge and learning opportunities provided.

❧

1

Introduction to Automation

Introduction

In this chapter we will talk about automation fundamentals and understand what is automation and need for automation. An important objective of this chapter is to understand the economics of automation, and determine when we should carry out automation in our projects. We will also discuss some popular commercial and open source automation tools available in the market.

Key objectives:

- What is automation?
- Why automate? What are the benefits of automation?
- Economics of automation.
- Commercial and Open Source automation tools.

1.1 What is Functional Automation?

Automation testing is to automate the execution of manually designed test cases, without any human intervention.

The purpose of automated testing is to execute manual functional tests quickly and in a cost effective manner. Frequently, we re-run tests that have been previously executed (also called regression testing) to validate functional correctness of the application. Think of a scenario where you need to validate the username and password for an application which has more than 10,000 users. It can be a tedious and monotonous task for a manual tester and this is where the real benefits of automation can be harnessed. We want to free up manual functional testers time so that they can perform other key tasks while automation provides extensive coverage to the overall test effort.

When we use the term "automation", there is usually confusion about whether automation scope includes functional and performance testing. Automation covers both.

- Functional Automation – Used for automation of functional test cases in the regression test bed.

- Performance Automation – Used for automation of non-functional performance test cases. An example of this is measuring the response time of the application under considerable (for example 100 users) load.

Functional automation and performance automation are two distinct terms and their automation internals work using different driving concepts. Hence, there are separate tools for functional automation and performance automation.

For the scope of this book, we will be only referring to **Functional Automation**.

1.2 Why do we Automate?

Find below key benefits of Functional Automation:

1. Effective Smoke (or Build Verification) Testing

Whenever a new software build or release is received, a test (generally referred to as "smoke test" or "shakedown test") is run to verify if build is testable for a bigger testing effort and major application functionalities are working correctly. Many times we can spend hours doing this only to discover that a faulty software build caused all the testing effort to go in vain. Testing has to now start all over again after release of a new build.

If the smoke test was automated, the smoke test scripts could be run by developers to verify the build quality before being released to the testing team.

2. Standalone - Lights Out Testing

Automated testing tools can be programmed to kick off a script at a specific time.

If needed, automated tests can be automatically kicked off overnight, and the testers can analyse the results of the automated test the next morning. This will save valuable test execution time for the testers.

3. Increased Repeatability

At times it becomes impossible to reproduce a defect which was found during manual testing. Key reason for this could be that tester forgot which combinations of test steps led to the error message, hence, unable to reproduce the defect. Automated testing scripts take the guess work out of test repeatability.

4. Testers can Focus on Advanced Issues

As tests are automated, automated scripts can be base-lined and re-run for regression testing. Regression tests generally yield fewer new defects as opposed to testing newly developed features. So, functional testers can focus on analysing and testing newer or more complex areas that have the potential for most of the defects while automated test scripts can be used for regression test execution.

5. Higher Functional Test Coverage

With automated testing large number of data combinations can be tested which might not be practically feasible with manual testing. We use the term 'Data driven testing' which means validating numerous test data combinations using one automated script.

6. Other Benefits

- **Reliable:** Tests perform precisely the same operations each time they are run, thereby eliminating human error.

- **Repeatable:** You can test how the software reacts under repeated execution of the same operations.

- **Programmable:** You can program sophisticated tests that bring out hidden information from the application.

- **Comprehensive:** You can build a suite of tests that cover every feature in your application.

- **Reusable:** You can re-use tests on different versions of an application, even if the user-interface changes.

- **Better Quality Software:** Because you can run more tests in less time with fewer resources.

- **Fast:** Automated tools run tests significantly faster than human users.

1.3 When should we Automate?
Economics of Automation

Let us take a scenario. If your Test Manager comes up to you and asks whether it is advisable for your company to automate an application, how would you respond?

In this scenario, the manager is interested in knowing if functional automation will deliver the organization a better return on investment (ROI) besides improving application quality and test coverage.

We can determine whether we should automate a given test if we can determine that the cost of automation would be less than the total cost of manually executing the test cases.

For example, if a test script is to run every week for the next two years, automate the test if the cost of automation is less than the cost of manually executing the test 104 times (2 years will have 104 weeks).

Calculating the **Cost of Test Automation**

Cost of Automation = Cost of tool + labour cost of script creation + labour cost of script maintenance

Automate if:

Cost of automation is lesser than the manual execution of those scripts.

The key idea here is to plan for the cost of script maintenance. I have seen a lot of automation projects fail because project managers did not plan for the labour costs involved in script maintenance.

Example

Let me give you an example from my personal experience.

I performed some automation work for one of our investment banking clients. We had a five-member team, which automated almost 3000 test cases in about six months time, which included around total 30 man months of effort. At the end of project, we gave client's testing team a hand-over of the entire automation suite created by our team. Our recommendation to them was that they would need at least a one or two member team to continuously maintain the scripts. This was because there were still functional changes happening to the application and scripts would need maintenance. But since the client project manager had no budget allocated for this activity; they skipped this advice and continued to execute automation scripts. After the first six months of the 3000 test cases, only 2000 test cases were passing, while the rest started failing. These scripts failures were because script fixes were needed due to application changes. The client team was okay with that and continued to execute those 2000 working test cases, and got rid of the remaining 1000 test cases, which were now executed manually. After another six months, only scripts corresponding to 1000 test cases were passing. So they got rid of another 1000 test cases and started executing them manually. After another six months (1.5 years in total), all the scripts were failing, and testing had to move back to manual functional testing.

In the above real-life scenario, the cost of automation and its benefits could have been reaped, if the client would have had allocated 1-2 automation testers (could have been part-time) to maintain the scripts and had properly planned and budgeted for it.

1.4 Commercial and Open Source Automation Tools

This section lists some of the popular Commercial and Open Source Automation Tools.

Vendor	Tool	Details
HP	Unified Functional Testing	HP UFT (previous version was called QTP) is the market leader in Test Automation in the commercial tools segment. It uses VBScript as the programming language and its ease of use makes it a tool of choice against other competing tools.
IBM	Rational Functional Tester	IBM Rational Functional tester is another popular test Automation Tool. We can program in VB.net or Java using this tool. Is recommended for technical testers.

Microfocus	SilkTest	Microfocus bought SilkTest from Borland. It is still a very popular automation tool which uses 4Test (propriety) language. Good for technical testers.
Microsoft	VSTP – Code UI tests	Code UI tests come with Microsoft Visual studio Ultimate or Premium version. You can program using VB.net or C# as languages of choice. Fairly good for technical testers.
SmartBear	TestComplete	Low cost alternative to other commercial tools with good features for automation. You have the option to program using VBScript, JScript, C++Script, C#Script or DelphiScript language.
OpenSource (free)	Selenium	Open source tools and market leader in open source segment. Primary for web-based automation. Support C#, Java, Python, and Ruby as programming language.
OpenSource (free)	Watir	Watir stands for "Web application testing in Ruby". It is again primarily for web application automation and uses Ruby as the programming language.

ভ৩

2

UFT Installation and Sample Application Walkthrough

In this chapter we will discuss how to install Unified Functional Testing (UFT). We will also introduce our customized sample application, which we will use as a part of our book.

We will also try to address some frequently found web application recording issues causing the UFT to malfunction with your application.

Key objectives:

- UFT Setup Instructions.
- Sample Application Walkthrough and sample scenario.
- Tips for web application recording issues.

2.1 HP Unified Functional Testing Software Setup Instructions

UFT Installation

1. Download HP Unified Functional Testing Trial version, from HP website. You can find the location of website by searching on Google.

2. Make sure to have admin rights on your machine.

3. If using Windows7 or Vista, it is good practice to disable User Account Control off, before your start the setup. You can do that from Control Panel → User Account → Change User Account Control Settings. Set them to never. Restart the PC.

4. Better to have internet on the machine, as UFT will download Microsoft script debugger.

5. To install, click on the **Installer Setup** file. You will see HP Unified Functional Testing 11.50 dialog box comes up.

6. Click on **Unified Functional Testing Setup** link.

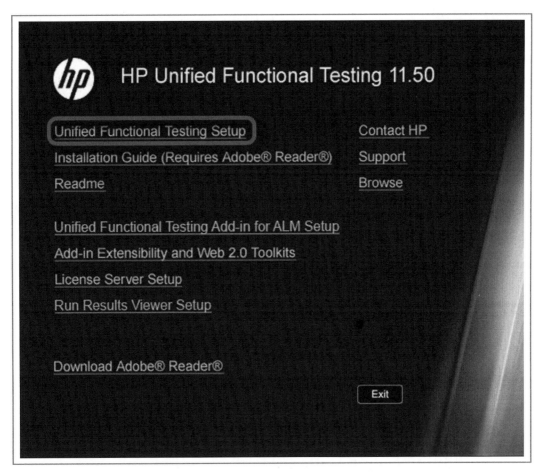

Figure 2-1 – HP UFT Installation window

7. UFT requires specific software, for example, Microsoft Visual C++ Run time components, to be installed before you install UFT. If Setup finds that the prerequisite software is not already installed on your computer, a screen is displayed listing the prerequisite programs.

    Click **OK** and follow the on-screen instructions to install the listed software, before continuing with the UFT installation. If you click Cancel, Setup stops, because UFT cannot be installed without the prerequisite software.

    In some situations, you may be prompted to restart your computer after installing the required software. To continue with the installation after restarting your computer, run the Setup program again.

8. Welcome to HP Unified Testing 11.50. Welcome window opens up. Click **Next** to proceed.

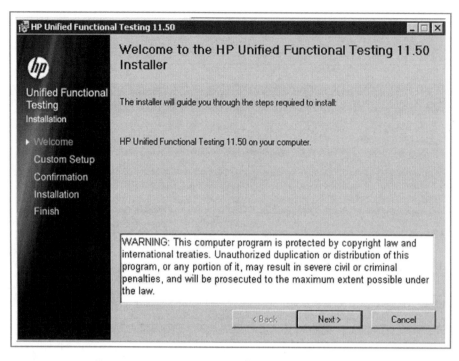

Figure 2-2 – HP UFT installation welcome screen

9. The **License Agreement** screen opens. Read the agreement.

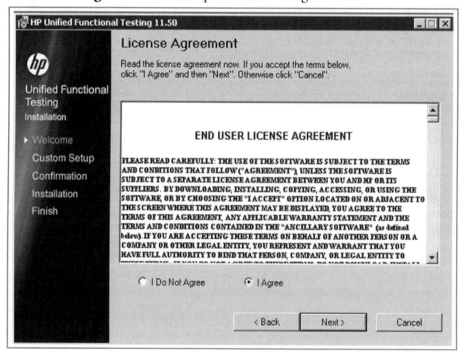

Figure 2-3 – HP UFT Installation – License Agreement

To install UFT, you must accept the terms of the license agreement by selecting **I Agree** and clicking **Next**.

10. In the **Customer Information** screen, type your **name** and the **name of your organization** and Click **Next**.

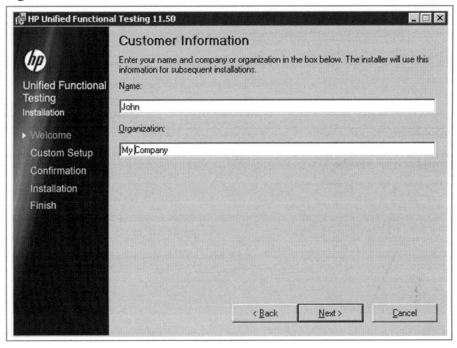

Figure 2-4– HP UFT Installation – Customer Information

11. In the **Custom Setup** screen, keep the default add-ins and click **Next** to proceed. As part of scope of this book, we will work with default add-ins.

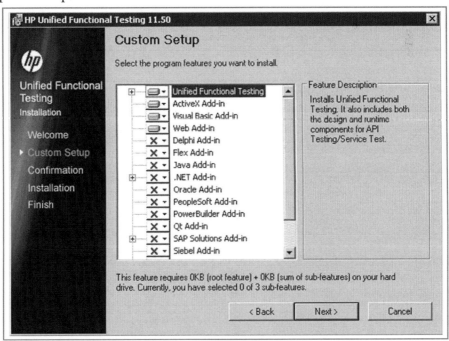

Figure 2-5– HP UFT Installation – Custom Setup

Note: Loading add-ins enables UFT to work with the corresponding environments. You can install the add-ins you require when you install UFT, or you can install them at a later time by running the installation again.

12. In the Select Installation Folder screen, select the location where you want to install UFT. Click **Next** to proceed.

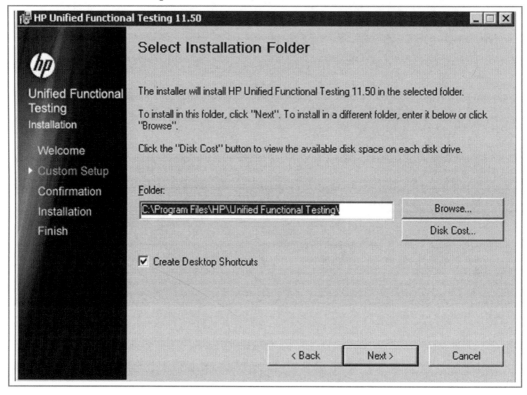

Figure 2-6– HP UFT Installation – Select Installation Folder

13. Confirm installation screen appears. Click **Next** to begin installation. The installing HP Unified Functional Testing screen displays the progress of the installation.

14. When the installation is complete, click **Finish**. Additional Installation Requirement screen opens.

Note: After the UFT installation is complete, the HP Run Results Viewer Installation is performed in the background. Therefore, it may take some time before the Additional Installation Requirements screen displays.

In addition to options to configure Internet Explorer and DCOM settings and running the License Wizard, the Additional Installation Requirements screen displays any prerequisite software that must be installed or configured to work with UFT, based on the options selected during installation.

15. Click **Run** in the Additional Installation Requirements screen to install or configure your selections.

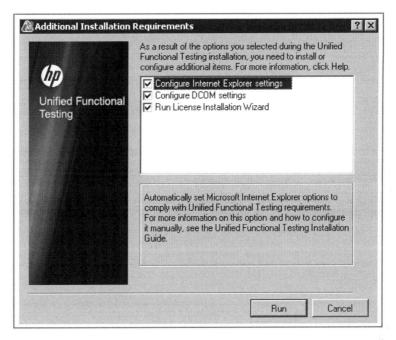

Figure 2-7– HP UFT Installation – Additional Installation Requirements

16. If you have selected to run the License Installation Wizard, the Unified Functional Testing License Installation - License Type screen displays. If you have a seat or concurrent license, enter the details. If you want to use the trial version, click **Cancel** on the License Installation Dialog.

17. **Close** the Additional Installation Requirement dialog, once all additional items are installed.

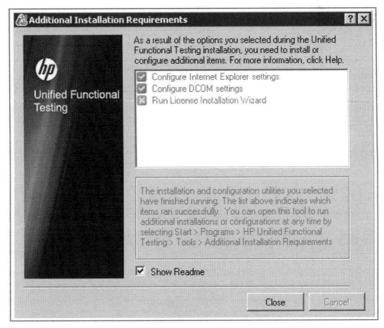

Figure 2-8– HP UFT Installation – Close Additional Installation Requirements

18. You can read the Readme file, which opens automatically.

19. You can now access HP UFT from Start -> All Programs → HP Software → HP Unified Functional Testing → HP Unified Functional Testing

20. If you are using the trial version of the software, you will get License Expiration warning dialog, once you launch HP UFT. Click on **Continue** to keep using the tool for the trial duration.

Note: If you do not see Continue button in the license expiry dialog (instead you see Cancel button), it is possible that you might have a previous version of HP QuickTest installed on the machine, because of which you would not be able to use the trial software. There is no workaround. In that case you cannot use the trial version of the software on that machine, and you would need to purchase the software.

Note: Refer to HP UFT Installation Guide, in case you need more detailed steps or face any issues with installation.

2.2 Sample Application Walkthrough

As part of this book, we will be working through a web based sample application. The reason why we planned to use our custom built web based application was that 80-90% of applications tested and automated are web based applications. So we will have a much closer and a better understanding of how we need to automate web-based application.

Our sample application is a simple hotel booking web application, which has the following key features:

- Search for Hotel
- Book a Hotel
- View Itinerary
- Cancel Booking

Let us browse through the application

1. Launch IE and enter URL www.adactin.com/HotelApp to see Login page.

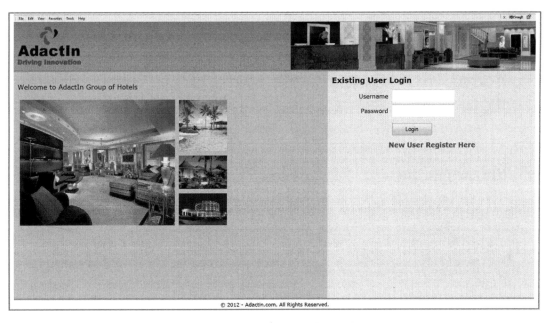

Figure 2-9 – Application Login Page

2. Click on "New User Register Here" to go to Registration page.

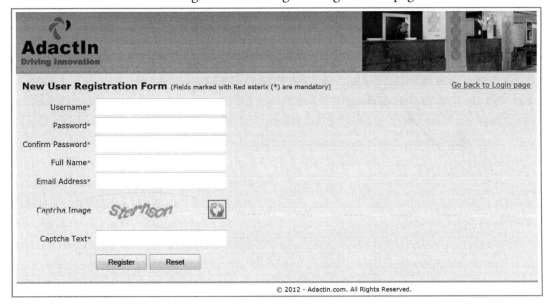

Figure 2-10 – Application Registration Page

3. Register yourself by entering all the fields. Remember the username and password as you will be using this username/password to login to application and remaining part of automation.

4. After you register, an automatic email will be sent to your email-id for confirmation. In case you do not receive the email, re-verify it in junk folder as email might have gone to your junk folder.

5. Click on the confirmation link in email.

6. Go to Login page link.

7. On the Login page use the username/password with which you have registered earlier, and click on the Login page. You will come to Search Hotel Page.

8. Search for Hotel-

   i. Select a location, e.g., Sydney

   ii. Select number of rooms, e.g., 2

   iii. Select adults per rooms, e.g., 2

   iv. Click on Search button

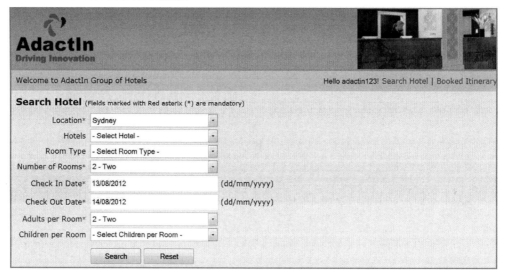

Figure 2-11 – Application Search Hotel Page

9. Select a Hotel-

   i. Select one of the Hotel Radio Buttons, e.g. select radio button next to Hotel Cornice

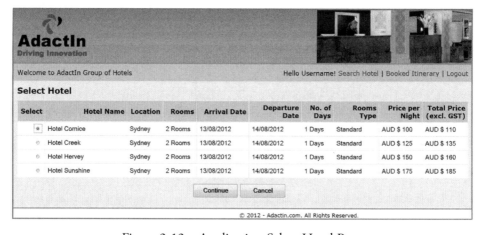

Figure 2-12 – Application Select Hotel Page

10. Book a Hotel-

    i.   Enter First Name

    ii. Enter Last Name

    iii. Enter Address

    iv. Enter 16-digit Credit Card number

    v. Enter Credit Card type

    vi. Enter Expiry Month

    vii. Enter Expiry Year

    viii. Enter CVV number

    ix. Click on **Book Now**

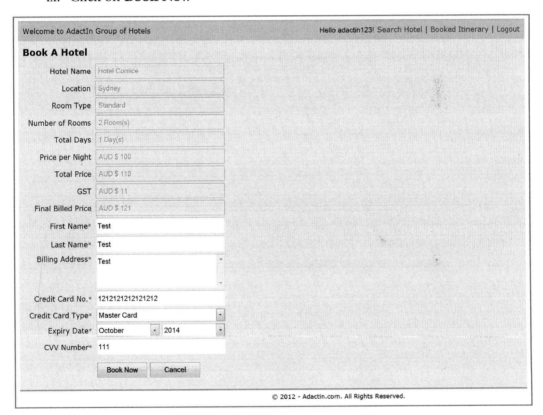

Figure 2-13 – Application Book a Hotel Page

11. After you see booking confirmation, you will notice that you get an Order No. generated.

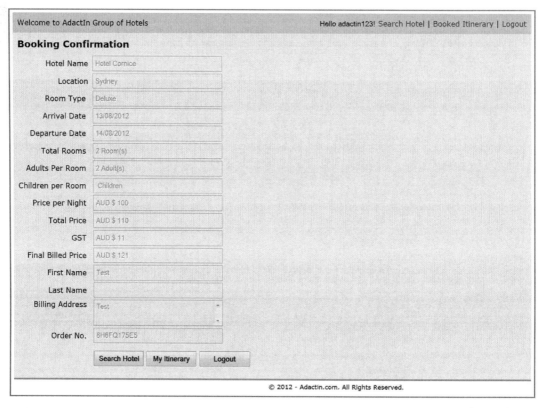

Figure 2-14 – Application Booking Confirmation Page

12. Copy the Order No. to clipboard. In our case it is 8H6FQ175E5.

13. Click on **My Itinerary** Button or Click on **Booking Itinerary** link at the top right corner of application. User will go to **Booked Itinerary** Page.

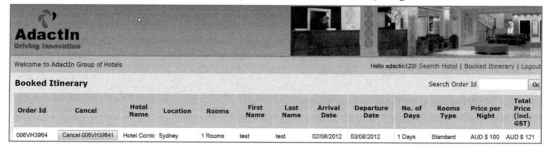

Figure 2-15 – Application Booked Itinerary Page

14. Enter the Order No. copied in previous step in search order Id field, and Click on **Go** button. You will see the order you recently created...

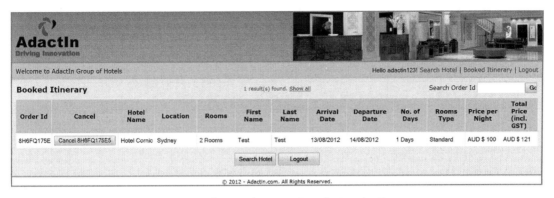

Figure 2-16 – Application Search Results Page

15. Click on **Logout** button or Logout link, on the top right corner to logout from the application. You will go to "**Click here to login again**" page.

Figure 2-17 – Application Click here to login again Page

16. Click on "**Click here to login again**" link to go to login page

> Note: Hotel Application has 2 builds:
>
> - Build 1 – Has been developed with known defects. Thus, few functional test cases and automation scripts will fail on this build.
>
> - Build 2 – Known defects have been fixed. Thus, functional test cases and automation test scripts should pass when executed on this build.
>
> User can access either of the build from the Login page of the Hotel Application.

ᘓᘔ

3

Planning Before Automation

Introduction

Before you actually start recording your scripts and doing automation, it is important to plan the recording of your scripts. You need to plan:

- The test cases which need to be automated.
- Define priority of the test cases and automate key test cases first.
- The stability of your application.
- The data dependency of the tests.
- If there are tests which use the same data?
- If the automation tester knows the steps of the tests to be automated?
- Whether the automation testers have permission to access application components and systems?
- Who is going to automate which test within the team?
- When should the automation tasks be accomplished?

In this chapter, we will try to understand what we need to plan before we start our recording.

Key objectives:

- To understand the pre-requisites before we record.
- To understand the Test Automation process.

3.1 Pre-requisites Before you Start Recording

Let us try to understand some of the pre-requisites before we start recording our scripts:

1. Prepare your Test Environment - Check whether your environment and application is stable

Determine that you have a test environment available in which you can record/replay and create your automation scripts.

Determine whether the application is stable from a development as well as functional point of view. Does the interface change very often?

As a recommendation, if the application interface is changing too often, or if the application is not stable from a functional point of view, or if the test environment is not stable, we should not start automation. It's important to understand the factual reason for that. Technically speaking, we can still perform automation, but it might increase maintenance and script modification effort later on, when functional issues or UI issues are fixed. So a better approach is to wait until the environment is stabilized.

2. Ensure that the automation tester has permission to access application components and systems

Ensure that the test suite and testers have permissions to access the database, host systems, and input/output data.

3. Execute the test case steps manually to determine the expected results

Execute the test case steps manually on the application, to verify that all steps are listed and ensure that you are able to understand the business process. One of the most important factors to take care in automated testing is to ensure that the test duplicates the test steps in the most straightforward manner possible. It is important to **capture the actions** stated in the test case **exactly as an end-user would perform** them in the business process.

Also, it helps you to understand if there is any **pre-data setup** required for the test. For example, if you need to automate login, you need to have a valid username and password. Rather than starting your recording first, you will realize that you need a valid login, when you first manually execute your tests.

Example

Let me give you another example from my personal experience:

Once we were implementing functional automation for a client and we had a test case which required us to verify that the login expires after two months. We thought of changing the system date of our PC to two months in the past and then verifying that the login expires. But the question was how do we change the system date using HP UFT? So we did some research and tried a couple of examples, and were able to figure out a way. But that took us about two days.

Now once we had implemented the solution, we found that whenever we ran the UFT script, the login did not actually expire and the user could still login. We ran the test case steps manually and found the login does not expire even when manually executed which got us perplexed. After some more investigations, we realised that we were changing the system date of our local PC and not the server. But as the expiry date was linked to the server date and not to the local machine, the login did not expire and the user could login. Also, we did not have access to the server, and due to authorization issues it was not possible to change the date of the server machine.

The question is - could we have foreseen this issue and saved our two days? If we would have manually tested this scenario, we would have realized our mistake and would not have spent two days trying to automate it.

4. Determine what data will be required to be used for test execution

Ensure that you understand what input data you would need for test creation. You need to understand valid and invalid input data. Also, a lot of times there are scenarios where you would need data in a specific format or type.

Example

Let me take an example here:

I used to work for a mortgage domain client. One of their applications required the input date to be greater than or equal to the current date. How do we design an automation script to take a date that's greater than the current date without the test case depending on the already defined data? It needs better planning. As a solution, instead of using hard-coded data, we used some VBScript function to generate date greater than today's date.

Apart from this, there might be scenarios where after the test verification has finished; you would need to roll back specific data that was earlier setup as part of test execution. So make sure to understand data dependencies before you start automation.

5. Determine the Start and End Point of the test and follow it for all your automation scripts

Make sure that for all your automation scripts, you determine where your script will start from and where it will end.

Why is this important? This is important as you are going to run your scripts as a suite or a batch and not individually. So your current script should know where your previous script ended.

For instance, say you are working on a web based application and you open your browser at the start of every test but fail to close the browser at the end of each test. If you are running 50 tests you will have 50 browser windows open at the end of your script run which will cause script execution issues.

The correct way is to determine the Start and End point of your test and follow it for all your scripts. This will ensure that any automation tester in your team would know which form or page of application will be open when they start creating their automation script and where they should finish their script.

A better solution for web based applications will be to open the browser at the start of every test and close the browser at the end of every test.

6. **Reset any Master Data, if data is modified as part of test**

Another important thing to do is to reset any master data to the default value, after data is modified as part of your test. The reason is that future test scripts would be looking for default data and not the data which you have modified as part of your current test.

Example

Let me give an example here:

I was once working on a manufacturing based application which had units (centimetres, millimetres, and inches) defined as master data to measure the length of various manufacturing components. As a part of one test case we automated, we changed the master data of Unit field from centimetres to inches, and verified that all the valid lengths are now in inches. Our automation script worked beautifully, and we integrated it with our automation suite and executed our overnight test run.

Next morning we found that all our scripts, following this script failed. We realized that its reason was that though we had changed the master data of Unit field from centimetres to inches, we never changed it back to default (which was centimetres). Hence, all the sequential scripts failed as they expected the unit to be centimetres, but found the unit in inches. So we had to fix the script to reset the unit field back to default value at the end of the script.

So as a thumb rule: Reset all the master data that you have modified at the end of your test to default values as it can impact other tests.

7. **Standardize naming conventions**

Create standards and conventions on how you are going to name your automation scripts, setup naming conventions for your temporary variables, functions, and other components of your automation framework.

This will help to ensure that the whole team is following standardized naming conventions and the complete framework can be easily maintained in the future.

8. **Plan and prioritize your test cases. Identify your automation candidates**

Plan and prioritize which test cases you should automate first. We use the term ***automation candidates*** for regression test cases, which we select for automation.

A few key criterions for selection of automation candidates include-

- Test cases which are high priority or linked to high priority requirements. Usually we automate Sanity or Build Acceptance test cases as a first step.

- Test cases which are data oriented or which need to be executed multiple times for different sets of data.

- Test cases which take long time to execute and their automation will free up functional testers to perform more key tasks.

- Existing or fixed defects in the systems which are now converted to test cases.

- Based on the frequency of execution of the test cases. Test cases which are executed very frequently are better candidates for automation giving more Return on Investment (ROI).

- Test cases for operating system compatibility or browser compatibility can be automated, as the same script can be executed for different operating systems or browsers.

9. Plan resources and schedule

Plan how many people will be automating the test cases, and what will be the delivery schedule.

3.2 Test Automation Process

This section describes automation processes usually followed as we automate the regression test cases.

1. Defining the scope for automation: Define the scope of test cases that should be automated, check feasibility, and confirm return on investment.

2. Selection of the Test Automation tool: Select right test automation tools, which will suit your application technology and fit into your budget. It can be an open source or a commercial tool.

3. Procurement of licenses: If a commercial tool is selected, procure the license for the commercial tool.

4. Training the testers to use the tool: If required, train the testing team on how to perform automation and use automation tool.

5. Automation strategy and plan: Design the automation strategy and plan on how and when regression test cases will be automated. Also, define data dependencies, environment needs and risks.

6. Identification and development of Automation Framework and Test Automation Lab: Automation framework is required to make sure automation scripts are maintainable. It involves setting up design and guidelines of automation components. This includes defining naming conventions, guideline document, structure of the automation scripts and setup of test machines in the test environment.

7. Creation of Automation Scripts: Actual recording or creation of automation scripts from regression test cases.

8. Peer Review and Testing: Review of Automation Scripts by peers to ensure that all conventions are followed and automation scripts are correctly mapped to functional test cases. Test case verification points are also verified as part of the review.

9. Integration of scripts: This involves integration of automation scripts into a larger automation suite for overnight test execution, to be executed as a batch process.

10. Script maintenance: Regular script maintenance that is required when an application undergoes functional changes and needs fixes in automation scripts.

૯૭

07/16/15

4

Create your First Script

Introduction

Many times, functional testers have a perception that we need to write programs to automate applications. This is not entirely true. Most of the automation tools come with record/replay features using which you can record user actions and can replay those actions back without writing a single line of program. Yes, you might need to make some enhancements to your script, which again can be accomplished without any programming.

In this chapter we will define how to record a basic script, replay the script, and save the script.

Key objectives:

- Understand UFT interface.
- Record a basic script.
- Replay script.
- Save script under test hierarchy.

4.1 Launch UFT and Understanding UFT Interface

In this section we will launch UFT and understand UFT interface in more detail.

1. Go to **Start** → **All Program Files** → **HP Software** → **HP Unified Functional Testing** → **HP Unified Functional Testing** and click.

2. UFT comes with below **Add-In Manager** Dialog Box. Select all the three **add-ins** and Click **OK** on this dialog box.

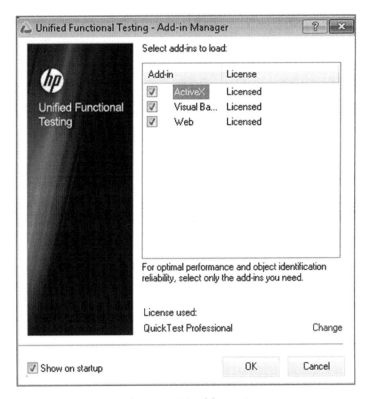

Figure 4-1 – UFT Add-In Manager

By default, user will see three Add-ins: Web, Visual Basic, and Active-X.

Why do we need Add-ins?

UFT needs to identify user interface controls in the application. For example, let us consider the button control, e.g., Login button, which was developed in Visual Basic Language and another button which was created in the Java Language. They are two different controls since the underlying technologies are different even though they might perform the same function. So UFT needs a way to recognise different technologies and specific user interface controls developed in those technologies.

Once you load any of the add-ins (VB, Web or Active-X), they work as an interface between UFT and the software application. It helps UFT to identify user controls in your application. Let us take another example. For web applications we always launch the web browser. The Browser, as a user interface control, has options to go back and forward. Once web-add-ins is loaded, it helps UFT to recognize the browser as a UI control and to perform back and forward operations on it.

So does UFT support other applications like Java, .Net, SAP etc. How do we get other add-ins?

Yes, UFT supports a variety of technologies including Java, .NET, SAP, Terminal Emulators, Silverlight, Delphi, Powerbuilder, Stringray, and many more. During UFT installation, it gives you an option to install UFT with default add-ins or extra add-ins. Even after you have installed UFT, you can launch the installer again and do a custom install of required add-ins.

3. UFT start page window opens.

On the Top Bar you will find various menu bar and title bar for the application.

Figure 4-2 – UFT Start-up Page

4. Create a new Test by going to **File** → **New** → **Test**.

This opens up the New Test Dialog Box.

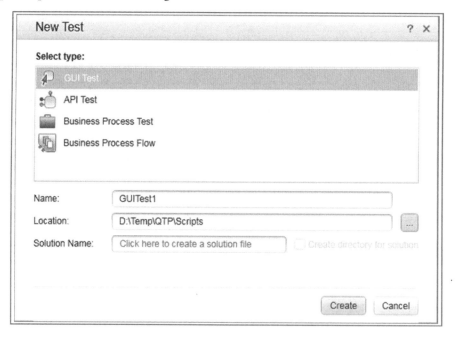

Figure 4-3 – New Test Dialog

5. Select **GUI Test** in Select type options.

6. Enter name of script as **MyFirstTest.**

7. Select/change **Location** where you would like to save your script (Example: Create a UFT folder in D: drive in which we can save all our scripts D:\UFT\).

8. Click on **Create** button.

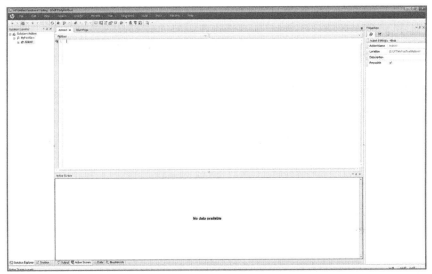

Figure 4-4 – UFT GUI Test Interface

Key tabs to note in this pane. We will discuss a few more tabs at a later stage:-

Editor View – This is the default view of the UFT GUI Test. In the Editor View, UFT displays each operation performed on your application in the form of a script, comprised of VBScript statements. The Editor View is a script editor with many script editing capabilities. For each object and method in an Editor View statement, a corresponding row exists in the Keyword View. This view is same as Expert View in QTP11.0 and earlier versions.

Data – Data pane is used to store the test data your test case will use. At the back-end, it is a excel sheet, which is stored with the UFT GUI Test.

Active Screen - The Active Screen provides a snapshot of your application as it appeared when you performed a certain step during a recording session. Make a note that this is not just a snapshot, it also stores information on object properties of the application, hence is called the Active Screen.

Solution Explorer – This pane maintains and shows the flow of UFT GUI Test with multiple actions (We will cover this later).

Keyword View – To view Keyword view, select **View → Keyword View.**

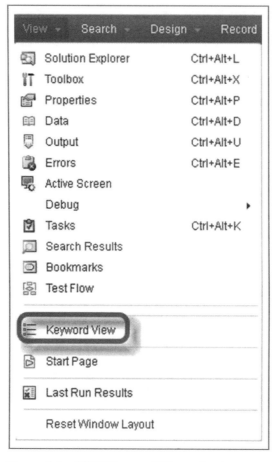

Figure 4-5 – UFT Keyword View selection menu

The Keyword View enables you to create and view the steps of your test in a keyword-driven, modular, table format. The Keyword View comprises a table-like view, in which each step is a separate row in the table, and each column represents different parts of the steps. You can modify the columns displayed to suit your requirements.

Click on **View → Keyword View** to display the view as Keyword View for the next section

4.2 Set UFT Web Page Frame Option Settings

In this section we will setup HP UFT web page frame settings:

1. Go to **Tools → Options → GUI Testing → Web → Page/Frame Options.**

2. Select **Different test object descriptions** option under label **Create a new Page test object for**.

3. Select **Different test object descriptions** option under label **Create a new Frame test object for**.

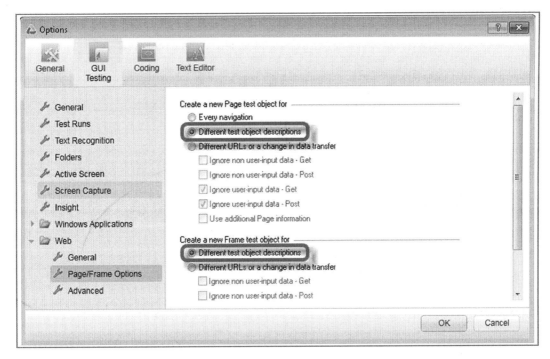

Figure 4-6 – Page/Frame Options

This setting will assist us later, by not having duplicate objects in our scripts.

4.3 Recording Script

Alright! Let us record our first script now.

> Note: Make sure web-ins are loaded and selected, in add-ins dialog box when you launch UFT.

> Note: Make sure all other applications and browsers except UFT are closed. This is not mandatory, but at a beginner level it helps you to make sure you do not incorrectly record.

1. Before we start recording, we will launch IE and enter URL. So launch IE and launch URL www.adactin.com/HotelApp in your browser page to see the websites login page.

Note: For our future exercises, we will assume application login page is visible and that the browser is launched.

2. Click on **Record** Button or Go to **Record** → **Record** and click.

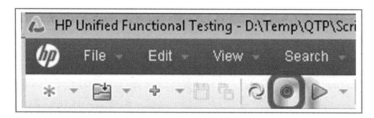

Figure 4-7 – Recording Icon

3. In the **Record and Run settings** dialog box, select Web Tab and select **Record and run test on any open browser**.

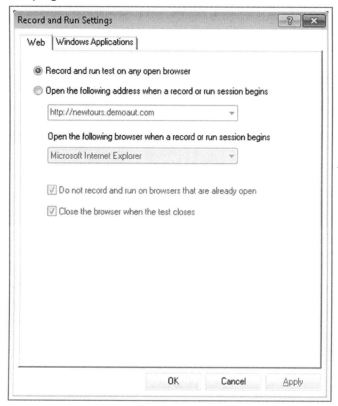

Figure 4-8 – Record and Run Setting Dialog Box

Record and run test on any open browser: This option enables you to record and run on any browsers which are open. This is the most common and widely used option.

Open the following address when a record or run session begins: You can define specific URL that you would like to open when your script records or runs. This is not a frequently used option.

4. Click **OK**.

Now you are in recording mode. Anything you do from now on will be recorded as an action in UFT script. You would see a red "Recording GUITest1" flashing dialog box come, giving an indication you are in recording mode.

Figure 4-9 – Record Toolbar

5. Assuming that application is already open in IE browser with login page visible, perform the following steps.

    a.   Login (Use the username/password with which you have registered earlier).

    b.   Search for Hotel.

        i.   Select a location, e.g., Sydney

        ii.   Select number of rooms, e.g., 2

        iii.   Select adults per rooms, e.g., 2

        iv.   Click on Search button

    c.   Select a Hotel.

        i.   Select one of the Hotel Radio buttons, e.g., select radio button next to Hotel Creek.

    d.   Book a Hotel.

        i.   Enter First Name

        ii.   Enter Last Name

        iii.   Enter Address

        iv.   Enter 16-digit Credit Card no:

        v.   Enter Credit Card type

        vi.   Enter Expiry Month

        vii.   Enter Expiry Year

        viii. Enter CVV number

        ix.   Click on Book Now

    e.   After you see the Booking confirmation page, click on Logout.

    f.   Click on "Click here to Login again" link to go back to Home page.

6. Stop recording by clicking on **Stop Recording** button in record toolbar.

Figure 4-10 – Stop Recording Icon

7. Verify the steps below that are recorded in HP UFT Keyword View. See steps as below that you see in Keyword View.

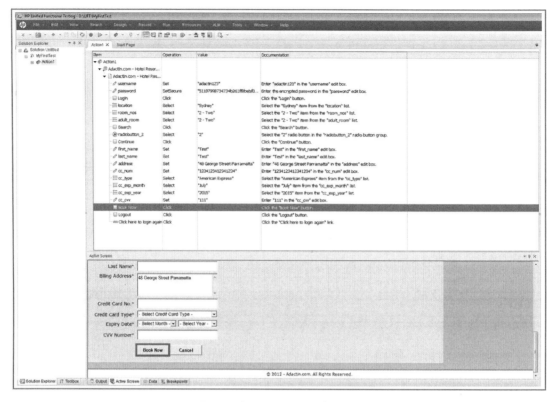

Figure 4-11 – Keyword View

If you look at the above steps, First column- "Item" represents the user controls of the application on which actions are done.

Second column "Operation" represents the operation or method performed on user controls. For example, Set method to enter value in username field.

Third column "Value" represents all the input data that has been entered into the application for testing.

Fourth column "Documentation" represents a detailed description of what each step is doing.

> **Note:** Note that all the actions which we performed are captured as separate steps in the UFT script. If you encounter any web recording issues look for possible fixes in section 4.4.

Exercise

Go through each step of the script you see in Keyword View and map them to actual manual steps you performed in the application.

8. Select item "location" in the Keyword View and then select Active Screen button in the bottom screen (if Active Screen is not already open you can open it from **View → Active Screen**)

Active Screen will show Location field highlighted in pink, which shows the actual control on which operation was performed. In Active Screen, you will see a snapshot of every action that is performed during recording.

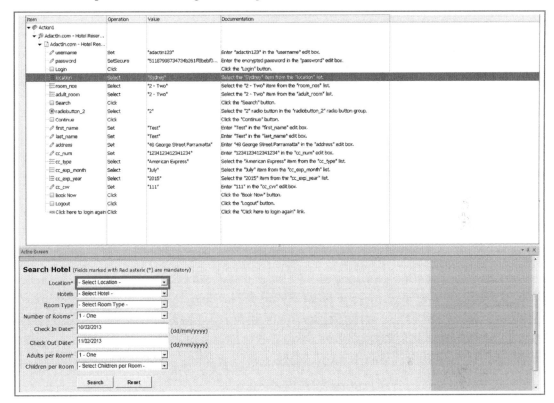

Figure 4-12 – Keyword View

9. Go to **View → Editor** and see the script in Editor View.

Editor View is the script view of UFT. It stores script in VBScript format which is the language UFT uses to script.

Editor View acts as a VBScript editor, and can store and execute any VBScript functions and commands.

Figure 4-13 – Editor View

4.4 Tips for Web Recording Issues

In the upcoming exercise, if you face issues with recording the sample application in QTP or UFT, try the following:

1. Make sure you always launch UFT first, and then the Browser. In case you already have Browser open, close the Browser and then relaunch after UFT has been started.

2. Ensure Web Add-ins are loaded (we will talk about them in coming chapters) when loading UFT.

3. Add the application URL to Internet Explorer, i.e., Trust Site link from Tools → Internet Options → Security -> Sites button.

4. If using QTP 11.0, install the latest QuickTest Professional Patch. There were few known issues with recording on 64bit IE which were resolved with QTP Patch 699. You can download the patch from HP Website.

5. If using QTP 11.0, try launching it in Administrator mode.

    a.   Right click QTP short cut>>Run As Administrator Mode.

6.   If the above does not work, then go to Control Panel and set User account setting to low level, i.e., not to notify, restart machine and then repeat step-1.

7. If above does not work, then go to IE →Tools → Internet Options→ Advanced> → Browsing → Enable Third Party Browser extension (usually it will be enabled by default in IE9) and then repeat step-1 and step-2.

4.5 Replay Script

Now that we have successfully recorded a script, let us replay the script to confirm all actions can be replayed back.

1. Click on **Run** button.

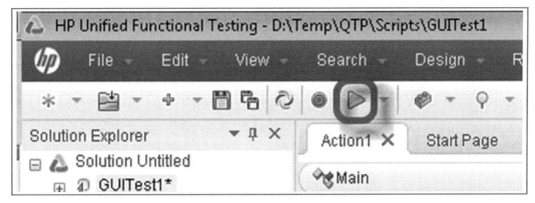

Figure 4-14 – Run Icon

2. In the **Run** Dialog box, select **Temporary Run result** option (which is selected by default). Click on the details **arrow** to see the Result options.

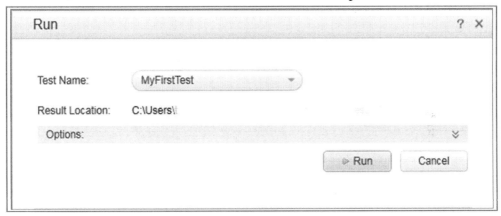

Figure 4-15 – Run Dialog

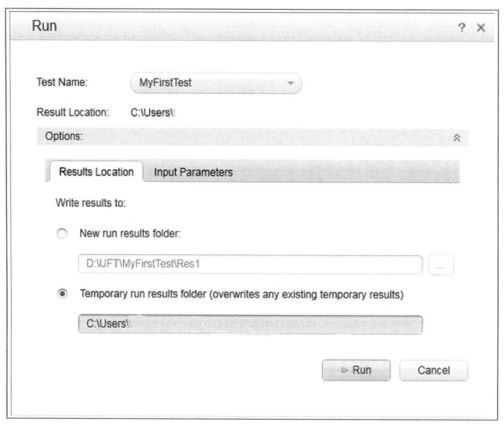

Figure 4-16 – Run Dialog Settings

New Run Results Folder: Use this option if you need to store results for future verification in a separate results folder location on your machine. This option should be used once the scripts are completed and you want to do actual execution on your application.

Temporary Run Result Folder: This is a temporary results folder and results are overwritten with the latest results next time when script is executed. We use this option when we are still developing our scripts, and saving our results for future reference is not important.

3. Click **Run.**

4. Verify the script executes and replays all the actions successfully.

5. Results View will pop-up automatically or can be opened from **View → Last Run Results**.

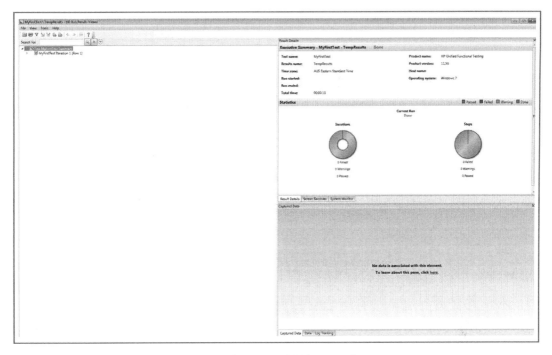

Figure 4-17 – UFT Test Results

6. Expand the results tree to confirm correct execution of steps.

7. **File** → **Exit** and close the results window.

> Note: Current status of Test Execution is "Done" and not "Passed". The reason behind that is that we have not yet added any verification points within the script.

Note: Current status of Test Execution is "Done" and not "Passed". The reason behind that is that we have not yet added any verification points within the script.

4.6 Save Script

In this section we will save our script and look at the scripts hierarchy.

1. Go to **File** → **Save MyFirstTest** or **Save MyFirstTest As**.

Figure 4-18 – Save Test option

2. Once the script is saved, go to D:\UFT\MyFirstTest Folder on the file system. You will see the below structure.

Figure 4-19 – UFT Test Hierarchy on file system

Action0 – It is the main calling Action which calls Action1

Action1 – This is the working action where entire script is recorded

Default.xls – This corresponds to DataTable which we see in the script

All other files store configuration information stored within the script

3. Now just click on **Action1** folder and get into Action1 folder.

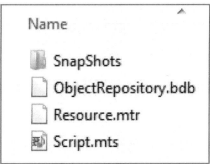

Figure 4-20 – UFT Action Hierarchy on file system

Snapshots – It stores the snapshots which we see in Active Screen

Resource.mtr – It corresponds to local Object Repository (which we will discuss in coming chapters)

Script.mts – It stores the actual script that we see in UFT Editor View

4. Right click on **Script.mts** file and Open it with **Notepad**.

You will see the same lines of code as you see in **Editor View**.

Also, after every line you will see text like "@@ hightlight id_" which links this step with snapshots in Active Screen.

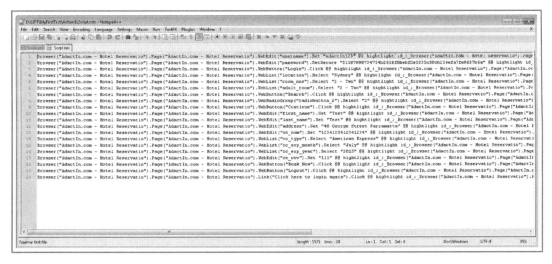

Figure 4-21 – UFT GUI Test script

> **Note:** Key thing to understand is that UFT stores script on the file system as a set of multiple files. Different automation tools store this information differently. A few of them store scripts either in database or as xml files. But UFT stores it as a folder in the file system.

Experienced automation testers use tools like VSS, CVS, or Subversion to maintain versions of UFT scripts, which are sets of multiple files.

&

5

Managing User Interface Controls

Introduction

In the last chapter we recorded a sample script and replayed it. You would be very curious to understand how UFT actually replayed the whole script. How could it identify the location field and enter the value that we had earlier recorded in the previous chapter? Was it like a video recording that got replayed?

Key objectives:

- Understanding Object Recognition fundamentals and how UFT replays.
- Using Object Repository.
- Highlighting Objects.
- Adding Objects in Object Repository.
- Using Object Spy.

5.1 How Does UFT Replay Scripts

Let us take a simple example:

Assume that you parked your car on some level of a big shopping mall before going for a party. For the sake of this example, say you had too many drinks at the party and so took a cab to get home. Next morning, you come back to the mall to pick up your car but you do not remember the location of the car apart from knowing the level on which your car was parked. How will you find your car? Assume that you do not have a remote control for the car!

Figure 5-1 – Sample Car

If I were to find my car, I will go looking for my car in the first row and look for the "Make" and "Colour" of my car. If I find a car with the same Make and Colour, I will go closer to the car and try to identify my car based on the registration number. If I can match all these three properties, I am sure I will find my car. So the three properties I will look for will be:

- Make of the car
- Colour of the car
- Registration No: of the car

I do not really need to care about height, width or any other details about my car.

This is what UFT as a tool does and as a matter of fact, this principle is followed by all other automation tools available in the market. They use some key properties of the objects to identify the user interface controls and then use those properties to identify the objects. For instance, if the user clicks on a button, UFT will store the label of the button and use that label to identify the object.

So below would be the process of how UFT will replay a script:

- While recording, UFT stores object property information somewhere (which is called Object Repository) in the script.
- When we replay the script, UFT will pick up the logical name (object name we see in the script), go to Object Repository and find the object and it properties for recognition.
- Once UFT gets the object properties, it will go to the application under test and try to find the object.
- Once it finds the object, it will perform the operation (click, select, etc.) on that object.

This is the basic automation fundamental required to understand how functional automation tools work. The key point to remember is that the UFT script is not a video recording of functionality, but a step by step execution of actions recorded in the script.

5.2 Using Object Repository

In the previous section, we understood that user interface controls (objects) information is stored in the Object Repository within UFT. In this section, let us try to see where exactly we can find this information in UFT.

1. Open your UFT script "MyFirstTest" which we created in the last exercise.
2. Go to **Resources → Object Repository...** and open **Object Repository** Dialog box.

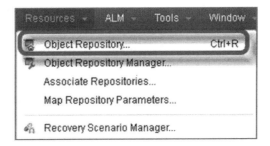

Figure 5-2 – Object Repository Selection menu

3. Expand the tree structure that you see in Object Repository. You will notice that there are objects defined which we have used in our script.

4. Select object "Book Now". In the right panel you will notice properties, which are used to identify the object.

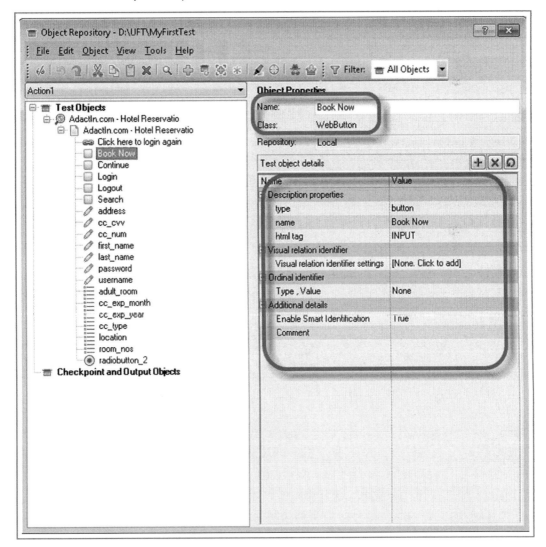

Figure 5-3 – Object Repository

In the top half of right pane –

Name - Name represents **logical name** of the object. This is how an object is called or referenced in UFT scripts. But it is important to understand that this is just a reference name. Object is actually identified by the description properties stored for the object.

Class – Class represents the "class" the object belongs to. For every technology, there are standard classes which are available. Any object that you will see will be part of that class. Based on the class of which the object is part of, an object gets access to methods and properties for that class.

In the bottom half of right pane –

Description Properties – This defines the actual properties and values, which are used to identify the object. In the above example you will notice there are three properties, type, name, and html tag, which are used to identify the object.

Ordinal identifier – At times you will find objects which have same description properties (e.g. Send button at top and bottom of your Yahoomail or Gmail account) . In that case how will UFT differentiate the objects? UFT uses Ordinal Identifier to identify the objects. You can have identifiers like Location and Index.

- Location – It checks the location of the object based on screen coordinates. If the object comes first on the script, it is given value 0 and second object will be given value 1.

- Index - The **value is based on the order in which the object appears within the source code while developing the application. This is defined by the developer of the application.**

> **Note:** You can update any property value of an object, by selecting the property value for the corresponding object and typing in the new value. It is that simple!

You might need to change the property value because of a new development that necessitates a need for the development team to change property values. For e.g., the developer might change the label of the login button from "Login" to Sign-In", which would require an update of the object property value.

5.3 Add Objects to Object Repository

One way to add objects to the Object Repository is by using the recording functionality. Can we add objects to the Object Repository without recording? Yes, we can!

Let us see how:

1. Let us manually navigate to the **Search Hotel** page of the application.

2. Open Object Repository (if it is not already open from previous exercise).

3. As part of this exercise we want to add "Reset" button into our object repository.

4. Click on **Add Objects to Local** icon and place the hand icon on the **Reset** button (important to note that the application object should be visible in the application).

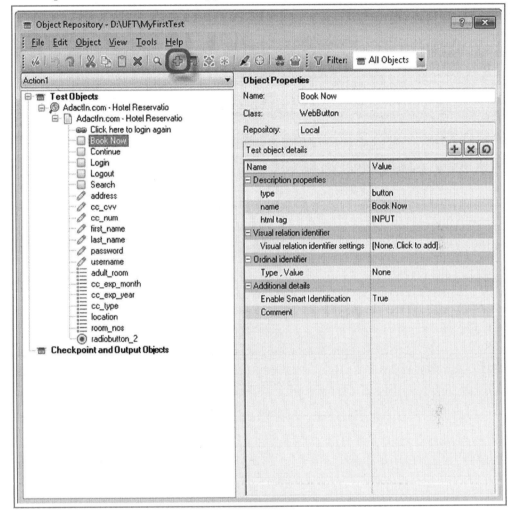

Figure 5-4– Add Objects icon

5. Verify the Reset button in **Object Selection – Add to Repository** dialog box and click **OK** with object selected.

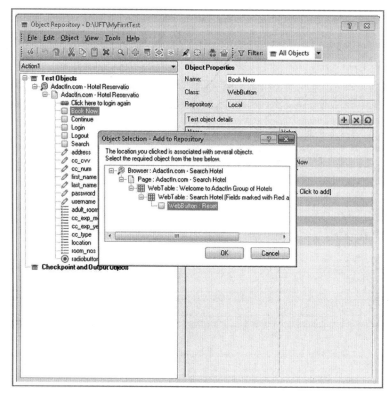

Figure 5-5– Object Selection Dialog

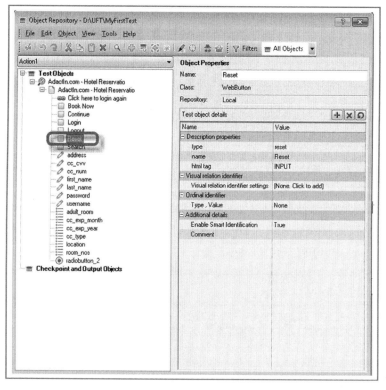

Figure 5-6– Added Object in Object Repository

You will notice that Reset button has been added to the Object Repository.

> Note: We will use Add Objects feature more often when we use shared Object Repository in the later sections.

5.4 Highlight Objects in Object Repository

How do you find out if a particular object does exist in your application, after it has been recorded? UFT provides us with the highlight feature, which helps us to highlight the object in the application if it exists.

> **Note:** Important to note that before we highlight the object, that object should be visible in the application under test so that it can be highlighted.

Let us see an example:

1. In the Hotel Reservation application, navigate to page in the application where you can see **Book Now** Button (which is in **Book Hotel** Page).

2. With the object repository already open from the previous exercise, select **Book Now** object.

3. Click on **Highlight** Button available in toolbar or alternatively select **View** → **Highlight in Application** (in Object Repository window).

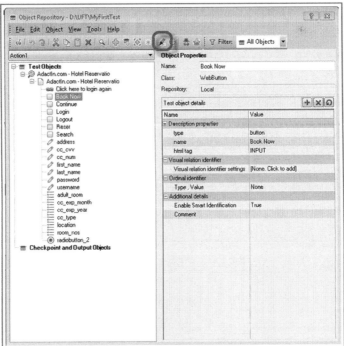

Figure 5-7– Highlight Object Icon

4. You will notice that **Book Now** button in the application gets highlighted.

> **Note:** Highlight represents a very good debugging feature in UFT, to trace which object has changed. It also helps in cases where any object has been changed (i.e., any object property has been changed) and script fails causing UFT to be not able to identify the object. In order to debug, the first thing you should try to do is to highlight the object in the application and check if UFT can recognize the object.

5.5 Using Object Spy

Object Spy is a tool, which is provided by UFT to identify run time objects (objects in real applications) properties.

Let us think of a scenario. If for some reason the developer changed the label for the "Reset" button to "Restore". If you had a UFT script which uses Reset object, your script will start failing. As a first step to isolate the issue you should try to highlight the object to find if you can identify the object. Since the object has been renamed you will not be able to highlight the object. As a next step, you should try to find out which property of the object has changed and if is different from one that exists in object repository. This is where Object Spy comes handy.

As a test scenario, let us try to get the properties of the Reset Button in Search Hotel Page

1. To use Object Spy, open object repository and select **Tools → Object Spy.**

Note: You can also get Object Spy by clicking on Object Spy icon in Object Repository toolbar or from UFT Toolbar.

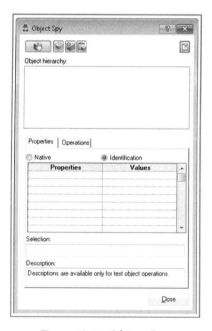

Figure 5-8– Object Spy

2. In the application under test, navigate to the page or window where you see the object for which you want to get property values.

3. Click on the Hand icon and place the Hand icon over the Reset button(in Search Hotel page). Left mouse click on the Reset Button.

4. You can look at all the possible property values for the **Reset** button object. Also you can find **operations** that can be performed on Reset button in **Operations** tab.

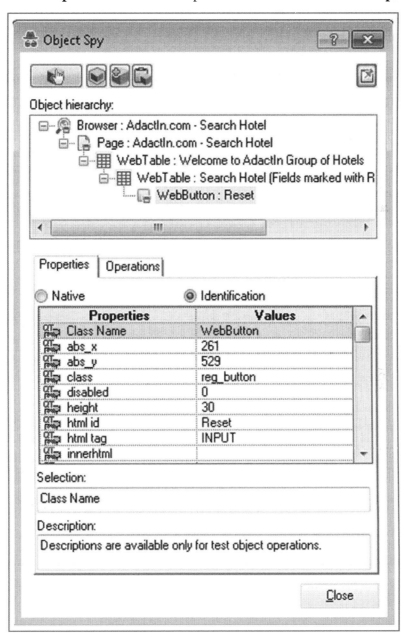

Figure 5-9– Object Spy Properties

☙

6

Parameterization – Data Driven Test

Introduction

In many instances, when we are performing regression testing, we need to repeat the same test case with different datasets. This can be a monotonous and time-consuming task, depending on how many different data sets are required to verify that data using the tests.

Example

Let us take an example:

I worked for one of our retail domain clients as part of the testing and automation team which had more than 2000 stores in the country, They had developed a point of sales system. Once this was manually tested, they gave us a list of more than 10000 usernames and password pairs, and asked us to set them up in the system. As a testing team, our task was to verify if all usernames and passwords are set up correctly. We were given a target of .01% failure threshold. If we had to verify all this manually, assuming we would verify 1 username/password combination every 1 minute (as there were couple of validations we had to do once logged in), it would have taken us 5000 minutes or approximately 20-24 days of man effort. Imagine how laborious and time-consuming that task would be?

Solution: Wouldn't it be great if you have an automated script using which could pick up the first username and password entered from an excel sheet, log the user in and perform all the validations without any manual intervention?

An even better solution would be to create a script to iterate across all the 10000 usernames and passwords. This is exactly what we did, we created an automation script using UFT, which took us less than 4 hours to develop, ran it overnight, got the failed records, again re-tested the records once fixed and delivered it to the customer with 0% issues. The concept of running the same script with multiple dataset values is called **Parameterization**.

Any test case which needs to be executed multiple times with different data values is an ideal candidate for automation.

Key objectives of this chapter are:

- How to Parameterize my Script.
- Script Execution and Result Analysis.

6.1 How to Parameterize a UFT Script

Scenario: As a test workflow, we need to book a Hotel for all the available cities, in our case Sydney, Melbourne, Brisbane, and Adelaide. So we want our script should be able to iterate once each for the above cities.

Should we create multiple scripts for every city?

The answer is 'No!'. We should use the same script and get it to be executed for multiple sets of data.

Let us see how to solve the above problem using Parameterization:

1. Open one of previously created scripts **MyFirstTest** which was created in your last exercise

2. Go to **File > Save As** and save the script as "**Parameterization**"

Figure 6-1– Save Test Option

3. Make sure you are in Keyword View of UFT (Select **View** → **Keyword View**).

4. Locate the line with Item **location** in the Keyword View.

5. Go to column **value** next to location line and click in the value column, and select the city.

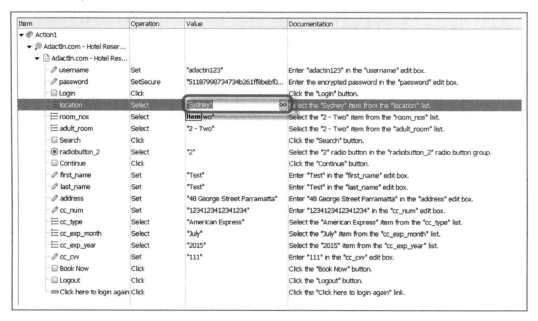

Figure 6-2 – Column selection for parameterization

6. Click on **<#>** icon

Figure 6-3 – # icon

7. In the **Value Configuration Options** dialog box, select **Parameter** radio button.

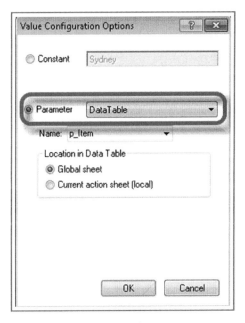

Figure 6-4 – Value Configuration Options

8. Keep the default selection of **Data Table.**

Other possible options in the drop-down menu are:

Environment – Enables you to use the system environments variable values or internal or externally defined environment variable in xml files. You could see system variables and create use defined variables in **File → Settings → Environment**.

Random Number - Enables you to insert random numbers as values in your test.

9. In the **Name** column, manually type name of column.

Figure 6-5 – Provide Name for Parameter

10. Keep the default selection of **Global Sheet** in **Location in Data Table** section.

Global Sheet – Use Global Sheet if you want to run the whole test (which can be comprised of multiple actions) to iterate for multiple data sets. This is the most frequently used option.

Current Action Sheet (local) – Use Local Sheet if you want a specific Action to iterate for multiple sets of data. For each global iteration, Action will be iterated for Data set defined in Local Sheet. This is not a very frequently used option.

For e.g. if you have 2 rows of data defined in Global sheet and 2 rows of data defined in Action sheet, the UFT script will run for total 4 iterations. It will run 2 times for first data row of Global sheet (because 2 rows are defined in Action sheet) and another 2 times for second data row of global sheet.

11. Click **OK.**

12. Go to **DataT**able pane (**View → Data**) at the bottom of the test. You would see your existing location data in **Location** Column.

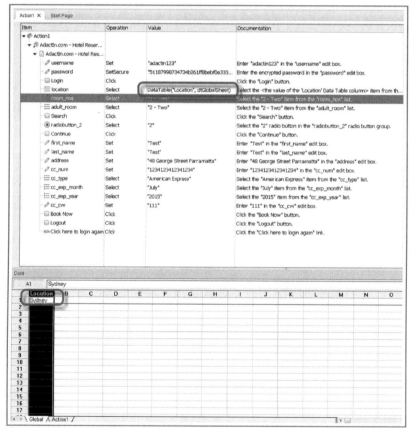

Figure 6-6 – Data column in Datasheet

13. Type more locations manually into the Excel driven DataTable.

Note: Make sure the locations used actually exist in the application as drop-down menu items.

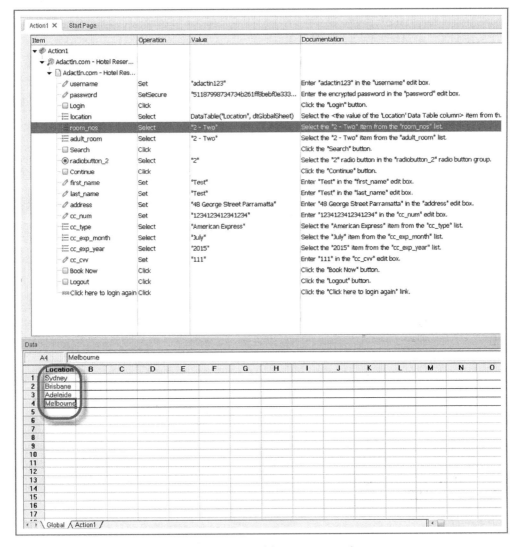

Figure 6-7 – Data addition in Datasheet

14. Observe the **Value** column which has been parameterized. Our previous constant value has been replaced with **"DataTable("Location", dtGlobalSheet).**

It means that parameter value will be picked up from the "Location" column, which is available in "Global" Sheet.

15. Go to **File** > **Save** and Save the script.

We are done with Parameterization!! Let us now run the script!

6.2 Script Execution and Result Analysis

In this section we will execute the above Parameterized script.

Note: Pre-requisite: Make sure application Login page is open.

1. Click on Run button or Go to **Run → Run**.

2. Select **Temporary Run results** option in **Run** Dialog box and Click **OK**.

Note: Moving forward, for all exercises we will be always selecting the "Temporary Run results option"

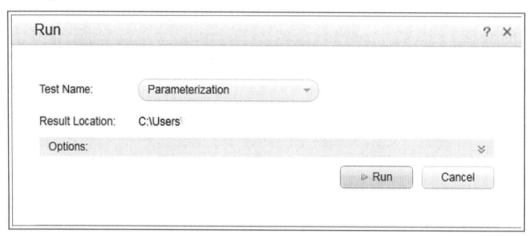

Figure 6-8 – Run Dialog box

3. You will observe that script executes 4 times for all the different location entered in Data table.

4. Go to **View → Last Run Results** (in case your results window do not automatically pop-up).

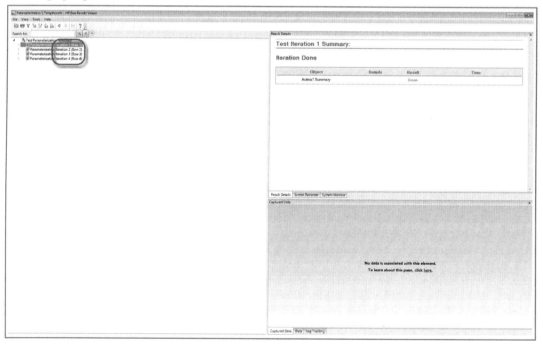

Figure 6-9 – Test Results

You will notice that the test ran for 4 iterations for each of the values setup in the Data Table.

5. Expand second iteration result tree and select location. Select statement, in the top right pane show the value for location that was entered in second iteration.

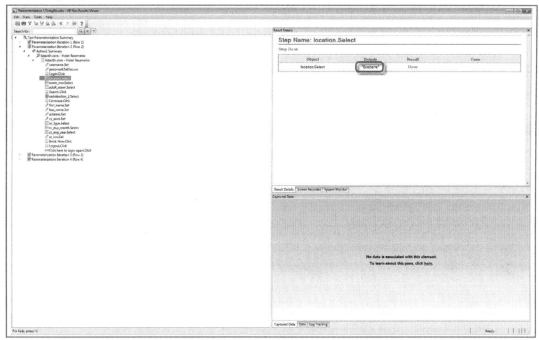

Figure 6-10 – Test Results

6. Select **Data** tab in bottom right pane.

You will see all the run time data values that were used during execution.

Note: During script execution, UFT copies all values from the **Design time** datatable (in which we had manually modified values) to the Run Time datatable. It uses Run Time DataTable values during script execution.

Figure 6-11 – Run Time Data table

Note: Any step in Keyword View which has entries in the value column can be parameterized.

Exercise

1. Parameterize first name, last name, and address and run the test for five different iterations.

ℰↄ

7

Verifying Tests -Checkpoints

Introduction

Till now, you would have noticed that the "Current Run" in results has the status "Done" and not "Passed". So why has the result not passed when our scripts have been executing perfectly?

The reason is that we do not have any verification points in our scripts, where we can compare expected results with actual results. An important use of test case automation is to compare expected results with actual results.

To accomplish this, in UFT we have a feature called Checkpoint. It compares expected result with the actual result and reports a pass or a fail in the results.

Key objectives:

- Need for Checkpoint.
- Type of Checkpoints.
- Insert Standard Checkpoint from Active Screen.
- Editing and renaming a Checkpoint.
- Analyse Checkpoint Results.
- Insert Standard Checkpoint during recording.

7.1 Need for Checkpoint

A checkpoint is a specialized step that compares two values and reports the result. A checkpoint compares the actual results from the test run, with the expected results in the test plan.

A basic test cannot be considered a valid functional test without some form of validation.

You use a checkpoint to:

- Verify the state of an object.
- Confirm that an application performs as expected.

A checkpoint checks whether an application responds appropriately when a user performs tasks correctly while testing the application. A checkpoint ensures that a user is barred from performing certain tasks and confirms that invalid or incomplete data flags appropriate messages.

- Example of validation is: Specifying limits, conditions, or boundaries.

Example

We were once testing an investment banking application where we could create varied instruments such as bonds, ADRs, etc. When creating an instrument, we would receive a "Save was successful" message and a unique instrument number. As part of our test case, we had to verify that "Save was successful" message appears. We also had to verify that we could search using the same instrument number and verify that all details were saved correctly. As part of our automation scripts, we had to verify both these conditions, so we used Checkpoints in UFT to verify this.

7.2 Types of Checkpoints

To see the different types of checkpoints in UFT, go to **Design → Checkpoint**

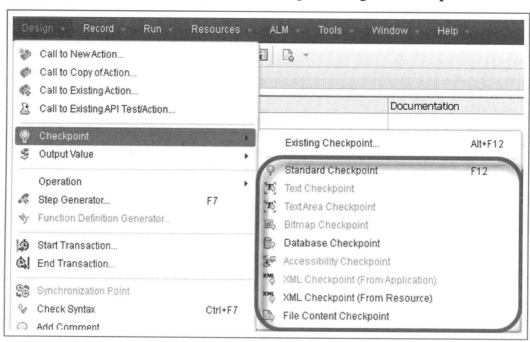

Figure 7-1 – Types of Checkpoints

You can insert the following checkpoint types to check objects in an application:

Checkpoint Type	Description
Standard Checkpoint	Checks property values of an object in your application. For example, you can check that a radio button is activated, after it is selected or you can check the value of an edit box. Standard Checkpoints are supported for all add-in environments
Image Checkpoint	Checks the value of an image in your application. For example, you can check that a selected image's source file is correct. You create an image checkpoint, by inserting a standard checkpoint on an image object. Image Checkpoints are supported for the Web add-in environment.
Bitmap Checkpoint	Checks an area of your application as a bitmap. For example, suppose you have a web site where you can display a map of a city that the user specifies. The map has control keys for zooming. Using the Bitmap Checkpoint, you can check that the map zooms in correctly. You can create a Bitmap Checkpoint for any area in your application. Bitmap checkpoints are supported for all add-in environments.
Table Checkpoint	Checks information within a table. For example, suppose your application contains a table listing all available flights from New York to San Francisco. You can add a Table Checkpoint to check that the time of the first flight in the table is correct. You create a table checkpoint by inserting a Standard Checkpoint on a table object. Table checkpoints are supported for all add-in environments that have a *Table test object.
Text Checkpoint	Checks that a text string is displayed in the appropriate place in an application. For example, suppose a web page displays the sentence "Flight departing from New York to San Francisco". You can create a text checkpoint that checks that the words "New York" are displayed between "Flight departing from" and "to San Francisco". Text checkpoints are supported for most add-in environments.

Text Area Checkpoint	Checks that a text string is displayed within a defined area in a Windows-based application, according to specified criteria. For example, suppose your Visual Basic application has a button that says View Doc <Num>, where <Num> is replaced by the four-digit code entered in a form elsewhere in the application. You can create a Text Area Checkpoint to confirm that the number displayed on the button is the same as the number entered in the form. Text Area Checkpoints are supported for all Windows-based environments, such as Standard Windows, Visual Basic, and ActiveX add-in environments.
Accessibility Checkpoint	Identifies areas of your web site that may not conform to the World Wide Web Consortium (W3C) Web Content Accessibility Guidelines. For example, guideline 1.1 of the W3C Web Content Accessibility Guidelines requires you to provide a text equivalent for every non-text element. You can add an **Alt** property check to check whether objects that require the **Alt** property under this guideline, do in fact have this tag. Accessibility Checkpoints are supported for the Web add-in environment.
Database Checkpoint	Checks the contents of a database accessed by your application. For example, you can use a Database Checkpoint to check the contents of a database containing flight information for your Web site. Database Checkpoints are supported for all add-in environments.
XML Checkpoint	Checks the data content of XML documents, in XML files or XML documents in Web Pages and frames. The **XML Checkpoint (Web Page/Frame)** option is supported for the Web add-in environment. The **XML Checkpoint** option is supported for all add-in environments.
File Content Checkpoint	Checks the text in a dynamically generated (or accessed) file. For example, suppose your application generates a PDF. You can check that the correct text is displayed on specific lines on specific pages in that PDF.

*Ref: HP UFT User guide

Note: For the scope of this book, we are going to discuss only Standard checkpoints in detail.

7.3 Insert Standard Checkpoint from Active Screen after Recording

Checkpoint can be inserted in the script during recording mode or after recording. We can insert a checkpoint in the script after recording from Active Screen.

Test Scenario

Let us take a simple test case for automation from our Hotel Application.

Test Objective: To Verify that when a location is selected in Search Hotel page, same location is displayed in Select Hotel page.

Test Steps:

1. Login to the application using User credentials.
2. Select Location as "Sydney" in Location field in Search Hotel Page.
3. Select Hotel as "Hotel Creek" in Hotels field.
4. Select Room Type as "Standard" in Room Type file.
5. Keep all the default selections.
6. Click on Search Button.
7. Verify that in the next Select Hotel Page Correct Location is displayed.

Expected Result

1. Correct location "Sydney" should appear in location column of select hotel search results.

How to Insert Checkpoint

Let us see how to insert checkpoints from Active Screen.

Pre-conditions

1. Create a new UFT **GUI Test** using **File → New → Test** and name the script as "Checkpoint".
2. Make sure your application (http://www.adactin.com/HotelApp/) login page is visible.

Steps to Insert Checkpoint

1. Record a basic script using following steps:
   a. Start Recording.
   b. User will login.

c. Search for Hotel with below values.

   i. Location : "Sydney"

   ii. Hotels: "Hotel Creek"

   iii. Room Type: "Standard"

   iv. Other fields: Default

d. Click on Search button.

e. Select first Radio button in search result and click on Continue.

f. Click logout (we do not need to book a hotel as my test case ends on Select a Hotel screen itself).

g. Click on Click here to Login link to go back to Login page.

h. Stop Recording (by clicking on Stop Recording button in Record toolbar) after recording the above workflow. You will notice below steps in Keyword View.

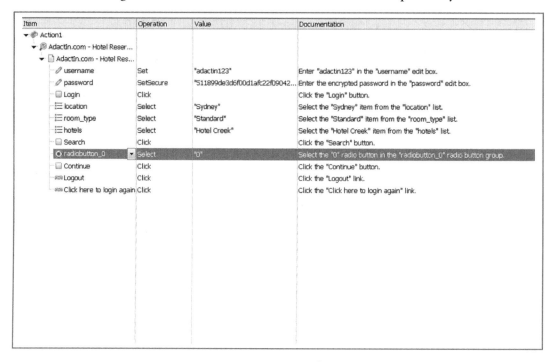

Figure 7-2 – Keyword View

2. Confirm correct playback of the script.

3. Save the script from **File → Save Checkpoint**.

4. Select the step in Keyword View where user selects Radio button in Select Hotel Screen.

5. Also select **Active Screen** Pane (if it is not already open you can open it from View → Active Screen). You will see Select Hotel Screen with highlight on Radio button.

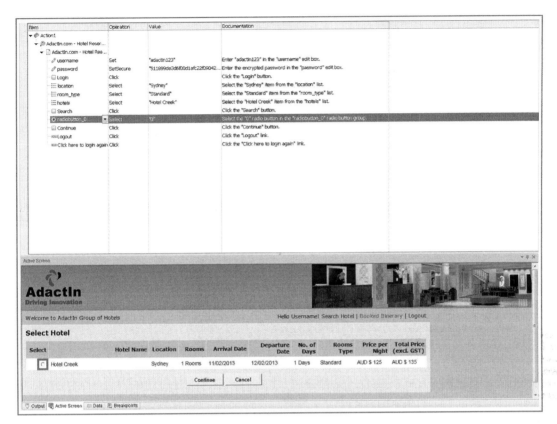

Figure 7-3 – Keyword View with Active Screen view

6. Go to **Active Screen**, and put the mouse cursor on top of "Sydney" **Location** which we need to Verify, **Right click** and Select **Insert Standard Checkpoint**.

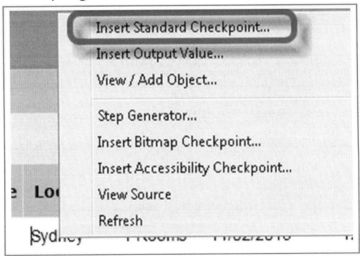

Figure 7-4 – Insert Standard Checkpoint

7. In **Object Selection** dialog box, make sure you see **Location_0** object. Select the object and press **OK**.

Figure 7-5 – Object Selection Dialog Box

8. In **Checkpoint properties** dialog box, select Property **Value**. You will see the property value after moving the vertical scroll bar in the dialog box. Make sure correct expected Value 'Sydney' is entered.

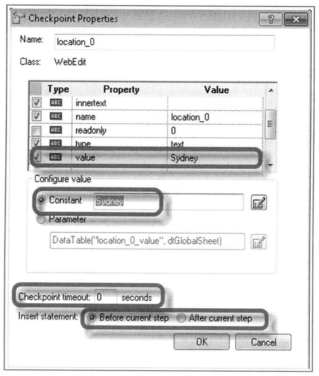

Figure 7-6 – Checkpoint Properties Dialog Box

In the above dialog box, if you would want to change your expected value, you can change it in the Constant field.

Checkpoint Timeout: This is the time UFT is going to wait if it does not find expected value. After timeout value if expected value is still not found, checkpoint will fail.

Insert Statement: You can choose to insert the checkpoint step before the current selected step in Keyword View (which in our case is selection of the Radio button) or after the current select step. It usually would depend on the test case we are trying to automate.

9. Uncheck other Properties in the dialog box for which we do not need to verify results. In our example, we just need **value** property.

Note: We can also verify multiple properties in one checkpoint itself by selecting multiple properties.

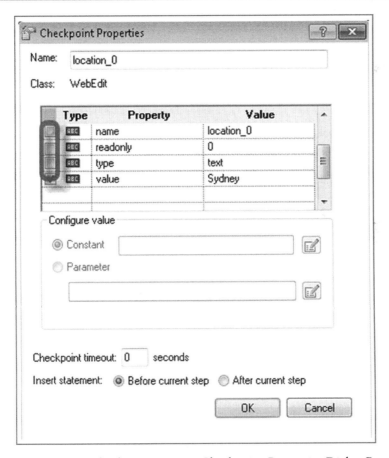

Figure 7-7 – Uncheck properties in Checkpoint Properties Dialog Box

De-select other properties except Value property in above dialog.

10. Press **OK** button.

11. Verify Checkpoint Step has been added in the script before Radio button selection.

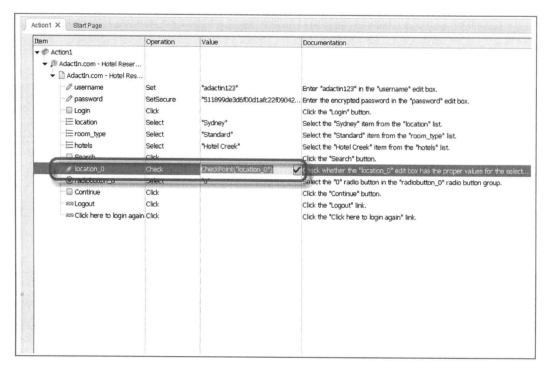

Figure 7-8 – Checkpoint Inserted

12. Save the Script using **File → Save.**

> Note: It is possible to drag the checkpoint to change the location of the checkpoint. Simply select checkpoint step, and drag it to place after Radio button_0 step.

7.4 Editing and Renaming the Checkpoint

Once saved, it is still possible to edit the checkpoint with expected result values and also rename the checkpoint. Let us see how:

1. Select the Checkpoint step in recently save script.

2. Right click and select **Checkpoint Properties**.

Figure 7-9 – Checkpoint Properties Option

3. In the **Checkpoint Properties** dialog box, rename checkpoint to SelectHotel_ Location_Checkpoint.

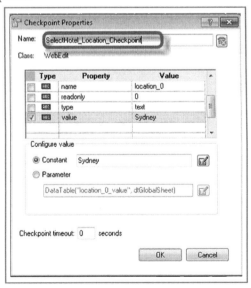

Figure 7-10 – Edit Checkpoint Name

Note: If required, you could also edit expected Result value.

4. Press **OK**.

5. Verify that Checkpoint Name get changed in the Keyword View.

7.5 Checkpoint Result Analysis

Let us now execute the script and look at the results:

1. Go to **Run** → **Run** and execute the script.

Note: Make sure application login window is open.

2. Open Results from **View** → **Last Run Results** and expand the result tree.

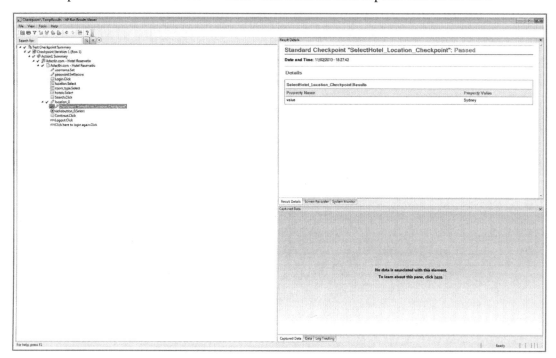

Figure 7-11 –Test Results

You will see the tick mark next to checkpoint that we have inserted and the end result shows as Passed.

3. Select the top of the result tree and you will see Current Run result as Passed.

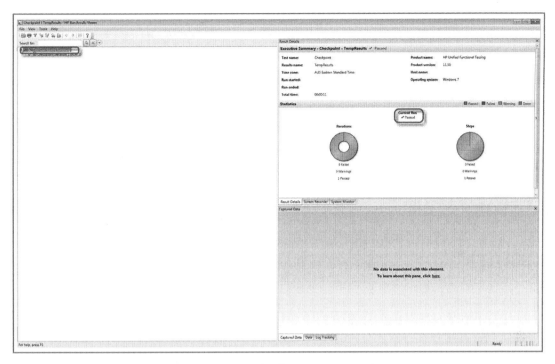

Figure 7-12 – Checkpoint Test Results

Exercise

1. Edit the Checkpoint to change the value to an incorrect value and see the results.

> Note: You will also see the snapshot of the application in a failed checkpoint.

7.6 Inserting Checkpoint during Recording

As mentioned earlier, checkpoint can be inserted both during and after recording. To insert a checkpoint during recording follow the below steps:

1. Create a new UFT GUI Test script.

2. Start recording.

3. Record steps up to point at where you want to insert checkpoint. Make sure your application is open and at the correct step for checkpoint insertion.

4. While in Recording mode, select **Design → Checkpoint → Standard Checkpoint**.

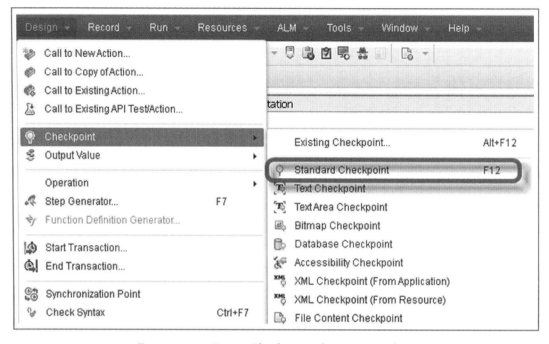

Figure 7-13 – Insert Checkpoint during Recording

Note: Standard Checkpoint might appear disabled if not in recording mode.

5. You will see a hand icon coming up. Move the hand icon to the top of the UI control (in our example Location field in Select a hotel page) and click.

Note: Be careful and hover over the hand icon on correct object in your application under test. As a good practice always keep application window in active state before trying to insert Checkpoint.

6. You will receive **Object Selection** dialog box. In this dialog select the correct object and click **OK**.

7. You will receive **Checkpoint Properties** dialog box, select the correct properties and provide expected results and Click **OK**.

8. Record the remaining script and stop recording.

9. Save your script.

10. Execute the script and analyse Test Results.

Inserting Checkpoint from Record Toolbar

Checkpoint can also be inserted, while recording using the Record Toolbar by clicking on Insert Checkpoint icon when in recording mode. QTP 11.0 and earlier version did not have this option.

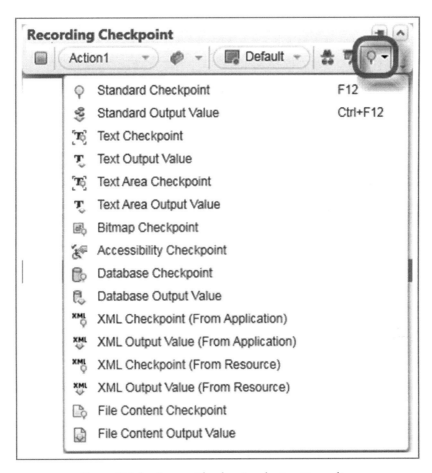

Figure 7-14 – Insert Checkpoint during Recording

8

Actions

Actions help divide your test into logical units, such as areas of key functionalities of the application. An action consists of its own test script, including all of the steps in that Action and any object definitions in its local object repository.

Each Action is stored together with the test in which you created it. You can insert a call to an Action that is stored within the test and also be able to call an external Action stored in another test.

When you open a test, you can choose to view the test flow (calls to actions) or you can view and edit the individual actions stored with your test.

Example

Let us consider an example here, where we can see effective use of actions:

While automating an accounting application, we found that the application had multiple components, like login, create account, sales, purchase, sales return, purchase return, and sales reports. Each component could have varied input values, and varied output values passed on to components down the chain. The functional testing team wanted to focus on end-to-end business processes from login to reports. So as an automation team, we created each of components as separate actions and called them sequentially based on business processes given to us by the test team. This greatly helped to achieve a wide test coverage using automation. This approach also utilized less time since our automation tests consisted of reusable components.

For every Action invoked in your test, UFT creates a corresponding Action Sheet in the data table so that you can enter data table parameters that are specific to that Action only.

By default, when you open a new test, one Action gets created for you. You can then, as required, insert as many Actions as you want.

Key objectives:

- Creating Reusable Actions.
- Calling Existing Actions.

8.1 Create Reusable Actions

Let us see how to create a reusable Action:

Test Scenario: User will login to the application, make a booking and logout.

We will record login, booking, and logout as separate Actions.

Pre-condition: Make sure application login page is available.

Business Action 1 - Login

1. Launch a new UFT GUI Test script and name is Login Script.

2. Start recording and record the following steps in application.

    a. Enter username

    b. Enter password

    c. Click Login

3. Stop recording and go to **Keyword View** of UFT.

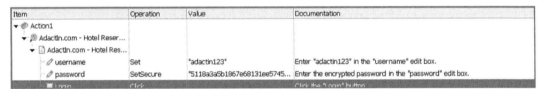

Item	Operation	Value	Documentation
▼ 🌀 Action1			
▼ 🌀 Adactin.com - Hotel Reser…			
▼ 📄 Adactin.com - Hotel Res…			
🖉 username	Set	"adactin123"	Enter "adactin123" in the "username" edit box.
🖉 password	SetSecure	"5118a3a5b1867e68131ee5745…	Enter the encrypted password in the "password" edit box.
🔲 Login	Click		Click the "Login" button

Figure 8-1 – Keyword View

4. Select Action1, and right click.

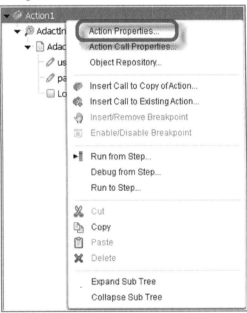

Figure 8-2 – Edit Action from Action Properties

5. Select **Action Properties** and Rename the Action to Login Action.

Figure 8-3 – Action Properties dialog Box

Also note that by default, Reusable Action checkbox is checked. This means that this Action is reusable and can be called from other scripts.

6. Click **OK** and then **Yes** on confirmation dialog box for renaming Action name.

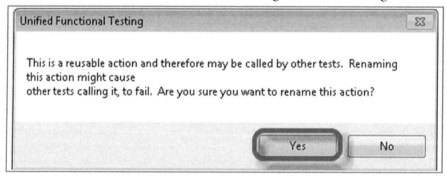

Figure 8-4 – UFT Message Pop-up

7. Select **File** → **Save** Login Script to save the script.

Business Action 2 – Booking

Pre-condition: Make sure user is already logged into the application.

8. Go to **File** → **New** → **Test** and create a new test and name it as Booking Script.

In this test we will be recording the entire booking process including Searching Hotel, Select hotel and Booking Hotel.

9. Record the following Steps.

    a. Search for Hotel

        i. Select a location, e.g., Sydney

        ii. Select number of rooms, e.g., 2

        iii. Select adults per room, e.g., 2

        iv. Click on Search button

    b. Select a Hotel

        i. Select one of the Hotel Radio buttons, e.g., select radio button next to Hotel Creek.

    c. Book a Hotel

        i. Enter First Name as "Test"

        ii. Enter Last Name as "Test"

        iii. Enter Address as "Test"

        iv. Enter 16-digit Credit Card number as "1212121212121212"

        v. Enter Credit Card type as "Mastercard"

        vi. Enter Expiry Month as "October"

        vii. Enter Expiry Year as "2015"

        viii. Enter CVV number as "111"

        ix. Click on Book Now

10. Once recording is finished **Stop** recording.

11. Select Action1, right click, select **Action properties** and rename the Action as "BookingAction".

12. Click **OK** on Action Properties dialog box and Yes on confirmation dialog box.

Item	Operation	Value	Documentation
▼ ⊚ BookingAction			
▼ ⊘ AdactIn.com - Search Hotel			
▼ ▢ AdactIn.com - Search H...			
⊟ location	Select	"Sydney"	Select the "Sydney" item from the "location" list.
⊟ room_nos	Select	"2 - Two"	Select the "2 - Two" item from the "room_nos" list.
⊟ adult_room	Select	"2 - Two"	Select the "2 - Two" item from the "adult_room" list.
▢ Search	Click		Click the "Search" button.
◉ radiobutton_2	Select	"2"	Select the "2" radio button in the "radiobutton_2" radio button group.
▢ Continue	Click		Click the "Continue" button.
⊘ first_name	Set	"Test"	Enter "Test" in the "first_name" edit box.
⊘ last_name	Set	"Test"	Enter "Test" in the "last_name" edit box.
⊘ address	Set	"Test"	Enter "Test" in the "address" edit box.
⊘ cc_num	Set	"1212121212121212"	Enter "1212121212121212" in the "cc_num" edit box.
⊟ cc_type	Select	"Master Card"	Select the "Master Card" item from the "cc_type" list.
⊟ cc_exp_month	Select	"October"	Select the "October" item from the "cc_exp_month" list.
⊟ cc_exp_year	Select	"2015"	Select the "2015" item from the "cc_exp_year" list.
⊘ cc_cvv	Set	"111"	Enter "111" in the "cc_cvv" edit box.
▢ Book Now	Click		Click the "Book Now" button.

Figure 8-5 – Keyword View

13. Save the script using **File → Save**.

Business Action 3 – Logout

Pre-condition: Make sure user is already logged into the application and Booking Confirmation page is visible.

14. Go to **File → New → Test** and create a new test and name it as LogoutScript.

In this test we will be recording Logout from the application.

15. Record the following steps

    a.   Click on Logout link

    b.   Click on link "Click here to login again"

16. Once recording is finished Stop recording.

17. Select Action1, right click, select **Action properties** and rename the Action as "LogoutAction".

18. Click **OK** on **Action Properties** dialog box and **Yes** on Confirmation dialog box. You will see script like the one given below in Keyword View.

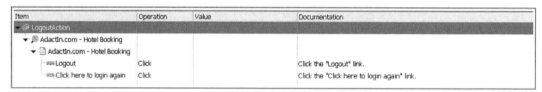

Item	Operation	Value	Documentation
▼ 🔗 LogoutAction			
▼ 🔗 Adactin.com - Hotel Booking			
▼ 🗋 Adactin.com - Hotel Booking			
⬛ Logout	Click		Click the "Logout" link.
⬛ Click here to login again	Click		Click the "Click here to login again" link.

Figure 8-6– Keyword View

19. Save the script using **File → Save**.

8.2 Call Existing Reusable Action in Script

Now that we have created reusable Actions, we will be using them all in one script.

Test Scenario: We will try to recreate the following test scenario and use previously created reusable Actions.

- Login
- Book a Hotel
- Logout

1. Launch a new GUI Test from **File → New → Test** and name it as CallingScript.

2. Go to **Design → Call to Existing Action**.

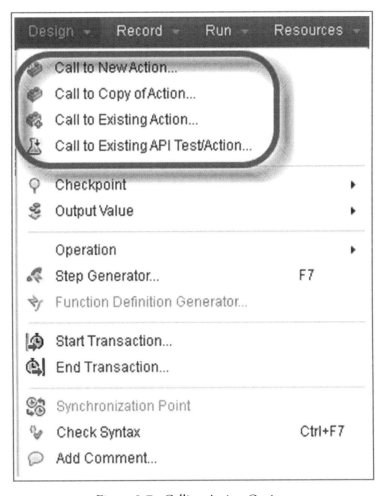

Figure 8-7– Calling Action Options

You will notice four possible options:

- **Call to New Action** – We can make a call to New Action within the same script.

- **Call to Copy of Action** – When you insert a call to a copy of an action into a test, the original action is copied in its entirety. This includes checkpoints, parameterization, the corresponding action tab in the data table, plus any defined action parameters. Once Action is copied, no linkage to original test takes place.

- **Call to Existing Action** - You can insert a call to a reusable Action that is stored in your current test (local action), or in any other test (external action). Inserting a call to an existing action is similar to linking to it. You can view the steps of the action in the action view, but you cannot modify them.

- **Call to Existing API Test/Action**– You can make a call to an Existing API Test or Action.

In our case, we will be using call to Existing Action and will select that option.

3. Browse to the LoginScript, which will have LoginAction.

Figure 8-8– Select Action dialog box

4. Click **Yes** on Relative path Conversion Pop-up.

Figure 8-9– Automatic Relative Path Conversion

5. You will see **Select Action** dialog and default **LoginAction** available.

Figure 8-10– Select Location of Action

6. Select **At the end of the Test** option to add this test at the end of the test and Click **OK**.

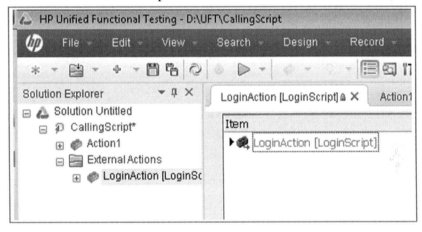

Figure 8-11– Solution Explorer view of Actions

7. Select **Action1** Pane and repeat the steps 2-6 for Booking Action

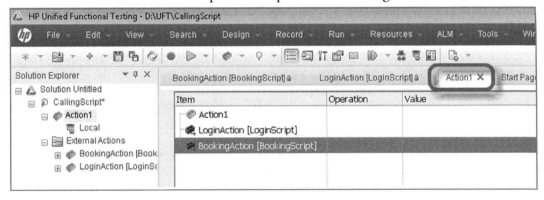

Figure 8-12– Multiple Actions added to Test

8. Repeat the steps 2-6 for Logout Action

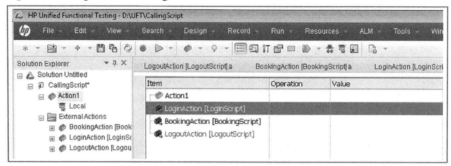

Figure 8-13– Multiple Actions added to Test

9. Select Action1, right click and **Delete** as we will not need Action 1

10. Verify the correct order of calling in Test Flow view (**View → Test Flow** View)

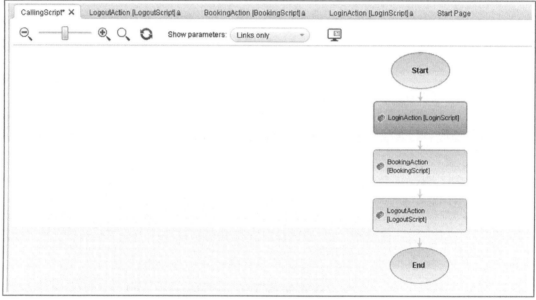

Figure 8-14– UFT Test Flow View

Note – You can drag/drop to change the order of called Actions.

11. Click on **Run** button and execute the Calling script, to verify successful playback. Make sure Login page is open in the application.

You will see that all the processes, Login, Booking and Logout are called and we can re-use all the actions created.

This exhibits the real advantage of using a modular framework, where we can re-use work done earlier, instead of re-creating the scripts again and again.

9

Multiple Choice Questions Set-1

Listed below are 10 multiple choice questions to test your understanding of the HP UFT this far. Please select the appropriate correct answer. The answer key and explanations are provided at the end of the test:

Start Questions

Q1. The following are the four main columns in the Keyword View

a) Item, Operation, Value, Comments

b) Item, Operation, Value, Documentation

c) Item, Operation, Property, Documentation

d) Number, Operation, Value, Documentation

Q2. Which pane contains information on open tests within UFT?

a) Output Pane

b) Properties Pane

c) Solution Explorer

d) UFT enables you to open and work on two tests at a time

Q3: The _____ are the highest level of the test hierarchy in the Keyword View.

a) Test

b) Steps

c) Call to Actions

d) Actions

Q4: In the Keyword View, you can also view properties for items such as checkpoints.

a) True

b) False

Q5: Object Spy can be found in?

a) Automation Menu

b) Tools Menu

c) Design Menu

d) Resource Menu

Q6: How can we add objects to the Local Object Repository?

a) While Recording

b) Using Add Objects feature in Object Repository

c) Using Active Screen

d) All of the above

Q7: From which option can you change Name of Action?

a) Action Properties

b) Action Call Properties

c) File → Settings

d) Tools → Option

Q8: Which are the default add-ins which are installed with UFT?

a) Web, VB, Dot-Net

b) Web, Java, Active-X

c) Web, VB, Active-X

d) VB, Active-X, Java

Q9: What are the different parameter types possible in UFT?

a) DataTable, Constant Number, Environment

b) DataTable, Random Number, Environment

c) Random Number, Environment, DataPool

d) Random Number, DataTable, User Variable

Q10: How can we insert a standard checkpoint in UFT?

a) From Active Screen

b) During Recording

c) Both of the above

d) None of the above

Answers

Q1. Answer: b

Explanation: Go to Keyword View and check the column names, which are Item, Operation, Value, and Documentation.

Q2. Answer: c

Explanation: In solution explorer user can see all open tests loaded within UFT.

Q3. Answer: d

Explanation: Action is the highest level in Keyword View. Go to Keyword View and you can expand or collapse an Action. Note that other views like solution explorer pane have test as the highest level.

Q4. Answer: a

Explanation: You can right click on a checkpoint and select checkpoint properties. So yes, you can view properties for items such as checkpoints.

Q5. Answer: b

Explanation" Object Spy can be found in Tools → Object Spy.

Q6. Answer: d

Explanation: Objects can be added to Object Repository using all the above methods.

Q7. Answer: a

Explanation: If you select Action, right click, and select Action properties, you can change Action name.

Q8. Answer: c

Explanation: Default Add-ins with UFT install are Web, VB, and Active-X. If need be, during installation of UFT, you can select and install other add-ins such as Java, Dot-net, and more.

Q9. Answer: b

Explanation: During parameterization, if you open Value Configuration Options dialog box, you could select anyone from 3 options in parameter field which are DataTable, Random Number, and Environment.

Q10. Answer: c

Explanation: Checkpoint can be inserted both from Active screen and during Recording.

 ❧

10

Working with Shared Repository

Introduction

We now know how UFT works as a tool, and recognizes objects based on object properties. When we perform recording, objects get added to the local object repository. For instance, when we login, username, and password objects get added to our local object repository. Now let us think, if we have more than 200 UFT scripts automated, these objects would be duplicated in each of these scripts. This means we are redundantly duplicating these objects in our scripts.

The problem does not end here. What if due to business requirements, the developer changes the property of these objects? This would result in all our 200 scripts failing. In order to fix this issue, we will need to go to each and every script, and change its local repository. This can be a nightmare to maintain!

A better solution would be if we kept all the required objects in an external shared location and all the scripts could just use these shared location objects. This will certainly avoid redundancy. Also, if any object changes, we would only need to change the object once and the script will be up and running again.

Example

At one of our clients, where we had to implement automation, we were given 100 existing automation scripts created using QTP/UFT. We were told script used to work 3 months earlier, but now, they fail on new builds. We were asked to fix the scripts. Guess what we found? All the scripts were using local object repository. When we identified the objects that were causing the script to fail, we discovered that the same object was used in all 100 scripts. So the object had to be modified at least 100 times as it was being used in all the scripts. But there were at least 100 objects, which had changed. Adding to this, they informed us that UI changes were still happening and that the objects will change again. Our recommendation to them was to hold on and to re-do the scripts using shared object repository. The advice stemmed from the fact that the same effort invested now would be required again when we get a new application build, with updated objects. Yes, it did mean that most of the previous efforts already made had been wasted. But our re-scripting approach, using a shared object repository approach, ensured that scripts maintenance was future proofed.

In this chapter we will discuss how to create and add objects to shared object repository, and how to maintain the shared object repository.

Key objectives:

- Create and add objects to Shared Object Repository.
- Rename logical names of objects.
- Associate Shared Repository to script.
- Recording of script using Shared Repository.

10.1 Create and Add Objects to Shared Object Repository

In this section we will see how to create, and add objects to Shared Object Repository.

1. Go to **Resources → Object Repository Manager**.

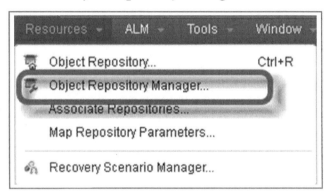

Figure 10-1 – Object Repository Manager Menu

2. You will see Object Repository Manager Dialog box opens up

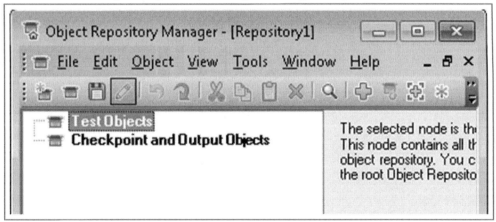

Figure 10-2 – Object Repository Manager (ORM) Dialog

Note: We will create/modify shared object repository using Object Repository manager.

As a next step, we will now add objects which we will use during our recording sessions, to the Shared Object Repository.

Note: Make sure your test application is open in the background and the Login page is open.

3. Click on **New Repository** button.

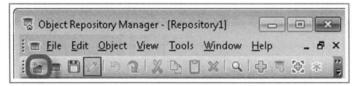

Figure 10-3 – Create new Object Repository

Note: We will be adding an object to the new Shared Repository. Later in the exercise, we will save this Shared Repository.

4. Click on **Add Objects** icon.

Figure 10-4 – Add Objects to Repository

5. This will give hand icon, which we need to place on that application object which we want to add to our shared OR. Place this **hand icon** on username field of Login page of our application. You will get an Object Selection dialog box.

Figure 10-5 – Add to Repository dialog

> Note: Make sure to click on Edit field where username is entered, and not on the label 'Username' in the application. Also, note that in the above dialog, you can correctly see the object you want to add. In our example, it is 'username' of Class WebEdit.

6. Verify that the object you want to add is highlighted and selected. Click **OK.**

7. Check that object username gets added to our Shared Repository.

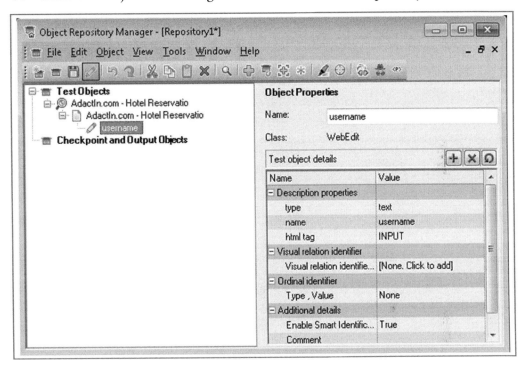

Figure 10-6 – Object added to Shared Object Repository

8. Similarly, add all the objects you will use for your application testing into shared object repository (manually browse through the application to add all objects to be used during recording). See below complete shared object repository.

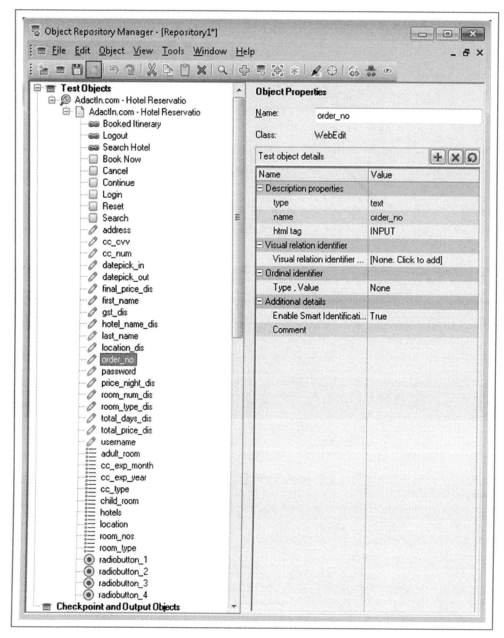

Figure 10-7 – Objects added to Shared Object Repository

9. Click on **Save** Button to Save the Repository in your UFT Folder with name "SharedOR.tsr".

Figure 10-8 – Save Button in ORM

10. Note the extension of Shared Repository file which is ".tsr".

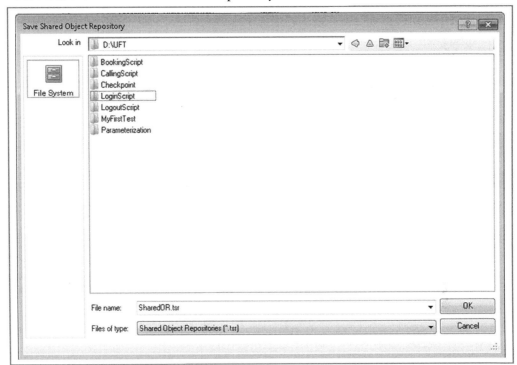

Figure 10-9 – Save Shared Repository

11. Click **OK** and close Object Repository Manager and Shared OR.

10.2 Renaming Added Test Objects

Many times, in applications, specifically the ones which are not coded using best coding practices, UI controls would have property values associated with them which are not very descriptive with proper explanations,. In cases like these, we would need to rename logical names of those objects to make our objects in the UFT script more readable and user friendly.

So the next step is to learn how to rename test objects so that objects added are more descriptive and a true reflection of what functionality they represent in the application.

Let us see how to rename added Test Object.

1. Open your shared OR which we just created in last exercise in Object Repository Manager (**Resources → Object Repository Manager**).

2. You will notice the Object Repository is in Read Only mode.

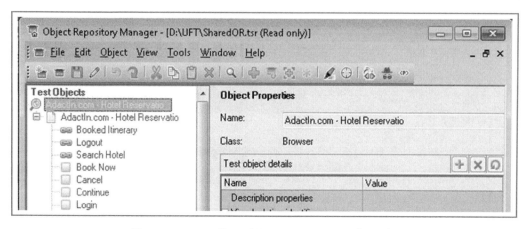

Figure 10-10 – Shared Repository in Read Mode

3. To activate editable mode, Click on **Enable Editing** button. You will notice that you can now edit the objects in Object Repository Manager.

Figure 10-11– Enable Editing

> **Note:** When we are working in a team environment where there are multiple automation testers working in the same team, you would usually keep the shared repository on a network drive. In order to prevent multiple users being able to open and edit the shared repository as the same time, it is essential to have the enable editing option. Otherwise, there can be conflict while saving and any one of the users editing the Object Repository can lose their changes. This is very similar to how Microsoft Excel Workbooks behave where two users cannot open and work on the same Excel sheet at the same time.

4. You will notice that Browser and Page title look incomplete. It is"AdactIn.com - Hotel Reservatio", instead of "AdactIn.com - Hotel Reservation".

5. Now let us rename the Logical Name of Browser and Page. Select the **Browser Object**, which is the topmost object in the tree.

6. In right pane in **Name** field, rename the object.

7. Click on **File → Save.**

8. Now select Child Object **Page** "AdactIn.com - Hotel Reservatio" and rename the logical name and save the changes.

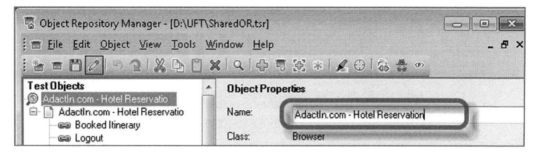

Figure 10-12– Rename Browser Object

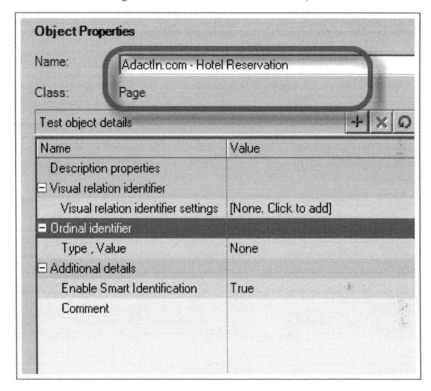

Figure 10-13– Rename Page

9. Save and Close Object Repository and Shared Object Repository.

So in this section, we have leant how to rename objects in a Shared Object Repository.

10.3 Associating Shared Repository with Script

We are only half way through now. We have Shared Repository created, but we still haven't used it yet. To use it, we need to associate it with the script.

Let us see how to associate Shared OR with a script.

1. Go to **File → New → Test** and create a new GUI test script and name is ORMScript.

2. Go to **Resource → Associate Repositories…**

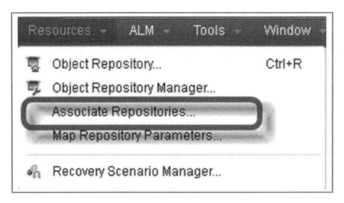

Figure 10-14– Associate Repositories

3. In the Associate Repositories dialog, click on **+ icon** to add path of Shared Object Repository.

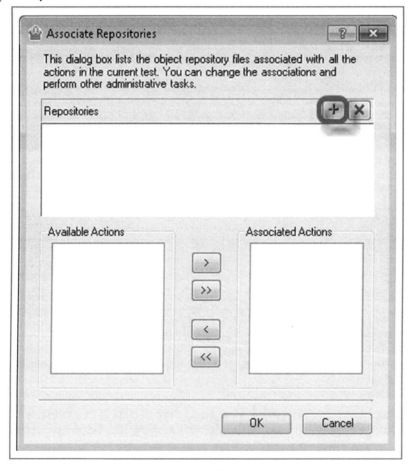

Figure 10-15– Add Repository

4. Select the Shared Repository file we created in last section and click **OK**.

5. Select Action1 in Available Actions and Click on the **">"** to move it to **Associated Actions**.

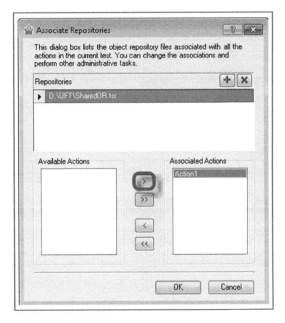

Figure 10-16– Associate Actions

6. Click **OK**.

7. Let us now verify in Object Repository that Shared Repository is visible. So go to **Resources → Object Repository** and open Object Repository.

Note: Object Repository is available within UFT GUI Test and shows all the objects, both local and shared. Object Repository Manager is used to maintain shared object repository, and is accessible from Resources menu. If an object is defined in both local and shared repository, the object in local repository gets preference.

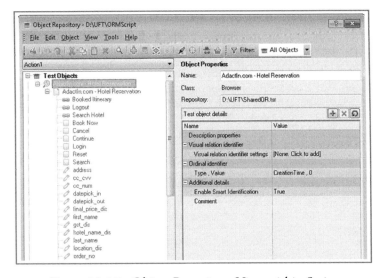

Figure 10-17– Object Repository View within Script

You will notice that all our objects, which we have added in shared object repository are visible.

8. In **Filter** dropdown, select SharedOR.tsr.

Figure 10-18– Object Repository Filter

You will see all objects we have added in shared object repository.

9. In Filter dropdown, select "Local Objects". You will notice that there is no local Object Repository.

10.4 Recording a Script with Shared OR

Now let us start recording our complete workflow again.

1. Launch IE browser, Enter URL, and perform the following steps.

    a. Login (Use the username/password with which you have registered earlier).

    b. Search for Hotel

        i. Select a location, e.g., Sydney

        ii. Select number of rooms, e.g., 2

        iii. Select adults per room, e.g., 2

        iv. Click on Search button

    c. Select a Hotel

        v. Select one of the Hotel Radio buttons, e.g., select radio button next to Hotel Creek.

    d. Book a Hotel

        vi. Enter First Name

        vii. Enter Last Name

        viii. Enter Address

        ix. Enter 16-digit Credit Card number

        x. Enter Credit Card type

        xi. Enter Expiry Month

        xii. Enter Expiry Year

        xiii. Enter CVV number

        xiv. Click on Book Now

e. After you see Booking confirmation page, click on Logout and go back to login page.

f. Stop Recording (by clicking on Stop Recording button in Record toolbar) after recording the above workflow.

2. Once the script is recorded verify the steps.

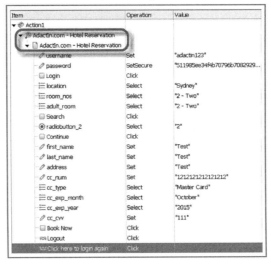

Figure 10-19– Objects used from Shared Repository

Note that Browser name and Page name are same, as we have setup in the Shared Object repository.

3. Open Object Repository from **Resources → Object Repository**.

4. Verify Local Object Repository is still empty by selecting Local Objects in Filter.

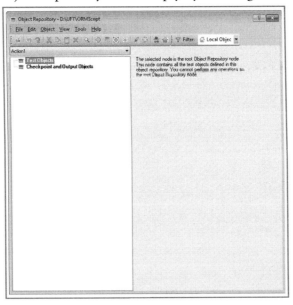

Figure 10-20– Local Objects in Object Repository

Note that when we recorded, all objects we used were from Shared OR and no local objects were added.

5. Run the script from **Run → Run** for verifying correct execution.

6. Save the script from **File → SaveAs** with name "ORMScript".

> **Note:** You can also use Object Repository Manager for merging two shared repositories using Object Repository Merge Tool (**Object Repository Manager → Tools → Object Repository Merge Tool**). In a team environment you might need to use Object Repository Merge tool to merge repositories created by different team members. The detailed use of merge tool is not included as part of the scope of this book.

Exercise

1. Rename all the objects, which you have added in Shared Repository with prefix of the object type it belongs to (for eg., Username which is a WinEdit object should be Ed_Username, or Book Now WinButton should be Btn_BookNow).

2. Create a new script and associate your updated repository with your new script.

3. Record the steps as we did in the chapter and verify that updated object logical names are being shown in the script. Also, confirm that your local Object Repository is empty after recording.

❧

11

UFT Editor View

As an alternative to using the Keyword View, if you prefer to work with VBScript statements, you can choose to work with your tests in Editor View. There are also a few advanced features of UFT for which you will need to use Editor View. For example, if you would need to connect to a database and run a query or read from a text file which stores data, you need to use Editor View.

You can move between the two views as you wish, by selecting the Editor View or Keyword View from View menu.

The Editor View displays the same steps and objects as the Keyword View, but in a different format:

- In the Keyword View, UFT displays information about each step and shows the object hierarchy in an icon-based table.

- In the Editor View, UFT displays each step as a VBScript line or statement. In object-based steps, the VBScript statement defines the object hierarchy.

Example

We were automating a VC++ application, where the logs were generated in text file format on the local machine. For our test we had to read those log files (text files) and verify that the events have been logged correctly. So we used UFT Editor View and VBScript statements to manually write code to read and parse text files.

To take another example, in many instances, we exercise a lot of effort in maintaining our existing automation scripts. If there is functional, workflow or test data changes, it might be more convenient to use the Editor View to perform the fixes. (Keep in mind that these types of changes can still be done from Keyword View, but you might find it easier to do it in Editor View once you understand its usage).

Key objectives:

- How Keyword View corresponds to Editor View.
- Auto completion of syntax using intellisense in Editor View.
- Automatic generation of code without recording.

11.1 How Editor View Corresponds to Keyword View

Each line of VBScript in the Editor View represents a step in the test.

Let us see in the example below:

1. Open your UFT GUI Test MyFirstTest. Go to **View** menu and select **Keyword View** (If you have already selected Keyword View you will see Editor View. Either Editor or Keyword View will be displayed at a time).

2. You would see below statements in Keyword View.

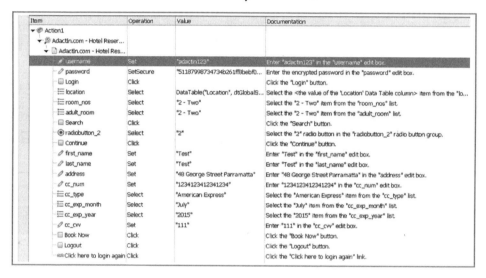

Figure 11-1 – Keyword view

3. Click on the **View** → **Editor** and see the statements in Editor View.

Figure 11-2 – View Editor

```
1   Browser("AdactIn.com - Hotel Reservatio").Page("AdactIn.com - Hotel Reservatio").WebEdit("username").Set "adactin123"
2   Browser("AdactIn.com - Hotel Reservatio").Page("AdactIn.com - Hotel Reservatio").WebEdit("password").SetSecure "51187998734734b261ff8bebf0e3335c50cb236efa7fa9637b6a"
3   Browser("AdactIn.com - Hotel Reservatio").Page("AdactIn.com - Hotel Reservatio").WebButton("Login").Click
4   Browser("AdactIn.com - Hotel Reservatio").Page("AdactIn.com - Hotel Reservatio").WebList("location").Select DataTable("Location", dtGlobalSheet)
5   Browser("AdactIn.com - Hotel Reservatio").Page("AdactIn.com - Hotel Reservatio").WebList("room_nos").Select "2 - Two"
6   Browser("AdactIn.com - Hotel Reservatio").Page("AdactIn.com - Hotel Reservatio").WebList("adult_room").Select "2 - Two"
7   Browser("AdactIn.com - Hotel Reservatio").Page("AdactIn.com - Hotel Reservatio").WebButton("Search").Click
8   Browser("AdactIn.com - Hotel Reservatio").Page("AdactIn.com - Hotel Reservatio").WebRadioGroup("radiobutton_2").Select "2"
9   Browser("AdactIn.com - Hotel Reservatio").Page("AdactIn.com - Hotel Reservatio").WebButton("Continue").Click
10  Browser("AdactIn.com - Hotel Reservatio").Page("AdactIn.com - Hotel Reservatio").WebEdit("first_name").Set "Test"
11  Browser("AdactIn.com - Hotel Reservatio").Page("AdactIn.com - Hotel Reservatio").WebEdit("last_name").Set "Test"
12  Browser("AdactIn.com - Hotel Reservatio").Page("AdactIn.com - Hotel Reservatio").WebEdit("address").Set "48 George Street Parramatta"
13  Browser("AdactIn.com - Hotel Reservatio").Page("AdactIn.com - Hotel Reservatio").WebEdit("cc_num").Set "1234123412341234"
14  Browser("AdactIn.com - Hotel Reservatio").Page("AdactIn.com - Hotel Reservatio").WebList("cc_type").Select "American Express"
15  Browser("AdactIn.com - Hotel Reservatio").Page("AdactIn.com - Hotel Reservatio").WebList("cc_exp_month").Select "July"
16  Browser("AdactIn.com - Hotel Reservatio").Page("AdactIn.com - Hotel Reservatio").WebList("cc_exp_year").Select "2015"
17  Browser("AdactIn.com - Hotel Reservatio").Page("AdactIn.com - Hotel Reservatio").WebEdit("cc_cvv").Set "111"
18  Browser("AdactIn.com - Hotel Reservatio").Page("AdactIn.com - Hotel Reservatio").WebButton("Book Now").Click
19  Browser("AdactIn.com - Hotel Reservatio").Page("AdactIn.com - Hotel Reservatio").WebButton("Logout").Click
20  Browser("AdactIn.com - Hotel Reservatio").Page("AdactIn.com - Hotel Reservatio").Link("Click here to login again").Click
```

Figure 11-3 – Editor View

4. Now let us try to map lines in Keyword View with lines in Editor View.

```
1   Browser("AdactIn.com - Hotel Reservatio").Page("AdactIn.com - Hotel Reservatio").WebEdit("username").Set "adactin123"
2   Browser("AdactIn.com - Hotel Reservatio").Page("AdactIn.com - Hotel Reservatio").WebEdit("password").SetSecure "51187998734734b261ff8bebf0e3335c50cb236efa7fa9637b6a"
3   Browser("AdactIn.com - Hotel Reservatio").Page("AdactIn.com - Hotel Reservatio").WebButton("Login").Click
```

Figure 11-4 – Keyword and Editor View comparison

The example above represents the login process. The hierarchy of the step enables you to see the type and name of the Browser, the type and name of the child objects of the Browser (Page and WebEdit), and the method performed on the object.

The table below explains how the different parts of the same step are represented in the Editor Vie

Editor View	Explanation
Browser("AdactIn.com - Hotel Reservatio")	The name of the current parent object Browser is "AdactIn.com - Hotel Reservatio".
Page("AdactIn.com - Hotel Reservatio").	The name of the current parent object Page is "AdactIn.com - Hotel Reservatio".
WebEdit("username")	The object type is WebEdit; the name of the edit box on which the operation is performed is "username".
Set	The method performed on the edit box is **Set**.
"adactin123"	Data entered into the WebEdit field.

In the Editor View, an object's description is displayed in parentheses, following the object type. For all objects stored in the object repository, the object's logical name is as used in the script. In the following example, the object type is Browser, and the logical name is "AdactIn.com - Hotel Reservatio":

Browser("AdactIn.com - Hotel Reservatio")

> Note: Note that though object's logical name is used in the script, the actual object properties are stored in the object repository.

> **Note:** Test object and method names are not case sensitive.

The objects in the object hierarchy are separated by a dot. In the following example, Browser and Page are two separate objects in the same hierarchy:

Browser("AdactIn.com - Hotel Reservatio").Page("AdactIn.com - Hotel Reservatio")

The operation (method) performed on the object is always displayed at the end of the statement, followed by any values associated with the operation. In the example below, "Set" is the method performed on object WebEdit("username") and "adactin123" is the data input for **Set** method.

Browser("AdactIn.com - Hotel Reservatio").Page("AdactIn.com - Hotel Reservatio"). WebEdit("username").Set "adactin123"

UFT relates to your application in terms of the objects in it. The steps you add to your test correspond to the operations, performed on the objects in your application.

The objects in UFT are based on the technical environment (Java, Dot-Net, SAP etc). By default, UFT supports objects from the standard Windows environments. You can work with additional environments by loading the relevant UFT add-ins in the Add-in Manager when you open UFT.

Most objects have corresponding special methods. For example, the **Back** method is associated with the **Browser** object, **Select** method for WinComboBox and **Set** for WinEdit.

For a complete list of objects and their associated methods and properties, choose **Help > HP Unified Functional Testing Help**, and open the **Object Model Reference for GUI Testing** from the Contents tab.

Exercise

Write Editor View statement for the following Keyword View steps:

Item	Operation	Value
▼ 🗐 Action1		
▼ 🔍 AdactIn.com - Hotel Reser...		
▼ 🗋 AdactIn.com - Hotel Res...		
✎ username	Set	"adactin123"
✎ password	SetSecure	"51187998734734b261ff8bebf0...
🗌 Login	Click	
☰ location	Select	DataTable("Location", dtGlobalS...
☰ room_nos	Select	"2 - Two"
☰ adult_room	Select	"2 - Two"
🗌 Search	Click	

Figure 11-5 – Exercise

For answers, you can see Editor View of your MyFirstTest.

> **Note:** You can encrypt the password using UFT Utility, which is available All Programs → HP Software → HP Unified Functional Testing → Tools → Password Encoder.

11.2 Manually Type the Steps in Editor View

You can generate statements in the following ways:

- You can manually type VBScript statements that use methods to perform operations.
- You can use the Step Generator to add steps that use methods and functions. We cover this in next section.

When you type in the Editor View, IntelliSense (the statement completion feature included with UFT) enables you to select the test object (Editor View (tests) only), method, property, or collection (tests only) for your statement from a drop down list and view the relevant syntax.

The **Statement Completion** option is enabled by default. You can disable or enable this option in the editor options dialog box.

When the **Statement Completion** option is enabled:

- If you type an object followed by an open parenthesis (, for example, Page (, UFT displays a list of all test objects of this type in the object repository. If there is only one object of this type in the object repository, UFT automatically enters its name in quotes after the open parenthesis.
- If you type a period after a test object in a statement, UFT displays a list of the relevant test objects (Editor View only), methods, properties, collections, and registered functions that you can add after the object you typed.

- If you type the name of a method or property, UFT displays a list of available methods and properties. Pressing CTRL+SPACE automatically completes the word if there is only one option, or highlights the first method or property (alphabetically) that matches the text you typed.

- If you type the name of a method or property, UFT displays the syntax for it, including its mandatory and optional arguments. When you add a step that uses a method or property, you must define a value for each mandatory argument associated with the method or property.

- If you press CTRL+SPACE, UFT displays a list of the relevant test objects (tests only), methods, properties, collections (tests only), VBScript functions, user-defined functions, VBScript constants, and utility objects that you can add. This list is displayed even if you typed an object that has not yet been added to the object repository. If the test contains a function, or is associated with a function library, the functions are also displayed in the list.

- If you use the **Object** property in your statement and if the object data is currently available in the Active screen (tests only) or the open application, UFT displays native methods, and properties of any run time object in your application.

To generate a statement using statement completion in the Editor View:

1. Confirm that the **Statement completion** option is selected
   (**Tools > View Options > General** tab).

2. Perform the following:
   - If you are working in the Editor View, type an object followed by an open parenthesis. If there is only one object of this type in the object repository, UFT automatically enters its name in quotes after the open parenthesis. If more than one object of this type exists in the object repository, UFT displays them in a list.

3. Double-click an object in the list or use the arrow keys to choose an object, and press ENTER. UFT inserts the object into the statement.

4. Perform the following:
   - If you are working in the Editor View, type a period (.) after the object on which you want to perform the method.

5. Type a period (.) after the object description, for example ("username"). UFT displays a list of the available methods and properties for the object.

   Tip: You can press CTRL+Space or choose **Edit > Advanced > Complete Word** after a period, or after you have begun to type a method or property name. UFT automatically completes the method or property name if only one method or property matches the text you typed. If more than one method or property matches the text, the first method or property (alphabetically) that matches the text you typed is highlighted.

6. Double-click a method or property in the list or use the arrow keys to choose a method or property and press ENTER. UFT inserts the method or property into the

statement. If the method or property contains arguments, UFT displays the syntax of the method or property in a tooltip.

Tip: You can also place the cursor on any method or function that contains arguments and press CTRL+SHIFT+SPACE or choose **Edit > Advanced > Argument Info** to display the statement completion (argument syntax) tooltip for that item.

7. Enter the method arguments after the method according to the displayed syntax.

> **Note:** After you have added a step in the Editor View, you can view the new step in the Keyword View. If the statement that you added in the Editor View contains syntax errors, UFT displays the errors in the Information pane when you select the Keyword View.

11.3 Using Step Generator

Apart from typing steps or using recording, another way to add steps in UFT is to use step generator.

Let us try to write a simple script to login to the application. Make sure that login window is open and visible.

> **Note:** You should know the manual steps that you would need to perform on your application to effectively use step generator.

1. Create a new UFT GUI Test script by selecting **File → New → Test** and name it StepGenerator.

2. Go to **Resources → Associate Repositories** and select the Shared Repository which we had created earlier in Shared Repository chapter.

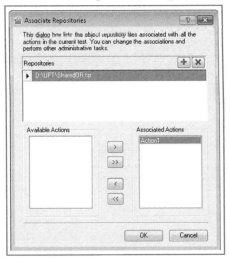

Figure 11-6 – Associate Repositories

3. Close the Associate Repository dialog box by clicking **OK**.

4. Go to **Design → Step Generator** which will open Step Generator Dialog Box.

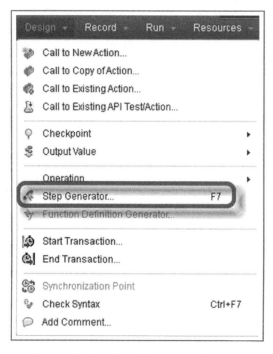

Figure 11-7 – Step Generator selection

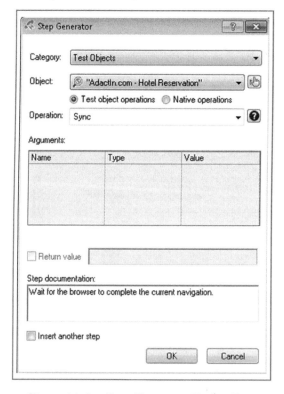

Figure 11-8 – Step Generator Dialog Box

Category – Shows which category of step you want to insert. It can be TestObjects, functions or utility functions.

5. In the Category Drop down select **Test Objects** options.

Possible Options

Test Objects – These are the objects, which are stored in your object repository. Choose this option if you want to insert your application based functional steps into the script.

Utility Objects – These are utility objects provided by UFT to enhance the scripts. Use this option to use objects like Data table, Reporter etc. (We will discuss these objects in later chapters).

Functions – These include local script function, external functions or VBScript functions (We will discuss about functions in later chapters).

6. In the Object Option, click on **colored square** icon which will open Object Repository view. We will use this view to add steps into the script.

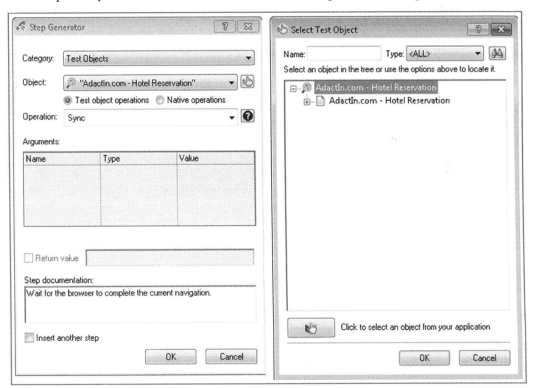

Figure 11-9 – Select Test Object

7. Click on the **Plus** icon and expand the object hierarchy to locate the correct object which is our case is username field.

Figure 11-10 – Expand Test Object Hierarchy

8. Select username object and Click **OK**.

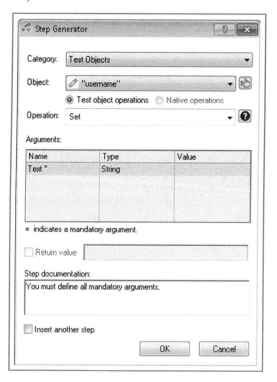

Figure 11-11 – Test Object Select

9. In the Operations field, select Operation "**Set**" (by default this operation is selected). Use this field to select what operation you would like to perform on the object.

10. You will now notice that Text field in Argument is mandatory. So Click on the **Value** column and enter Username value.

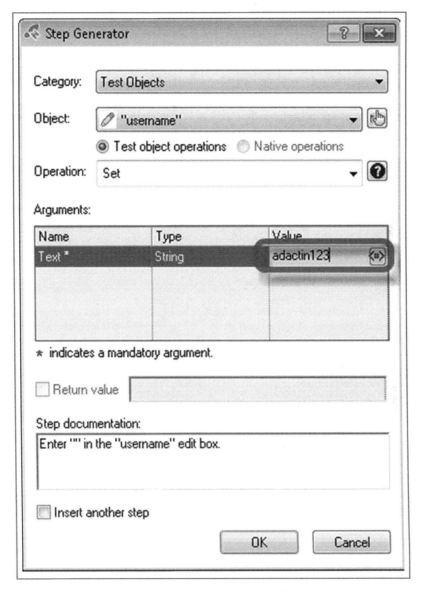

Figure 11-12 – Enter Input data

11. Check the checkbox **Insert another step** (OK button changes to Insert button) as you will add more steps and click **Insert**.

12. You will notice that the line below will be added in the script.

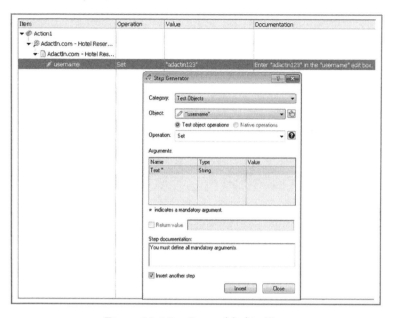

Figure 11-13 – Step added in Test

13. Now repeat the same steps by clicking on square icon (next to Object field dropdown) and select password object.

14. We can select Set as method for password and enter password value in Text field. Click **Insert** to add steps. We are deliberately not using SetSecure method, for password as in that case you would need to encrypt the password value.

> **Note:** You could actually encrypt the password using UFT Utility which is available All Programs → HP Software → HP Unified Functional Testing → Tools → Password Encoder.

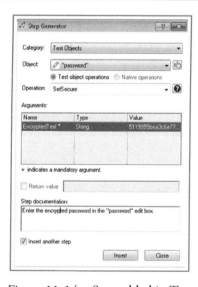

Figure 11-14 – Step added in Test

15. Repeat the steps for clicking on Login button. The default operation is click and there is no mandatory value.

16. Close the Step Generator dialog box once you have clicked on Login button.

17. You will see below lines of code in Editor View.

```
Browser("AdactIn.com - Hotel Reservation").Page("AdactIn.com - Hotel Reservation").WebEdit("username").Set "adactin123"
Browser("AdactIn.com - Hotel Reservation").Page("AdactIn.com - Hotel Reservation").WebEdit("password").SetSecure "5119955bea3c6e776b6bbdf4fc1c20473ccab796d8d00e80e7f6"
Browser("AdactIn.com - Hotel Reservation").Page("AdactIn.com - Hotel Reservation").WebButton("Login").Click
```

Figure 11-15– Editor View script

Note: Make sure to replace the password value to your password value.

18. Execute the script to verify successful playback.

> **Note:** Many Automation Testers use Step Generator to create their own scripts which is easy instead of just typing the steps.

Exercise

1. Recreate the steps of Booking Hotel workflow using Step Generator (It should give steps similar to recorded MyfirstTest.

2. Replay the script and confirm correct execution.

> **Note:** Do not forget to associate your shared repository with you test before you start using Step Generator.

೧

12

VBScript Fundamentals

VBScript is the scripting language used in UFT Editor View. We can write VBScript statements in UFT Editor View and execute them, making UFT very powerful. VBScript being a global language, we can find plenty of sample code on Google and use it in our UFT GUI script.

Example

Recently we automated some scenarios where we had to create an automation test report in a MS Word document format with snapshots of all application pages. We had to forward this document to the development and business team. We used VBScript (in UFT) and MS Word object model to easily accomplish this.

Using VBScript, we can interact with external third party applications (Word, Excel, PDF, Text file, Database), and write custom code in our script, which makes our script more intelligent and worthwhile.

Having said this, VBScript is still a very simple language. We do not use any complex pointers, data structures, exception handing blocks or object instantiation constructs. Many testers fear using complicated programming principles. This makes UFT a simple tool to use, not only for programmers but also for functional testers and business analysts.

Key objectives:

- VBScript Basics and data types.
- VBScript Conditional Statement, Loop Statements, Procedures.
- Commonly used VBScript string functions.
- Sample VBScript programs.

12.1 VBScript Basics and Data Types

What is VBScript?

- VBScript is a scripting language.
- A scripting language is a lightweight programming language.
- It is primarily used for client side scripting within html pages.
- VBScript is a light version of Microsoft's programming language, Visual Basic.

VB is different from VBScript. VB is a programming language with a full blown programming environment like integrated development environment and VBScript is a simpler scripting language, which is normally written in a text editor like notepad.

HP UFT acts as an editor for VBScript. Any VBScript code can be written in HP UFT editor view and executed. Using VBScript, we can read/write from excel sheets, text files, word documents, databases, and other external sources. It's important to understand that these are accomplished by the VBScript language and not by UFT. We can however find such read/write code snippets by doing a Google search and just copy pasting them in UFT editor view to execute the scripts.

Windows Script

VBScript interacts with a host of applications using Windows script. With windows script, browsers, and other host applications do not require special integration code for each scripting component. Windows script enables a host to compile scripts, obtain and call entry points, and manage the namespace available to the developer. Microsoft provides run time support for VBScript.

Data Types:

What is a Variable?

A variable is a name given to a location in memory, where some data used by a program is stored. You can refer to a variable by name to see or to change its value.

Variables can hold different types of data: numbers, characters, strings, and some special complex data. These categories are called data types.

VBScript keeps it simple. In VBScript there is only one data type "**Variant**". In this variant type, you can store numbers, characters, strings, boolean and other data types. Surely this makes things simpler!

For example: The books detail of a library, stores the id of the book, and name of the book and for storing these data sets it uses variables.

| book_id |
| book_name |

VBScript is a loosely typed language, which means you do not have to declare the variables before using them in your scripts.

Rules for Variable Names:

- Must begin with a letter
- Cannot contain a period (.)

- Cannot exceed 255 characters

Declaring Variables

- You can declare variables with the Dim, Public or the Private statement. For e.g.

Dim bookname
bookname= "Software Testing"

You can also declare variables by using its name in your script. For e.g.

bookname= "Test Automation"

However, the second method is not good practice because you can misspell the variable name later in your script. This can cause unexpected results when your script is running.

For example, on assigning the "bookname" variable to value "bikename", the script will automatically create a new variable called "bikename". To prevent your script from doing this, you can use the **Option Explicit** statement. When you use this statement, you will have to declare all your variables with the dim, public or private statement. Put the Option Explicit statement on the top of your script. Option Explicit makes the declaration of variables mandatory. For example:

Example

option explicit

dim bookname

bookname="Software Testing"

Array Variables

You can create a variable that can contain a series of values. This is called an array variable. The declaration of an array variable uses parentheses ( ) following the variable name. In the following example, an array containing 3 elements is declared:

dim marks(2)

We start at zero so this array contains 3 elements. This is a fixed-size array.

marks (0)= "100"
marks (1)= "70"
marks (2)= "50"

VBScript Constants

You create user-defined constants, in VBScript using the Const statement. Using the **Const** statement, you can create string or numeric constants with meaningful names and assign them literal values. For example:

Const address = "125/7 XYZ"

Const phone = "222222222"

12.2 VBScript Conditional Statements, Looping Statements and Procedures

Conditional Statements

Decision-making in programs is what programming is all about. You have to tell the program what to do at every step. Very often when you write code, you want to perform different actions for different decisions. You can use conditional statements in your code to a this.

In VBScript we have four conditional statements:

- **if statement** - use this statement if you want to execute a set of code when a condition is true.

- **if...then...else statement** - use this statement if you want to select one of two sets of lines to execute.

- **if...then...elseif statement** - use this statement if you want to select one of many sets of lines to execute.

- **select case statement** - use this statement if you want to select one of many sets of lines to execute.

Example:

```
if  i<5 Then msgbox "smaller"
```

If you want to execute **more than one** statement when a condition is true, you must put each statement on separate lines and end the statement with the keyword "End If":

```
if marks>80 Then
msgbox "Distinction"
i = i+1
end If
```

If you want to execute a statement if a condition is true and execute another statement if the condition is not true, you must add the "Else" keyword:

if marks>80 then
msgbox "Grade A"
else
msgbox "Grade B"
end If

Looping Statements

Very often we want the same steps of program to be repeatedly executed, for this we can use looping statements.

VBScript supports four types of looping statements:

- **For...Next statement** - runs statements a specified number of times.
- **For Each...Next statement** - runs statements for each item in a collection or each element of an array.
- **Do...Loop statement** - loops while or until a condition is true.
- **While...Wend statement** - executes a series of statements as long as a given condition is true.

Example:

For i=1 to 5

Msgbox(i)

Next

The **For** statement specifies the counter variable (**i**) and its start and end values. The **Next** statement increases the counter variable (**i**) by one.

> **Note:** I personally prefer to use For Next statement for looping as there is less scope of confusion at boundary values even though technically, we can use any of the looping statements.

VBScript Procedures

We need procedures so that we do not need to re-write or re-script common and repeatable component in our application (e.g. Login).

We have two kinds of procedures: The Subroutines and the Functions.

A Subroutine:

- Is a series of statements, enclosed by the Sub and End Sub statements.
- Can perform actions, but **does not return** a value.
- Can take arguments that are passed to it by a calling procedure.
- Without arguments, must include an empty set of parentheses ().

Sub sub1()
Msgbox("hello")
End Sub
or
Sub sub2(argument1,argument2)

End Sub

A Function procedure:

- Is a series of statements, enclosed by the Function and End Function statements.
- Can perform actions and **can return** a value.
- Can take arguments that are passed to it by a calling procedure.
- Without arguments, must include an empty set of parentheses ().

Function sum1()
A=10+20
Sum1=A
End Function

or

Function sum1(arg1,arg2)
Res=arg1+arg2
Sum1=Res
End Function

12.3 VBScript String Manipulation Functions

Find below a list of the most used VBScript string manipulation functions.

Note: Ones marked with * are very important ones.

Function	Description
InStr	*Returns the position of the first occurrence of one string within another. The search begins at the first character of the string
InStrRev	Returns the position of the first occurrence of one string within another. The search begins at the last character of the string
LCase	*Converts a specified string to lowercase
Left	Returns a specified number of characters from the left side of a string
Len	*Returns the number of characters in a string
LTrim	Removes spaces on the left side of a string
RTrim	Removes spaces on the right side of a string
Trim	*Removes spaces on both the left and the right side of a string
Mid	Returns a specified number of characters from a string
Replace	Replaces a specified part of a string with another string a specified number of times
Right	Returns a specified number of characters from the right side of a string
StrComp	Compares two strings and returns a value that represents the result of the comparison
StrReverse	Reverses a string
Ubound	*Returns the number of elements in an array
Split	*Splits the string based on delimiter and stores the result in an array
&	*Concatenates two strings

Note: Ones marked with * are very important ones.

Example:

InStr- Returns the position of the first occurrence of one string within another. The search begins at the first character of the string.

Syntax: InStr([optional] startpos, string, searchvalue, [optional] compare)

Parameter	Description
start	Optional. Specifies the starting position for each search. The search begins at the first character position (1) by default. This parameter is required if compare is specified
string1	Required. The string to be searched
string2	Required. The string expression to search for
compare	Optional. Specifies the string comparison to use. Default is 0 Can have one of the following values: 0 = vbBinaryCompare - Perform a binary comparison 1 = vbTextCompare - Perform a textual comparison

searchstring="this is an searchtext"

position=instr(1,searchstring, "is", 0)

Output: 6

Explanation - "is" starts at 6th position in the system

Replace

Syntax:replace(string, search, replacewith)

replace("HExxO","xx","LL")

Output:HELLO

Strcomp

Syntax:strcomp(string, search, replacewith)

Example: strcomp("Hello","Hello")
Output:0 (0 means the strings are identical)

Example 2: strcomp("Hello","Helloxxx")
Output:-1 (-1 means the value of "Hello" is smaller than "Helloxxx")

Example 3: strcomp("60","40")
Output:-1 (1 means the value "60" is higher than "40")

Ltrim - Removes spaces on the left side of a string

Syntax:Ltrim(string)

Example: ltrim("   HELLO")

Output:HELLO

Rtrim - Removes spaces on the right side of a string

Syntax:Rtrim(string)

Example: ltrim("HELLO   ")

Output:HELLO

Trim - Removes spaces on both the left and the right side of a string

Syntax: Trim(string)

Example: ltrim("   HELLO   ")

Output:HELLO

Strreverse -Reverses a string

Syntax: Strreverse(string)

Example:strreverse("HELLO")
Output:OLLEH

Mid - returns characters from the center of an string,

Syntax: mid(inputstring, startpos, lengh_of_the_output_string)

Example: mid("HELLO",2,3)

Output:ELL (beginning at character 2, 3 characters long)

Len - Returns the number of characters in a string

Syntax - Len(string)

Example

txt="This is a beautiful day!"
Len(txt)

Output: 24

Split - Splits the string based on delimiter and stores the result in an array

Syntax – Split (string, delimiter)

Example

txt="Split;a;string"
arrSplit = Split(txt, ":")

x = arrSplit (0)

y= arrSplit (1)

z= arrSplit(2)

Output:

x = Split

y = a

z = string

& - Concatenate Strings

String1 = "Hello"
String2 = "User"

String3 = String1 & String2

Output in String3:

"HelloUser"

12.4 Sample VBScript Programs

Note: Apostrophe is used to comment a statement in VBScript.

You can copy the programs below in UFT Editor View and execute them to view the output. *Please take care* while doing so, you might need to delete and add apostrophe (for Comments) again as existing ones might indicate syntax errors once copied to UFT Editor View.

1. String Reversal

'About Program - This program will get input from the user and reverse the string

'Comment - Get Input from User
sInputString = Inputbox("Enter the String:","String Reverse")

'Comment – Get Length of the string
iStringLength= Len(sInputString)

For i = 1 to iStringLength
' Mid will get one character at a time and by concatenating it with the Reversed string a string reversal is obtained

RevString = Mid(sInputString,i,1)&RevString

Next

Msgbox RevString

2. Fibonacci -

'About Program - This program shows series of fibonacci numbers in total, upto number specified by users. For instance, if users enter 6, 6 numbers of fibonacci series will be shown.

'By definition, the first two numbers in the Fibonacci sequence are 0 and 1 (alternatively, 1 and 1), and each subsequent number is the sum of the previous two.

'In mathematical terms, the sequence Fn of Fibonacci numbers, is defined by the recurrence relation.

'Comment - Get Input from User
sInputval=InputBox("enter a number","Fibonacci",0)

'Comment - Check if the number is blank and set it to zero to integer value

if(sInputval="") Then

   sInputval=0

else

   sInputval=cint(sInputval)

End if

dim temp1,temp2, temp3

   temp1=0

   temp2=1

   temp3=temp1+temp2

'Comment - Create a basic informational string and store in variable

   sReportString="The fibonacci series of a given number "&sInputval&" is :
"&vbnewline

   sReportString=sReportString &" "&temp1&" "&temp2

'Comment - Loop through based in input value to get all the fibonacci series numbers

   For i = 3 to sInputval

      sReportString=sReportString&" "&temp3

```
                temp1=temp2
                temp2=temp3
                temp3=temp1+temp2
                next
        msgbox sReportString
```

3. Sample Factorial Program

'About Program - In mathematics, the **factorial** of a non-negative integer *n*, denoted by *n!*, is the product of all positive integers less than or equal to *n*. For example,

'5! = 5*4*3*2*1 = 120

'Comment - Get Input from User
sInputValue=inputbox("Enter a number","Factorial",0)

'Comment - Check if the number is blank and set it to zero to integer value

if (sInputValue= "") Then

        sInputValue=0

else

        sInputValue=cint(sInputValue)

End if

        dim iCounter

        iCounter=1

        'Comment - Check if the number is <0 it is an invalid number

        if sInputValue<0 then

            msgbox "Invalid number"

        'Comment - Check if the number is 0 or 1 factorial value is 1

        elseif sInputValue=0 or sInputValue=1 then

            msgbox "The factorial of given number "&sInputValue&" is :
"&iCounter

        else

        'Comment - Check if the number is greater than 1 then calculate factorial

            for i=sInputValue to 2 step -1

$$iCounter=iCounter*i$$

next

msgbox "The factorial of given number "&sInputValue&" is :
"&iCounter

end if

Note: Please note that there can be multiple ways this program can be accomplished.

Exercise

1. Write a VBscript program, which will accept your first name, middle name (s), and last name and then reverse just first name, middle name, and last name.

For example:

Input String = "John Parker Smith"

Output String = "nhoJ rekraP htimS"

Note: Keep in consideration that a few people might have more than one word of middle name like "John Parker Dellar Smith". Avoid hard-coding it for 3-word names.

2. If you have a Input string which is in format "a=1;b=2;c=4;d:=9;" write a program to which if you input c it will return 4 (which is what c equals in the string). Assume and recreate you own string.

For example:

Search String (this is hard-code in program) : "a=1;b=2;c=4;d:=9;"

Input: d

Output: 9

13

Using Functions

In one of the previous sections, we discussed about making our scripts modular and reusable, which will save us maintenance effort and also help us improve productivity.

We could use Actions as a UFT feature to make our scripts and framework modular.

Another advanced way to make scripts modular will be to use functions. UFT allows users to create a separate function library, which can store all the functions. These functions can then be re-used in a different script.

For example, all our scripts will have to login to the application. Now, instead of recording login steps repeatedly in every script, if we keep an external login function, we can re-use that function in all our scripts.

Example

Let us see another practical example here:

At one of our client places, we were automating an investment banking application. As a first step of every test case, we had to create investment instruments after which we had to validate, and add details in later steps (we had more than 100 test cases for each instrument type). Creating an instrument was a tedious step with up to 50 field values to be entered. Based on the test scenario, input data would change. Now recording the steps of investment instrument creation in each and every script would have been a nightmare and time consuming. It would have also been a maintenance issue, if in later development stages the application workflow is changed or new fields were added.

So we created functions to create instruments and for each of the test case that was automated, we just invoked the same function in every script. This helped us reduce the overall time to automate. This also assisted in maintenance down the line, when the investment instrument creation workflow changed.

Key objectives:

- Create Functions
- Creating Function Library File
- Calling Functions from UFT script

13.1 How to Create Functions

In this section let us see how to create functions and syntax of function.

Part – 1 – Record Basic Script

1. Launch a new UFT GUI Test script and name is FunctionScript.
2. Start Recording and record the following steps in application.

    i.   Enter username

    ii. Enter password

    iii. Click Login

   a. Search for Hotel

    iv. Select a location, e.g., Sydney

    v.   Select number of room, e.g., 2

    vi. Select adults per room, e.g., 2

    vii. Click on Search button

   b. Select a Hotel

    viii. Select one of the Hotel Radio buttons, e.g., select radio button next to Hotel Creek.

   c. Book a Hotel

    ix. Enter First Name

    x.   Enter Last name

    xi. Enter Address

    xii. Enter 16 digit Credit Card number

    xiii. Enter Credit Card type

    xiv. Enter Expiry Month

    xv. Enter Expiry Year

    xvi. Enter CVV number

    xvii. Click on Book Now

   d. After you see booking confirmation. Notice that you get an Order No. generated.

   e. Click on Logout button or Logout link on top right corner to logout from the application. You will go to "Click here to login again" page.

   f. Click on "Click here to Login again" link to go to login page.

   g. Stop recording.

3. You will get the script below recorded.

```
1   Browser("AdactIn.com - Hotel Reservatio").Page("AdactIn.com - Hotel Reservatio").WebEdit("username").Set "adactin123"
2   Browser("AdactIn.com - Hotel Reservatio").Page("AdactIn.com - Hotel Reservatio").WebEdit("password").SetSecure "51187998734734b261ff8bebf0e3335c50cb236efa7fa9637b6a"
3   Browser("AdactIn.com - Hotel Reservatio").Page("AdactIn.com - Hotel Reservatio").WebButton("Login").Click
4   Browser("AdactIn.com - Hotel Reservatio").Page("AdactIn.com - Hotel Reservatio").WebList("location").Select DataTable("Location", dtGlobalSheet)
5   Browser("AdactIn.com - Hotel Reservatio").Page("AdactIn.com - Hotel Reservatio").WebList("room_nos").Select "2 - Two"
6   Browser("AdactIn.com - Hotel Reservatio").Page("AdactIn.com - Hotel Reservatio").WebList("adult_room").Select "2 - Two"
7   Browser("AdactIn.com - Hotel Reservatio").Page("AdactIn.com - Hotel Reservatio").WebButton("Search").Click
8   Browser("AdactIn.com - Hotel Reservatio").Page("AdactIn.com - Hotel Reservatio").WebRadioGroup("radiobutton_2").Select "2"
9   Browser("AdactIn.com - Hotel Reservatio").Page("AdactIn.com - Hotel Reservatio").WebButton("Continue").Click
10  Browser("AdactIn.com - Hotel Reservatio").Page("AdactIn.com - Hotel Reservatio").WebEdit("first_name").Set "Test"
11  Browser("AdactIn.com - Hotel Reservatio").Page("AdactIn.com - Hotel Reservatio").WebEdit("last_name").Set "Test"
12  Browser("AdactIn.com - Hotel Reservatio").Page("AdactIn.com - Hotel Reservatio").WebEdit("address").Set "48 George Street Parramatta"
13  Browser("AdactIn.com - Hotel Reservatio").Page("AdactIn.com - Hotel Reservatio").WebEdit("cc_num").Set "1234123412341234"
14  Browser("AdactIn.com - Hotel Reservatio").Page("AdactIn.com - Hotel Reservatio").WebList("cc_type").Select "American Express"
15  Browser("AdactIn.com - Hotel Reservatio").Page("AdactIn.com - Hotel Reservatio").WebList("cc_exp_month").Select "July"
16  Browser("AdactIn.com - Hotel Reservatio").Page("AdactIn.com - Hotel Reservatio").WebList("cc_exp_year").Select "2015"
17  Browser("AdactIn.com - Hotel Reservatio").Page("AdactIn.com - Hotel Reservatio").WebEdit("cc_cvv").Set "111"
18  Browser("AdactIn.com - Hotel Reservatio").Page("AdactIn.com - Hotel Reservatio").WebButton("Book Now").Click
19  Browser("AdactIn.com - Hotel Reservatio").Page("AdactIn.com - Hotel Reservatio").WebButton("Logout").Click
20  Browser("AdactIn.com - Hotel Reservatio").Page("AdactIn.com - Hotel Reservatio").Link("Click here to login again").Click
```

Figure 13-1 – Editor View script

Part – 2 – Divide the Script into Functions

4. See below the syntax of how we use function in VBScript.

Function function_name [(arglist)]

[statements]

[function_name = expression]

[Exit Function]

[statements]

[function_name = expression]

End Function

Function Name: Required. The name of the newly created function.

Arglist: List of variables representing arguments that are passed to the **Function** procedure when it is called. Commas separate multiple variables.

Statements: Any group of statements to be executed within the body of the **Function** procedure.

Exit Function - Exit out of the function. Remaining steps in the function are not executed.

Expression: Return value of the **Function**.

Example

See below the example of Function:

Function **Multiply** (a, b)

    c = a * b

    Multiply = c

End Function

5. Let us divide our script into 3 separate functions – Login, Looking and Logout. Let us create Login Function. In the Editor View, **put your cursor in the first row** and write the following line of code. 'sUsername' is variable name (Move down your previously recording lines of code).

Function Login (sUsername)

'Statements to be added

End Function

6. Copy the first 3 lines where we login to the application within this function.

```
1
2  Function Login (sUsername)
3      Browser("AdactIn.com - Hotel Reservatio").Page("AdactIn.com - Hotel Reservatio").WebEdit("username").Set "adactin123"
4      Browser("AdactIn.com - Hotel Reservatio").Page("AdactIn.com - Hotel Reservatio").WebEdit("password").SetSecure "51187998734734b261ff8bebf0e3335c50cb236efa7fa9637b6a"
5      Browser("AdactIn.com - Hotel Reservatio").Page("AdactIn.com - Hotel Reservatio").WebButton("Login").Click
6  End Function
```

Figure 13-2 – Login Function declaration

7. Replace the argument's username with variable value.

```
1  Function Login (sUsername)
2      Browser("AdactIn.com - Hotel Reservatio").Page("AdactIn.com - Hotel Reservatio").WebEdit("username").Set sUsername
3      Browser("AdactIn.com - Hotel Reservatio").Page("AdactIn.com - Hotel Reservatio").WebEdit("password").SetSecure "51187998734734b261ff8bebf0e3335c50cb236efa7fa9637b6a"
4      Browser("AdactIn.com - Hotel Reservatio").Page("AdactIn.com - Hotel Reservatio").WebButton("Login").Click
5  End Function
```

Figure 13-3 – Replace Function arguments

8. Follow the steps 5-6-7 for Booking Function and Logout Function. You will see a script like below.

```
1  Function Login (sUsername)
2      Browser("AdactIn.com - Hotel Reservatio").Page("AdactIn.com - Hotel Reservatio").WebEdit("username").Set sUsername
3      Browser("AdactIn.com - Hotel Reservatio").Page("AdactIn.com - Hotel Reservatio").WebEdit("password").SetSecure "51187998734734b261ff8bebf0e3335c50cb236efa7fa9637b6a"
4      Browser("AdactIn.com - Hotel Reservatio").Page("AdactIn.com - Hotel Reservatio").WebButton("Login").Click
5  End Function
6
7  Function Booking (sLocation, sFirstName, sLastName)
8
9      Browser("AdactIn.com - Hotel Reservatio").Page("AdactIn.com - Hotel Reservatio").WebList("location").Select sLocation
10     Browser("AdactIn.com - Hotel Reservatio").Page("AdactIn.com - Hotel Reservatio").WebList("room_nos").Select "2 - Two"
11     Browser("AdactIn.com - Hotel Reservatio").Page("AdactIn.com - Hotel Reservatio").WebList("adult_room").Select "2 - Two"
12     Browser("AdactIn.com - Hotel Reservatio").Page("AdactIn.com - Hotel Reservatio").WebButton("Search").Click
13     Browser("AdactIn.com - Hotel Reservatio").Page("AdactIn.com - Hotel Reservatio").WebRadioGroup("radiobutton_2").Select "2"
14     Browser("AdactIn.com - Hotel Reservatio").Page("AdactIn.com - Hotel Reservatio").WebButton("Continue").Click
15     Browser("AdactIn.com - Hotel Reservatio").Page("AdactIn.com - Hotel Reservatio").WebEdit("first_name").Set sFirstName
16     Browser("AdactIn.com - Hotel Reservatio").Page("AdactIn.com - Hotel Reservatio").WebEdit("last_name").Set sLastName
17     Browser("AdactIn.com - Hotel Reservatio").Page("AdactIn.com - Hotel Reservatio").WebEdit("address").Set "48 George Street Parramatta"
18     Browser("AdactIn.com - Hotel Reservatio").Page("AdactIn.com - Hotel Reservatio").WebEdit("cc_num").Set "1234123412341234"
19     Browser("AdactIn.com - Hotel Reservatio").Page("AdactIn.com - Hotel Reservatio").WebList("cc_type").Select "American Express"
20     Browser("AdactIn.com - Hotel Reservatio").Page("AdactIn.com - Hotel Reservatio").WebList("cc_exp_month").Select "July"
21     Browser("AdactIn.com - Hotel Reservatio").Page("AdactIn.com - Hotel Reservatio").WebList("cc_exp_year").Select "2015"
22     Browser("AdactIn.com - Hotel Reservatio").Page("AdactIn.com - Hotel Reservatio").WebEdit("cc_cvv").Set "111"
23     Browser("AdactIn.com - Hotel Reservatio").Page("AdactIn.com - Hotel Reservatio").WebButton("Book Now").Click
24
25 End Function
26
27 Function Logout
28
29     Browser("AdactIn.com - Hotel Reservatio").Page("AdactIn.com - Hotel Reservatio").WebButton("Logout").Click
30     Browser("AdactIn.com - Hotel Reservatio").Page("AdactIn.com - Hotel Reservatio").Link("Click here to login again").Click
31
32 End Function
```

Figure 13-4 – Script for all functions

9. Edit the Script to call Function. Add below three lines in code.

Login "adactin123"

'Note: Use your own username instead of regular adactin123

Booking """Sydney", "Test", "Test"

Logout

You script will look like that given below.

```
 Main
 1    Login "adactin123"
 2    Booking "Sydney", "Test", "Test"
 3    Logout
 4
 5  ⊟ Function Login (sUsername)
 6        Browser("AdactIn.com - Hotel Reservatio").Page("AdactIn.com - Hotel Reservatio").WebEdit("username").Set sUsername
 7        Browser("AdactIn.com - Hotel Reservatio").Page("AdactIn.com - Hotel Reservatio").WebEdit("password").SetSecure "51187998734734b261ff8bebf0e3335c50cb236efa7fa9637b6a"
 8        Browser("AdactIn.com - Hotel Reservatio").Page("AdactIn.com - Hotel Reservatio").WebButton("Login").Click
 9    End Function
10
11  ⊟ Function Booking (sLocation, sFirstName, sLastName)
12
13        Browser("AdactIn.com - Hotel Reservatio").Page("AdactIn.com - Hotel Reservatio").WebList("location").Select sLocation
14        Browser("AdactIn.com - Hotel Reservatio").Page("AdactIn.com - Hotel Reservatio").WebList("room_nos").Select "2 - Two"
15        Browser("AdactIn.com - Hotel Reservatio").Page("AdactIn.com - Hotel Reservatio").WebList("adult_room").Select "2 - Two"
16        Browser("AdactIn.com - Hotel Reservatio").Page("AdactIn.com - Hotel Reservatio").WebButton("Search").Click
17        Browser("AdactIn.com - Hotel Reservatio").Page("AdactIn.com - Hotel Reservatio").WebRadioGroup("radiobutton_2").Select "2"
18        Browser("AdactIn.com - Hotel Reservatio").Page("AdactIn.com - Hotel Reservatio").WebButton("Continue").Click
19        Browser("AdactIn.com - Hotel Reservatio").Page("AdactIn.com - Hotel Reservatio").WebEdit("first_name").Set sFirstName
20        Browser("AdactIn.com - Hotel Reservatio").Page("AdactIn.com - Hotel Reservatio").WebEdit("last_name").Set sLastName
21        Browser("AdactIn.com - Hotel Reservatio").Page("AdactIn.com - Hotel Reservatio").WebEdit("address").Set "48 George Street Parramatta"
22        Browser("AdactIn.com - Hotel Reservatio").Page("AdactIn.com - Hotel Reservatio").WebEdit("cc_num").Set "1234123412341234"
23        Browser("AdactIn.com - Hotel Reservatio").Page("AdactIn.com - Hotel Reservatio").WebList("cc_type").Select "American Express"
24        Browser("AdactIn.com - Hotel Reservatio").Page("AdactIn.com - Hotel Reservatio").WebList("cc_exp_month").Select "July"
25        Browser("AdactIn.com - Hotel Reservatio").Page("AdactIn.com - Hotel Reservatio").WebList("cc_exp_year").Select "2015"
26        Browser("AdactIn.com - Hotel Reservatio").Page("AdactIn.com - Hotel Reservatio").WebEdit("cc_cvv").Set "111"
27        Browser("AdactIn.com - Hotel Reservatio").Page("AdactIn.com - Hotel Reservatio").WebButton("Book Now").Click
28
29    End Function
30
31  ⊟ Function Logout
32
33        Browser("AdactIn.com - Hotel Reservatio").Page("AdactIn.com - Hotel Reservatio").WebButton("Logout").Click
34        Browser("AdactIn.com - Hotel Reservatio").Page("AdactIn.com - Hotel Reservatio").Link("Click here to login again").Click
35
36    End Function
```

Figure 13-5 – Call the Functions

Note: If we want to return values from function we will need to use syntax FunctionName = [returnvalue] For example:

Login = "pass"

This will return pass from login function.

10. Save the script

13.2 Create Function Library File and Linking with Script

The functions that we created in the last section are called local functions, because they are available only within the scripts, and not accessible to other scripts.

To make these functions accessible to other scripts, we need to copy these functions in an external function library file.

Let us see how to create external function library file.

1. Go to **File → New → Function Library**. Name the function library as Functions. qfl and open the new file. This will open new Function library functions window alongside already open FunctionScript.

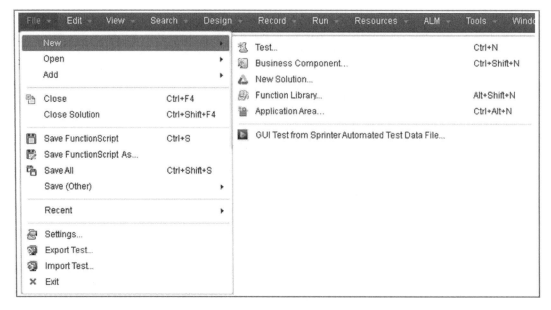

Figure 13-6 – Create New Function Library

2. Select you FunctionScript tab and cut all the three functions and paste them in Function Library file.

```
Function Login (sUsername)
    Browser("AdactIn.com - Hotel Reservatio").Page("AdactIn.com - Hotel Reservatio").WebEdit("username").Set sUsername
    Browser("AdactIn.com - Hotel Reservatio").Page("AdactIn.com - Hotel Reservatio").WebEdit("password").SetSecure "51187998734734b261ff8bebf0e3335c50cb236efa7fa9637b6a"
    Browser("AdactIn.com - Hotel Reservatio").Page("AdactIn.com - Hotel Reservatio").WebButton("Login").Click
End Function

Function Booking (sLocation, sFirstName, sLastName)

    Browser("AdactIn.com - Hotel Reservatio").Page("AdactIn.com - Hotel Reservatio").WebList("location").Select sLocation
    Browser("AdactIn.com - Hotel Reservatio").Page("AdactIn.com - Hotel Reservatio").WebList("room_nos").Select "2 - Two"
    Browser("AdactIn.com - Hotel Reservatio").Page("AdactIn.com - Hotel Reservatio").WebList("adult_room").Select "2 - Two"
    Browser("AdactIn.com - Hotel Reservatio").Page("AdactIn.com - Hotel Reservatio").WebButton("Search").Click
    Browser("AdactIn.com - Hotel Reservatio").Page("AdactIn.com - Hotel Reservatio").WebRadioGroup("radiobutton_2").Select "2"
    Browser("AdactIn.com - Hotel Reservatio").Page("AdactIn.com - Hotel Reservatio").WebButton("Continue").Click
    Browser("AdactIn.com - Hotel Reservatio").Page("AdactIn.com - Hotel Reservatio").WebEdit("first_name").Set sFirstName
    Browser("AdactIn.com - Hotel Reservatio").Page("AdactIn.com - Hotel Reservatio").WebEdit("last_name").Set sLastName
    Browser("AdactIn.com - Hotel Reservatio").Page("AdactIn.com - Hotel Reservatio").WebEdit("address").Set "48 George Street Parramatta"
    Browser("AdactIn.com - Hotel Reservatio").Page("AdactIn.com - Hotel Reservatio").WebEdit("cc_num").Set "123412341234"
    Browser("AdactIn.com - Hotel Reservatio").Page("AdactIn.com - Hotel Reservatio").WebList("cc_type").Select "American Express"
    Browser("AdactIn.com - Hotel Reservatio").Page("AdactIn.com - Hotel Reservatio").WebList("cc_exp_month").Select "July"
    Browser("AdactIn.com - Hotel Reservatio").Page("AdactIn.com - Hotel Reservatio").WebList("cc_exp_year").Select "2015"
    Browser("AdactIn.com - Hotel Reservatio").Page("AdactIn.com - Hotel Reservatio").WebEdit("cc_cvv").Set "111"
    Browser("AdactIn.com - Hotel Reservatio").Page("AdactIn.com - Hotel Reservatio").WebButton("Book Now").Click

End Function

Function Logout

    Browser("AdactIn.com - Hotel Reservatio").Page("AdactIn.com - Hotel Reservatio").WebButton("Logout").Click
    Browser("AdactIn.com - Hotel Reservatio").Page("AdactIn.com - Hotel Reservatio").Link("Click here to login again").Click

End Function
```

Figure 13-7 – Function Library

3. So your script will now have only three function calls.

```
Login "adactin123"
Booking "Sydney", "Test", "Test"
Logout
```

4. Save the FunctionScript.

5. Save the Function Library file.

> **Note:** Note that the extension of function library file is .qfl.

Now we need to link the function library file with the UFT script so that when UFT script makes a function call it can reach the correct function.

6. To link the Function Library file, go to **File → Settings → Resources**. You can link the library file with the script, by clicking on the **Plus** icon and navigating to the path of Library file.

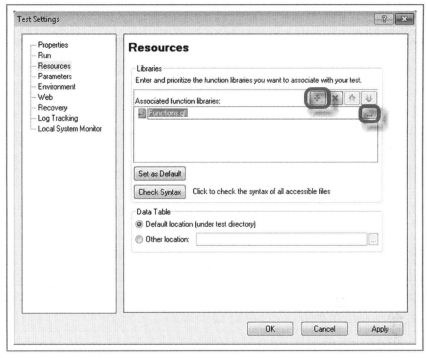

Figure 13-8 – Link Function Library to Test

7. Click **OK** to Close Settings Dialog.

> **Note:** You could also de-link the library file from above **Test Settings** by clicking on delete button.

13.3 Execution of Script with Function Calls

Let us now execute script and see if is runs:

1. Execute the script and verify correct calling of all the functions and script execution.

> **Note:** If you create a completely new script and would want to use functions in function library file. Make sure that you perform 2 steps.

- Link library file with Script
- Associate Shared Repository

> **Note:** Note that function library file does not have a repository of its own. It uses the object repository of script, which is calling the functions. So you would need to make sure objects used in function library file are associated with the script.

Exercise

1. Create separate functions for Search Hotel, Select Hotel, and Book a Hotel (this function should return new order number value).

2. Add them to the same script so that the workflow is Login, Search Hotel, Select Hotel Booking Hotel, and Logout.

3. Create a new script in which we call the functions in below order.

    i.   Login

    ii. Search Hotel (with search condition)

    iii. Select Hotel

    iv. Book Hotel

    v.   Search Hotel (now with different search conditions)

    vi. Select Hotel

    vii. Book Hotel

    viii. Logout

❧

14

Capture Dynamic Values

Many times you will notice that values in the application are created at run time. For example, if you are testing a banking application and you need to test a scenario where you create a new bank account, search for this account number in admin section and update the address. You will notice that the account number that you are using is dynamically generated every time and is not static. When you perform your search account operation, you would need this dynamically generated value instead of a static value.

Values in the application which are dynamically generated at run time are called dynamic values.

Example

We once were automating an Insurance application, where a user can login and buy insurance. The system will generate an insurance number for the new insurance policy, which would be dynamic and random. The user could then re-login at a later stage and view his existing insurances, search based on the new insurance number, and make changes to the order. To test this insurance scenario, it was important that we should be able to capture dynamic data (which is the insurance number) from the application and that search based on this dynamically generated insurance number once we re-login into the application.

UFT provides us two ways of how we can capture these values. We can either use UFT feature **Output Values** to capture Dynamic Values, or use scripting way and use **GetROProperty** method to capture order number value. In this chapter we will see both ways to capture dynamic values.

Key objectives:

- Understanding the problem.
- Using Output Values to capture Dynamic Values.
- Using GetROProperty to capture Dynamic Values.

14.1 Understanding the Problem

To understand the problem let us consider a test scenario.

Test Scenario

- Login
- Search a Hotel
- Select a Hotel
- Book a Hotel and get the order number generated
- Search for Booked Order in Booked Itinerary to confirm correct booking details
- Logout

Pre-condition – Make sure Login page of application is available

1. Create a new UFT Test by **File → New → Test** and name it as 'DynamicValueBasedscript'.
2. Start recording and record below workflow.

   a. Login (Use the username/password with which you have registered earlier).

   b. Search for Hotel

      i. Select a location, e.g., Sydney

      ii. Select number of rooms, e.g., 2

      iii. Select adults per rooms, e.g., 2

      iv. Click on Search button

   c. Select a Hotel

      v. Select one of the hotel Radio Buttons, e.g., select Radio Button next to Hotel Creek.

   d. Book a Hotel

      vi. Enter First Name as "Test"

      vii. Enter Last Name as "Test"

      viii. Enter Address as "Test"

      ix. Enter 16-digit Credit Card number as "1212121212121212"

      x. Enter Credit Card type as "Mastercard"

      xi. Enter Expiry Month as "October"

      xii. Enter Expiry Year as "2015"

      xiii. Enter CVV number as "111"

      xiv. Click on Book Now (manually note the order number generated).

e. Click on "My Itinerary" button.

f. In the Search Order field enter the order number just created.

g. Click on "Go" button.

h. Logout from the application.

3. Stop Recording after recording the above workflow. You will notice the script given below.

```
1   Browser("AdactIn.com - Hotel Reservatio").Page("AdactIn.com - Hotel Reservatio").WebEdit("username").Set "adactin123"
2   Browser("AdactIn.com - Hotel Reservatio").Page("AdactIn.com - Hotel Reservatio").WebEdit("password").SetSecure "511ad1d7cd12af284f4d687efa251c9222a67b655ec8b6000e36"
3   Browser("AdactIn.com - Hotel Reservatio").Page("AdactIn.com - Hotel Reservatio").WebButton("Login").Click
4   Browser("AdactIn.com - Hotel Reservatio").Page("AdactIn.com - Hotel Reservatio").WebList("location").Select "Sydney"
5   Browser("AdactIn.com - Hotel Reservatio").Page("AdactIn.com - Hotel Reservatio").WebList("room_nos").Select "2 - Two"
6   Browser("AdactIn.com - Hotel Reservatio").Page("AdactIn.com - Hotel Reservatio").WebList("adult_room").Select "2 - Two"
7   Browser("AdactIn.com - Hotel Reservatio").Page("AdactIn.com - Hotel Reservatio").WebButton("Search").Click
8   Browser("AdactIn.com - Hotel Reservatio").Page("AdactIn.com - Hotel Reservatio").WebRadioGroup("radiobutton_2").Select "2"
9   Browser("AdactIn.com - Hotel Reservatio").Page("AdactIn.com - Hotel Reservatio").WebButton("Continue").Click
10  Browser("AdactIn.com - Hotel Reservatio").Page("AdactIn.com - Hotel Reservatio").WebEdit("first_name").Set "Test"
11  Browser("AdactIn.com - Hotel Reservatio").Page("AdactIn.com - Hotel Reservatio").WebEdit("last_name").Set "Test"
12  Browser("AdactIn.com - Hotel Reservatio").Page("AdactIn.com - Hotel Reservatio").WebEdit("address").Set "Test"
13  Browser("AdactIn.com - Hotel Reservatio").Page("AdactIn.com - Hotel Reservatio").WebEdit("cc_num").Set "121212121212121212"
14  Browser("AdactIn.com - Hotel Reservatio").Page("AdactIn.com - Hotel Reservatio").WebList("cc_type").Select "Master Card"
15  Browser("AdactIn.com - Hotel Reservatio").Page("AdactIn.com - Hotel Reservatio").WebList("cc_exp_month").Select "October"
16  Browser("AdactIn.com - Hotel Reservatio").Page("AdactIn.com - Hotel Reservatio").WebList("cc_exp_year").Select "2015"
17  Browser("AdactIn.com - Hotel Reservatio").Page("AdactIn.com - Hotel Reservatio").WebEdit("cc_cvv").Set "111"
18  Browser("AdactIn.com - Hotel Reservatio").Page("AdactIn.com - Hotel Reservatio").WebButton("Book Now").Click
19  Browser("AdactIn.com - Hotel Reservatio").Page("AdactIn.com - Hotel Reservatio").WebButton("My Itinerary").Click
20  Browser("AdactIn.com - Hotel Reservatio").Page("AdactIn.com - Hotel Reservatio").WebEdit("order_id_text").Set "5U12V6IQ50"
21  Browser("AdactIn.com - Hotel Reservatio").Page("AdactIn.com - Hotel Reservatio").WebButton("Go").Click
22  Browser("AdactIn.com - Hotel Reservatio").Page("AdactIn.com - Hotel Reservatio").Link("Logout").Click
23  Browser("AdactIn.com - Hotel Reservatio").Page("AdactIn.com - Hotel Reservatio").Link("Click here to login again").Click
```

Figure 14-1 – Editor View Script

4. Go to Editor View and add a delay of 8 seconds before you click on My Itinerary button and a delay of 5 seconds, before you click on the Go button to search for order number. To add delay statements, you can just type wait (8) and wait (5) which will make the script wait that many seconds.

Note: We are adding these wait statements so that when we run the script, we will notice the values being generated, when we book the order as also the value we use to search the order number in My Order Page. There is no technical reason for adding these wait statements.

```
15  Browser("AdactIn.com - Hotel Reservatio").Page("AdactIn.com - Hotel Reservatio").WebList("cc_exp_month").Select "October"
16  Browser("AdactIn.com - Hotel Reservatio").Page("AdactIn.com - Hotel Reservatio").WebList("cc_exp_year").Select "2015"
17  Browser("AdactIn.com - Hotel Reservatio").Page("AdactIn.com - Hotel Reservatio").WebEdit("cc_cvv").Set "111"
18  Browser("AdactIn.com - Hotel Reservatio").Page("AdactIn.com - Hotel Reservatio").WebButton("Book Now").Click
19  wait(8)
20  Browser("AdactIn.com - Hotel Reservatio").Page("AdactIn.com - Hotel Reservatio").WebButton("My Itinerary").Click
21  Browser("AdactIn.com - Hotel Reservatio").Page("AdactIn.com - Hotel Reservatio").WebEdit("order_id_text").Set "5U12V6IQ50"
22  Browser("AdactIn.com - Hotel Reservatio").Page("AdactIn.com - Hotel Reservatio").WebButton("Go").Click
23  wait(5)
24  Browser("AdactIn.com - Hotel Reservatio").Page("AdactIn.com - Hotel Reservatio").Link("Logout").Click
25  Browser("AdactIn.com - Hotel Reservatio").Page("AdactIn.com - Hotel Reservatio").Link("Click here to login again").Click
```

Figure 14-2 – Wait Statements added

5. Save the script.

6. Now run the script by clicking on run button. Notice the new order number generated and the value we use to search this order number in My Itinerary Page.

You will notice that the new order number generated is different from the one we are using to search in the search order number field.

This presents a problem since as part of our test scenario; we would like to search for an order number which we have just inserted. Let us see how we can resolve this issue in our next section.

14.2 Using Output Value to Capture Dynamic Values

It's important for us is to capture the generated order number and use that while searching.

1. Go to script "DynamicValueBasedscript" created in last section and do a **File →** **Save As** and save the script as "Outputvaluescript".

2. Now select the Keyword View of the script (Select **View → Keyword View**).

3. Select the step where user clicks on **My Itinerary** button.

4. Open **Active Screen** pane (if it is not already open you can open it from **View →** **Active Screen**).

> **Note:** We can add Output Values either from Active Screen or while recording from **Insert → Standard Output Value** menu option. As part of this exercise we will use Active Screen to add Output Value.

> **Note:** While selecting Active Screen, you might be prompted for username/ password which you could use to securely view active screen. Enter any username and password for future reference to the script.

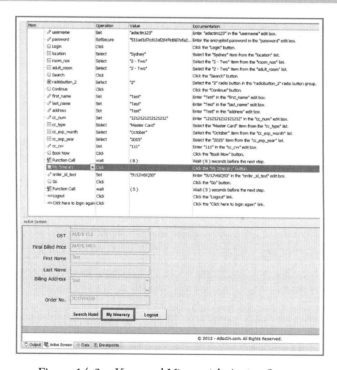

Figure 14-3 – Keyword View with Active Screen

5. Place the cursor on the Order No. edit field, right click and select **Insert Output Value**.

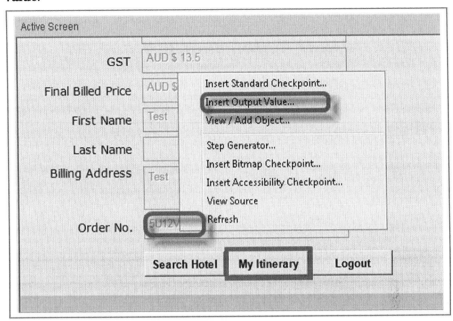

Figure 14-4 – Insert Output Value from Active Screen

6. You will notice an **Object Selection** Dialog box. Click **OK** in the dialog box

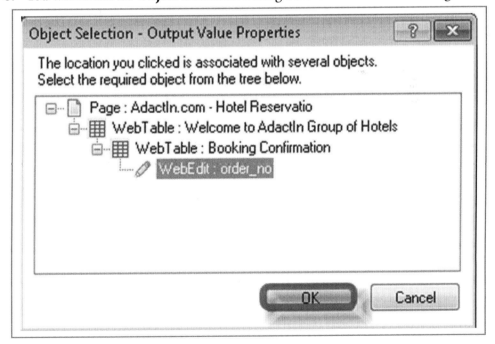

Figure 14-5 – Object Selection Dialog box

7. In the **Output Value Properties** dialog box, select the checkbox for property **value** (this property stores newly generated order number)

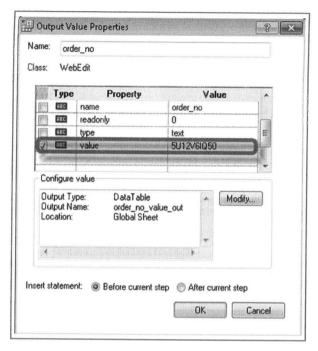

Figure 14-6 – Output Value Properties

8. Click on **Modify** button to modify the **name** of column in DataTable in which extracted value will be stored. You can remove the default value and type your own name.

Note: You will need to manually type name of the column instead of selecting from dropdown.

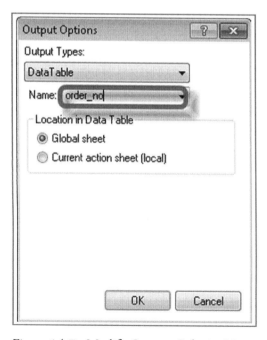

Figure 14-7– Modify Output Column Name

9. Click **OK** on the Output Options dialog box

10. Notice that we have 2 options for Insert Statement, Before Current Step and After Current Step. Since our current step is My Itinerary button, let us keep the default selection of **Before Current Step**, since we need to capture order no. before clicking on My Itinerary button.

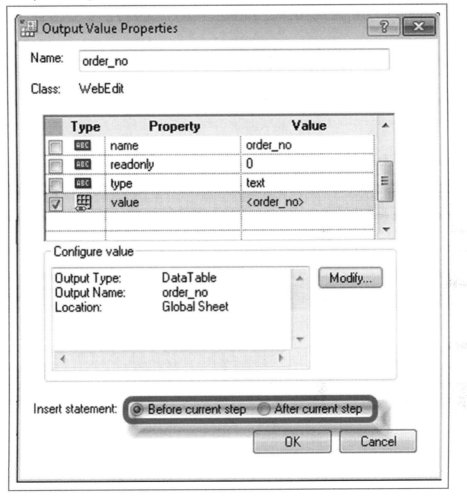

Figure 14-8– Before or After Current Step Selection

11. Click **OK** on Output Value Properties dialog box. You will notice that a new statement has been added in the script with Operation "Output"

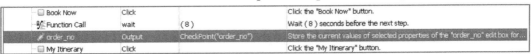

Figure 14-9– Output Value step in Keyword View

12. Also click on Data tab (in case you do not see DataTable window go to **View** → **Data**) and notice that a new column with name "order_no" is added.

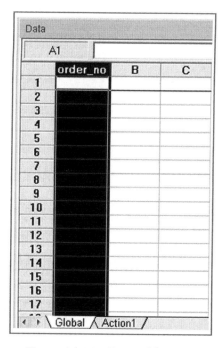

Figure 14-10– Data table View

The first half of our job is done, that is to capture the Dynamic Output Value, which will be captured and stored in the DataTable.

Now we need to use the value captured. Let us see how:

13. Select the step where we enter order_id_text for Search Order No.

☐ My Itinerary	Click		Click the "My Itinerary" button.
✎ order_id_text	Set	"5U12V6IQ50"	Enter "5U12V6IQ50" in the "order_id_text" edit box.
☐ Go	Click		Click the "Go" button.

Figure 14-11– Order-id input step

You will notice that in the value we are trying to set we are using a static value "5U12V6IQ50". We need to replace this value with the newly created Dynamic Value we have output/exported into the Data Table,

14. Click on static order number value you see and click on "<#>" icon to open.

☐ My Itinerary	Click		Click the "My Itinerary" button.
✎ order_id_text	Set	"5U12V6IQ50"	Enter "5U12V6IQ50" in the "order_id_text" edit box.
☐ Go	Click	Text	Click the "Go" button.

Figure 14-12– Parameterize Order-id value

15. In the Value Configuration Options dialog box select **Parameter**.

16. In the Name field from the dropdown, select **Order No**

Figure 14-13– Select column name

17. Click **OK** on the dialog box.

18. You will notice your script in Keyword View will look like this.

Book Now	Click		Click the "Book Now" button.
Function Call	wait	(8)	Wait (8) seconds before the next step.
order_no	Output	CheckPoint("order_no")	Store the current values of selected properties of the "order_no" edit box for...
My Itinerary	Click		Click the "My Itinerary" button.
order_id_text	Set	<order_no>	Enter "5U12V6IQ50" in the "order_id_text" edit box.
Go	Click		Click the "Go" button.
Function Call	wait	(5)	Wait (5) seconds before the next step.
Logout	Click		Click the "Logout" link.

Figure 14-14– Final Parameterized Script

19. Save the script.

20. Now execute the script and verify that the new generated order number is searched in Order Number field.

Note: We can further enhance this script with checkpoints to verify that data for the searched order is the same as that we had entered earlier.

14.3 Using GetROProperty to Capture Dynamic Values

Capturing Dynamic Values using Output Value method is an UFT feature to capture dynamic value using the UFT user interface. It is more relevant for automation testers who are not well-versed with scripting.

GetROProperty method presents another alternative but very popular method to capture Dynamic Values in the application. "RO" in GetROProperty method stands for "Run time Object".

Let us look at how we can capture and resolve problems presented earlier in this chapter.

1. Open script "DynamicValueBasedscript" created in section 14.1 and do a **File →
Save As** and save the script as "GetROpropertyscript".

2. Go to Editor View. (Go to **View → Editor**) You will notice the script below.

```
1   Browser("AdactIn.com - Hotel Reservatio").Page("AdactIn.com - Hotel Reservatio").WebEdit("username").Set "adactin123"
2   Browser("AdactIn.com - Hotel Reservatio").Page("AdactIn.com - Hotel Reservatio").WebEdit("password").SetSecure "511ad1d7cd12af284f4d687efa251c9222a67b655ec8b6000e36"
3   Browser("AdactIn.com - Hotel Reservatio").Page("AdactIn.com - Hotel Reservatio").WebButton("Login").Click
4   Browser("AdactIn.com - Hotel Reservatio").Page("AdactIn.com - Hotel Reservatio").WebList("location").Select "Sydney"
5   Browser("AdactIn.com - Hotel Reservatio").Page("AdactIn.com - Hotel Reservatio").WebList("room_nos").Select "2 - Two"
6   Browser("AdactIn.com - Hotel Reservatio").Page("AdactIn.com - Hotel Reservatio").WebList("adult_room").Select "2 - Two"
7   Browser("AdactIn.com - Hotel Reservatio").Page("AdactIn.com - Hotel Reservatio").WebButton("Search").Click
8   Browser("AdactIn.com - Hotel Reservatio").Page("AdactIn.com - Hotel Reservatio").WebRadioGroup("radiobutton_2").Select "2"
9   Browser("AdactIn.com - Hotel Reservatio").Page("AdactIn.com - Hotel Reservatio").WebButton("Continue").Click
10  Browser("AdactIn.com - Hotel Reservatio").Page("AdactIn.com - Hotel Reservatio").WebEdit("first_name").Set "Test"
11  Browser("AdactIn.com - Hotel Reservatio").Page("AdactIn.com - Hotel Reservatio").WebEdit("last_name").Set "Test"
12  Browser("AdactIn.com - Hotel Reservatio").Page("AdactIn.com - Hotel Reservatio").WebEdit("address").Set "Test"
13  Browser("AdactIn.com - Hotel Reservatio").Page("AdactIn.com - Hotel Reservatio").WebEdit("cc_num").Set "121212121212121"
14  Browser("AdactIn.com - Hotel Reservatio").Page("AdactIn.com - Hotel Reservatio").WebList("cc_type").Select "Master Card"
15  Browser("AdactIn.com - Hotel Reservatio").Page("AdactIn.com - Hotel Reservatio").WebList("cc_exp_month").Select "October"
16  Browser("AdactIn.com - Hotel Reservatio").Page("AdactIn.com - Hotel Reservatio").WebList("cc_exp_year").Select "2015"
17  Browser("AdactIn.com - Hotel Reservatio").Page("AdactIn.com - Hotel Reservatio").WebEdit("cc_cvv").Set "111"
18  Browser("AdactIn.com - Hotel Reservatio").Page("AdactIn.com - Hotel Reservatio").WebButton("Book Now").Click
19  wait(8)
20  Browser("AdactIn.com - Hotel Reservatio").Page("AdactIn.com - Hotel Reservatio").WebButton("My Itinerary").Click
21  Browser("AdactIn.com - Hotel Reservatio").Page("AdactIn.com - Hotel Reservatio").WebEdit("order_id_text").Set "5U12v6IQ50"
22  Browser("AdactIn.com - Hotel Reservatio").Page("AdactIn.com - Hotel Reservatio").WebButton("Go").Click
23  wait(5)
24  Browser("AdactIn.com - Hotel Reservatio").Page("AdactIn.com - Hotel Reservatio").Link("Logout").Click
25  Browser("AdactIn.com - Hotel Reservatio").Page("AdactIn.com - Hotel Reservatio").Link("Click here to login again").Click
```

Figure 14-15– Editor View

3. Next step is to add Order No. field into Object Repository. Manually browse through the application so that you can see Order No. object.

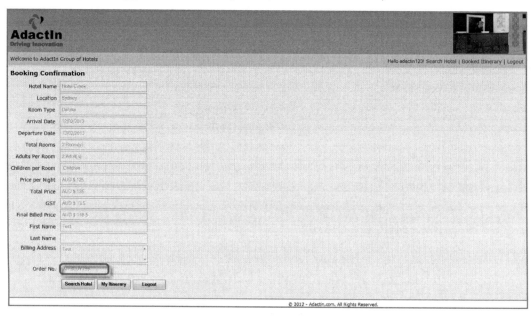

Figure 14-16– Order No. object visible

4. Go to **Resources → Object Repository** and Click on **Add Objects** button and add Order Number object.

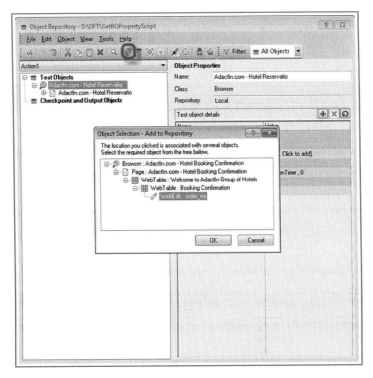

Figure 14-17– Add Object to Repository Selection dialog box

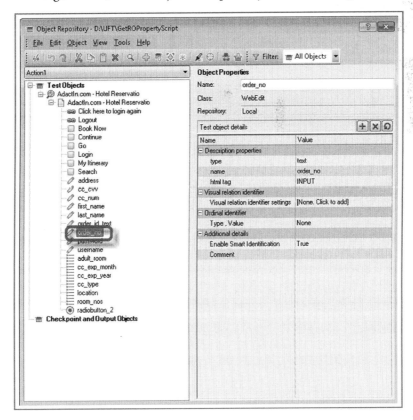

Figure 14-18– Object added to Repository

5. **Close** Object Repository.

6. Now we need to know which property of the Order No. object will store order number information. So we use Object Spy (Go to **Tools** → **Object Spy**) and spy on the order number field.

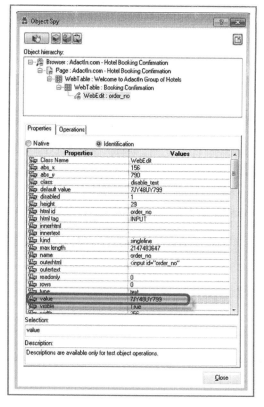

Figure 14-19– Object Spy

We see that "value" property of Order No" object stores order number information.

7. Close Object Spy window.

8. In the Editor View place the cursor before step "My Itinerary".

```
1  Browser("AdactIn.com - Hotel Reservatio").Page("AdactIn.com - Hotel Reservatio").WebEdit("username").Set "adactin123"
2  Browser("AdactIn.com - Hotel Reservatio").Page("AdactIn.com - Hotel Reservatio").WebEdit("password").SetSecure "511ad1d7cd12ef284f4d687efa251c9222a67b655ec8b6000e36"
3  Browser("AdactIn.com - Hotel Reservatio").Page("AdactIn.com - Hotel Reservatio").WebButton("Login").Click
4  Browser("AdactIn.com - Hotel Reservatio").Page("AdactIn.com - Hotel Reservatio").WebList("location").Select "Sydney"
5  Browser("AdactIn.com - Hotel Reservatio").Page("AdactIn.com - Hotel Reservatio").WebList("room_nos").Select "2 - Two"
6  Browser("AdactIn.com - Hotel Reservatio").Page("AdactIn.com - Hotel Reservatio").WebList("adult_room").Select "2 - Two"
7  Browser("AdactIn.com - Hotel Reservatio").Page("AdactIn.com - Hotel Reservatio").WebButton("Search").Click
8  Browser("AdactIn.com - Hotel Reservatio").Page("AdactIn.com - Hotel Reservatio").WebRadioGroup("radiobutton_2").Select "2"
9  Browser("AdactIn.com - Hotel Reservatio").Page("AdactIn.com - Hotel Reservatio").WebButton("Continue").Click
10 Browser("AdactIn.com - Hotel Reservatio").Page("AdactIn.com - Hotel Reservatio").WebEdit("first_name").Set "Test"
11 Browser("AdactIn.com - Hotel Reservatio").Page("AdactIn.com - Hotel Reservatio").WebEdit("last_name").Set "Test"
12 Browser("AdactIn.com - Hotel Reservatio").Page("AdactIn.com - Hotel Reservatio").WebEdit("address").Set "Test"
13 Browser("AdactIn.com - Hotel Reservatio").Page("AdactIn.com - Hotel Reservatio").WebEdit("cc_num").Set "1212121212121212"
14 Browser("AdactIn.com - Hotel Reservatio").Page("AdactIn.com - Hotel Reservatio").WebList("cc_type").Select "Master Card"
15 Browser("AdactIn.com - Hotel Reservatio").Page("AdactIn.com - Hotel Reservatio").WebList("cc_exp_month").Select "October"
16 Browser("AdactIn.com - Hotel Reservatio").Page("AdactIn.com - Hotel Reservatio").WebList("cc_exp_year").Select "2015"
17 Browser("AdactIn.com - Hotel Reservatio").Page("AdactIn.com - Hotel Reservatio").WebEdit("cc_cvv").Set "111"
18 Browser("AdactIn.com - Hotel Reservatio").Page("AdactIn.com - Hotel Reservatio").WebButton("Book Now").Click
19 wait(8)
20
21 Browser("AdactIn.com - Hotel Reservatio").Page("AdactIn.com - Hotel Reservatio").WebButton("My Itinerary").Click
22 Browser("AdactIn.com - Hotel Reservatio").Page("AdactIn.com - Hotel Reservatio").WebEdit("order_id_text").Set "5U12V6IQ50"
23 Browser("AdactIn.com - Hotel Reservatio").Page("AdactIn.com - Hotel Reservatio").WebButton("Go").Click
24 wait(5)
25 Browser("AdactIn.com - Hotel Reservatio").Page("AdactIn.com - Hotel Reservatio").Link("Logout").Click
26 Browser("AdactIn.com - Hotel Reservatio").Page("AdactIn.com - Hotel Reservatio").Link("Click here to login again").Click
```

Figure 14-20– Cursor Position Editor View

9. Use Step Generator (**Design → Step Generator**) to create a step using GetROProperty to get property value of "value" property. Also add Return Value as sOrder_No in, which extracted value will be stored.

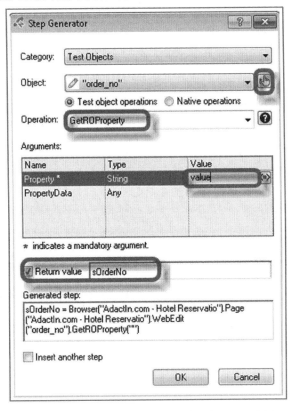

Figure 14-21– Step Generator dialog box to add Step

10. You will see below line in the **Editor View**.

```
18   Browser("AdactIn.com - Hotel Reservatio").Page("AdactIn.com - Hotel Reservatio").WebButton("Book Now").Click
19   wait(8)
20   sOrderNo = Browser("AdactIn.com - Hotel Reservatio").Page("AdactIn.com - Hotel Reservatio").WebEdit("order_no").GetROProperty("value")
21   Browser("AdactIn.com - Hotel Reservatio").Page("AdactIn.com - Hotel Reservatio").WebButton("My Itinerary").Click
22   Browser("AdactIn.com - Hotel Reservatio").Page("AdactIn.com - Hotel Reservatio").WebEdit("order_id_text").Set "5U12V6IQ50"
23   Browser("AdactIn.com - Hotel Reservatio").Page("AdactIn.com - Hotel Reservatio").WebButton("Go").Click
24   wait(5)
```

Figure 14-22– Editor View with new line of code

GetROproperty method will capture the Order number value and store it in the variable sOrder_No.

11. Now we need to use the order number value captured in search field. Replace the static value in above snapshot from "5U12V6IQ50" with variable value sOrder_No.

```
18   Browser("AdactIn.com - Hotel Reservatio").Page("AdactIn.com - Hotel Reservatio").WebButton("Book Now").Click
19   wait(8)
20   sOrderNo = Browser("AdactIn.com - Hotel Reservatio").Page("AdactIn.com - Hotel Reservatio").WebEdit("order_no").GetROProperty("value")
21   Browser("AdactIn.com - Hotel Reservatio").Page("AdactIn.com - Hotel Reservatio").WebButton("My Itinerary").Click
22   Browser("AdactIn.com - Hotel Reservatio").Page("AdactIn.com - Hotel Reservatio").WebEdit("order_id_text").Set sOrderNo
23   Browser("AdactIn.com - Hotel Reservatio").Page("AdactIn.com - Hotel Reservatio").WebButton("Go").Click
24   wait(5)
```

Figure 14-23– Replace static value with variable

12. Execute the script to verify correct order number value is captured and used in the script while searching.

> **Note:** I have noticed that once automation testers are more familiar with UFT and with using editor view, most of them tend to use GetROProperty method, instead of output value feature to capture dynamic values.

Exercise

1. Create a new function for Booking Search with input parameter of Order Number

2. Add it to your function library file created in last chapter.

3. Create a new script and call function in following order: Login, Search Hotel, Select Hotel, Book Hotel, Search Order, and Logout.

 e/s

15

Reporter Object and Custom Checkpoint

In one of the previous chapters, we looked into how UFT provides the Standard Checkpoint and other types of checkpoints, to verify functional correctness of the application. This is done at the elementary level.

At an advanced level, we use Custom Checkpoints to verify the correctness of the application. What we mean by Custom Checkpoint is that using scripting; we can manually compare our expected value with actual value and pass/fail the script. Why do we need to do that when we have UFT Checkpoint feature? The reason is that it gives us more flexibility to manipulate the expected and actual values and compare values as required.

Example

We were once automating an accounting based application package. We had to test the reports feature of the application. A sample test scenario included verifying the profit and loss report for a particular account. In order to achieve this we had to first calculate the expected value from what was set up in various forms in the application, and fetch the actual value from reports and then perform comparisons. We had to do this for a large number of values in the report. Custom Checkpoint made it a lot simpler and flexible for us to perform these kinds of checks, because we could perform computations on expected values and also create loop statements to verify multiple values in the same script. This would have been difficult using Standard Checkpoint as it did not allow run time computations on expected values and we would have to add too many standard checkpoints.

> Note: You can replace Standard Checkpoints and use just Custom Checkpoints.

In this chapter, we will discuss how to add a Custom Checkpoint. One of the key utility objects which we will learn will be the Reporter Object. This object helps us to report pass, fail, or informational messages from within the script.

Key objectives:

- Reporter Object and ReportEvent Method Syntax
- Apply Custom Checkpoints on a Test Scenario

15.1 Reporter Object and ReportEvent Method Syntax

Reporter Object: The object used for sending information to the test results.

ReportEvent Method: It is the method of Reporter Object, which reports an event to the test results.

Syntax

Reporter.ReportEvent *EventStatus, ReportStepName, Details* [, *Reporter*

Argument	Type	Description
EventStatus	Number or pre-defined constant	Status of the report step: **0** or **micPass:** Causes the status of this step to be passed and sends the specified message to the report. **1** or **micFail:** Causes the status of this step to be failed and sends the specified message to the report. When this step runs, the test fails. **2** or **micDone:** Sends a message to the report without affecting the pass/fail status of the test. **3** or **micWarn**ing: Sends a warning message to the report, but does not cause the test to stop running, and does not affect the pass/fail status of the test.
ReportStepName	String	Name of the intended step in the report (object name).
Details	String	Description of the report event. The string will be displayed in the step details frame in the report.
ImageFilePath	String	**Optional**. Path and filename of the image to be displayed in the **Captured Data** pane of the Run Results window. Images in the following formats can be displayed: BMP, PNG, JPEG, and GIF.

Note: ImageFilePath is one of the latest features added in UFT so that keeps a snapshot of result screens in your script.

Example

The following examples use the **ReportEvent** method to report a failed step.

Reporter.ReportEvent 1, "Step Name", "This Step failed" or

Reporter.ReportEvent micFail, "Step Name", "This Step failed".

15.2 Custom Checkpoint

Let us take a test scenario for which we will try to apply a Custom Checkpoint.

Test Objective: To verify that when a location is selected in search hotel, same location is displayed in select hotel page.

Test Steps:

1. Login to the application using User credentials.
2. Select Location as "Sydney" in location field in search hotel page.
3. Select Hotel as "Hotel Creek" in hotels field.
4. Select Room type as "Standard" in room type file.
5. Keep all the default selections.
6. Click on Search button.
7. Verify that in the next Select Hotel Page, correct location is displayed.

Expected Result

8. Correct location "Sydney" should appear in Location Column of Select Hotel search results.

Let us see how to insert Custom Checkpoint-

Pre-conditions -

1. Create a new UFT Test using **File → New → Test** and name the script as CustomCheckpointScript
2. Make sure your application (http://www.adactin.com/HotelApp/) login page is visible

Steps to Insert Custom Checkpoint

1. Record a basic script using following steps.
   a. User will login.
   b. Search for Hotel with below values.
      i. Location: "Sydney"
      ii. Hotels: "Hotel Creek"
      iii. Room Type: "Standard"
      iv. Other fields: Default
   c. Click on Search button.

d. Select first Radio button in search result and click Continue.

e. Click Logout (we do not need to book a hotel as my test case ends on select a hotel screen itself).

f. Click on "Click Here to Login" link to go back to Login page.

g. Stop Recording (by clicking on Stop Recording button in Record toolbar) after recording the above workflow. You will notice the following script in Editor View.

```
1  Browser("AdactIn.com - Hotel Reservatio").Page("AdactIn.com - Hotel Reservatio").WebEdit("username").Set "adactin123"
2  Browser("AdactIn.com - Hotel Reservatio").Page("AdactIn.com - Hotel Reservatio").WebEdit("password").SetSecure "511ae62e36071396c7c05cc05d5bfb082bdc7185e376247ce510"
3  Browser("AdactIn.com - Hotel Reservatio").Page("AdactIn.com - Hotel Reservatio").WebButton("Login").Click
4  Browser("AdactIn.com - Hotel Reservatio").Page("AdactIn.com - Hotel Reservatio").WebList("location").Select "Sydney"
5  Browser("AdactIn.com - Hotel Reservatio").Page("AdactIn.com - Hotel Reservatio").WebList("room_type").Select "Standard"
6  Browser("AdactIn.com - Hotel Reservatio").Page("AdactIn.com - Hotel Reservatio").WebList("hotels").Select "Hotel Creek"
7  Browser("AdactIn.com - Hotel Reservatio").Page("AdactIn.com - Hotel Reservatio").WebButton("Search").Click
8  Browser("AdactIn.com - Hotel Reservatio").Page("AdactIn.com - Hotel Reservatio").WebRadioGroup("radiobutton_0").Select "0"
9  Browser("AdactIn.com - Hotel Reservatio").Page("AdactIn.com - Hotel Reservatio").WebButton("Continue").Click
10 Browser("AdactIn.com - Hotel Reservatio").Page("AdactIn.com - Hotel Reservatio").Link("Logout").Click
11 Browser("AdactIn.com - Hotel Reservatio").Page("AdactIn.com - Hotel Reservatio").Link("Click here to login again").Click
```

Figure 15-1 – Editor View

2. Save the script.

3. Confirm correct playback of the script.

4. Go to Editor View (**View → Editor**). Inserting a Custom Checkpoint will use the following features.

   a. Add object to Object Repository.

   b. GetROProperty to capture object value.

   c. If-Else conditional statement

   d. Reporter Object

5. So first step is to add Location Object in Object Repository, since this object will not be automatically present in our repository as we have not recorded on this object (if you are using Shared Repository you might already have this object in your Shared Repository).

   a. Make sure Location Object on Select Hotel page is visible. Manually login to the application and follow the steps mentioned above in Test Objective and go to Select Hotel page (in case you are logged out).

Figure 15-2 – Application Select Hotel page

   b. Open **Resources → Object Repository** and click on **Add objects** icon to add Location Object. Note that you need to click on Location "Sydney" (if that is the location you have selected in Search Hotel page). Click **Ok** in the Object Selection Dialog box.

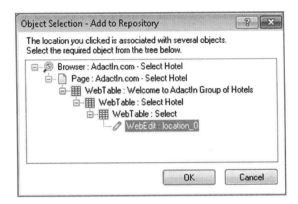

Figure 15-3– Location Object Selection

c. You will see that object location_0 gets added into the repository.

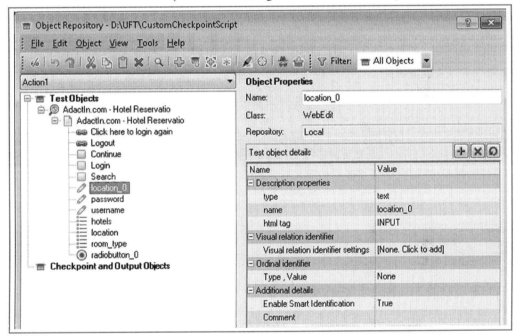

Figure 15-4– Object added in repository

d. Close Repository

6. Now we will use GetROProperty to capture run time object value from location field.

Note: Using Object Spy, we can find out that "value" property of the location_0 object stores actual value of location.

a. Go to **Editor View** in your script

b. Put your cursor just after click on Search button to move to Select Hotel page and press Enter.

```
1  Browser("AdactIn.com - Hotel Reservatio").Page("AdactIn.com - Hotel Reservatio").WebEdit("username").Set "adactin123"
2  Browser("AdactIn.com - Hotel Reservatio").Page("AdactIn.com - Hotel Reservatio").WebEdit("password").SetSecure "511ae62e36071396c7c05cc05d5bfb082bdc7185e376247ce510"
3  Browser("AdactIn.com - Hotel Reservatio").Page("AdactIn.com - Hotel Reservatio").WebButton("Login").Click
4  Browser("AdactIn.com - Hotel Reservatio").Page("AdactIn.com - Hotel Reservatio").WebList("location").Select "Sydney"
5  Browser("AdactIn.com - Hotel Reservatio").Page("AdactIn.com - Hotel Reservatio").WebList("room_type").Select "Standard"
6  Browser("AdactIn.com - Hotel Reservatio").Page("AdactIn.com - Hotel Reservatio").WebList("hotels").Select "Hotel Creek"
7  Browser("AdactIn.com - Hotel Reservatio").Page("AdactIn.com - Hotel Reservatio").WebButton("Search").Click
8  |
9  Browser("AdactIn.com - Hotel Reservatio").Page("AdactIn.com - Hotel Reservatio").WebRadioGroup("radiobutton_0").Select "0"
10 Browser("AdactIn.com - Hotel Reservatio").Page("AdactIn.com - Hotel Reservatio").WebButton("Continue").Click
11 Browser("AdactIn.com - Hotel Reservatio").Page("AdactIn.com - Hotel Reservatio").Link("Logout").Click
12 Browser("AdactIn.com - Hotel Reservatio").Page("AdactIn.com - Hotel Reservatio").Link("Click here to login again").Click
```

Figure 15-5– Cursor Position

c. We will use step generator to add GetROProperty Step. Go to **Design → Step Generator**, and select location_0 object from test object and select **Operation** 'GetROProperty'.

d. Enter the name of **property** we want to capture as 'value'.

e. Check the checkbox for **Return Value** and use variable as sLocation.

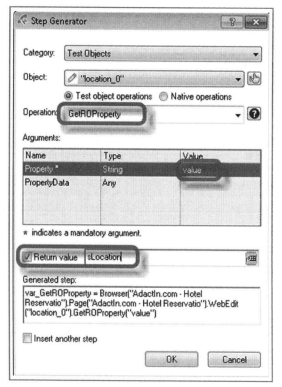

Figure 15-6– Step Generator setup

f. Click **OK**. You will see the following line in code.

```
5  Browser("AdactIn.com - Hotel Reservatio").Page("AdactIn.com - Hotel Reservatio").WebList("room_type").Select "Standard"
6  Browser("AdactIn.com - Hotel Reservatio").Page("AdactIn.com - Hotel Reservatio").WebList("hotels").Select "Hotel Creek"
7  Browser("AdactIn.com - Hotel Reservatio").Page("AdactIn.com - Hotel Reservatio").WebButton("Search").Click
8  sLocation = Browser("AdactIn.com - Hotel Reservatio").Page("AdactIn.com - Hotel Reservatio").WebEdit("location_0").GetROProperty("value")
9  Browser("AdactIn.com - Hotel Reservatio").Page("AdactIn.com - Hotel Reservatio").WebRadioGroup("radiobutton_0").Select "0"
10 Browser("AdactIn.com - Hotel Reservatio").Page("AdactIn.com - Hotel Reservatio").WebButton("Continue").Click
11 Browser("AdactIn.com - Hotel Reservatio").Page("AdactIn.com - Hotel Reservatio").Link("Logout").Click
```

Figure 15-7– Step added in Editor View

7. Type below If--Else conditional statement in the code which will be used to pass or fail the script if captured value is "Sydney".

```
1   Browser("AdactIn.com - Hotel Reservatio").Page("AdactIn.com - Hotel Reservatio").WebEdit("username").Set "adactin123"
2   Browser("AdactIn.com - Hotel Reservatio").Page("AdactIn.com - Hotel Reservatio").WebEdit("password").SetSecure "511ae62e36071396c7c05cc05d5bfb082bdc7185e376247ce510"
3   Browser("AdactIn.com - Hotel Reservatio").Page("AdactIn.com - Hotel Reservatio").WebButton("Login").Click
4   Browser("AdactIn.com - Hotel Reservatio").Page("AdactIn.com - Hotel Reservatio").WebList("location").Select "Sydney"
5   Browser("AdactIn.com - Hotel Reservatio").Page("AdactIn.com - Hotel Reservatio").WebList("room_type").Select "Standard"
6   Browser("AdactIn.com - Hotel Reservatio").Page("AdactIn.com - Hotel Reservatio").WebList("hotels").Select "Hotel Creek"
7   Browser("AdactIn.com - Hotel Reservatio").Page("AdactIn.com - Hotel Reservatio").WebButton("Search").Click
8   sLocation = Browser("AdactIn.com - Hotel Reservatio").Page("AdactIn.com - Hotel Reservatio").WebEdit("location_0").GetROProperty("value")
9
10  If sLocation = "Sydney" Then
11      'Pass the script
12  Else
13      'Fail the script
14  End If
15
16  Browser("AdactIn.com - Hotel Reservatio").Page("AdactIn.com - Hotel Reservatio").WebRadioGroup("radiobutton_0").Select "0"
17  Browser("AdactIn.com - Hotel Reservatio").Page("AdactIn.com - Hotel Reservatio").WebButton("Continue").Click
18  Browser("AdactIn.com - Hotel Reservatio").Page("AdactIn.com - Hotel Reservatio").Link("Logout").Click
19  Browser("AdactIn.com - Hotel Reservatio").Page("AdactIn.com - Hotel Reservatio").Link("Click here to login again").Click
```

Figure 15-8– Step with If-Else statements

Note: We have intentionally commented out steps for passing or failing the script, which we will add in next step.

8. Now we use Reporter Object to pass or fail the script

   a. With cursor at step where you see Pass the script, go to **Design → Step Generator…**

   b. Select **Utility Objects** from the '**Category**' Dropdown.

   c. In the '**Object**' field select **Reporter** Object.

   d. By default the Operation is **ReportEvent.**

   e. In the Event Status, Value column select **micPass.**

   f. In **ReportStepName** manually Type Step Value – "Verify Location Field".

   g. In the **Details** field manually type step value – "Location Field is correct".

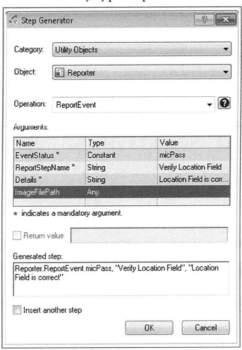

Figure 15-9– Add Reporter Object using Step Generator

h.   Click **OK** and in the script you will see the following line of code.

```
1   Browser("AdactIn.com - Hotel Reservatio").Page("AdactIn.com - Hotel Reservatio").WebEdit("username").Set "adactin123"
2   Browser("AdactIn.com - Hotel Reservatio").Page("AdactIn.com - Hotel Reservatio").WebEdit("password").SetSecure "511ae62e36071396c7c05cc05d5bfb082bdc7185e376247ce510"
3   Browser("AdactIn.com - Hotel Reservatio").Page("AdactIn.com - Hotel Reservatio").WebButton("Login").Click
4   Browser("AdactIn.com - Hotel Reservatio").Page("AdactIn.com - Hotel Reservatio").WebList("location").Select "Sydney"
5   Browser("AdactIn.com - Hotel Reservatio").Page("AdactIn.com - Hotel Reservatio").WebList("room_type").Select "Standard"
6   Browser("AdactIn.com - Hotel Reservatio").Page("AdactIn.com - Hotel Reservatio").WebList("hotels").Select "Hotel Creek"
7   Browser("AdactIn.com - Hotel Reservatio").Page("AdactIn.com - Hotel Reservatio").WebButton("Search").Click
8   sLocation = Browser("AdactIn.com - Hotel Reservatio").Page("AdactIn.com - Hotel Reservatio").WebEdit("location_0").GetROProperty("value")
9
10  If sLocation = "Sydney" Then
11      'Pass the script
12      Reporter.ReportEvent micPass, "Verify Location Field", "Location Field is correct"
13  Else
14      'Fail the script
15  End If
```

Figure 15-10– Reporter Step in Editor View

i.   Placing the cursor at comment for fail the script, follow the steps a-h for the fail reporter function. In the event status, select micFail.

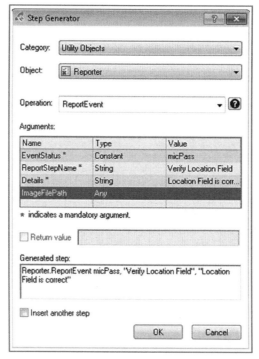

Figure 15-11– Step for reporting Fail

j.   Click **OK** and you will see below final script.

```
1   Browser("AdactIn.com - Hotel Reservatio").Page("AdactIn.com - Hotel Reservatio").WebEdit("username").Set "adactin123"
2   Browser("AdactIn.com - Hotel Reservatio").Page("AdactIn.com - Hotel Reservatio").WebEdit("password").SetSecure "511ae62e36071396c7c05cc05d5bfb082bdc7185e376247ce510"
3   Browser("AdactIn.com - Hotel Reservatio").Page("AdactIn.com - Hotel Reservatio").WebButton("Login").Click
4   Browser("AdactIn.com - Hotel Reservatio").Page("AdactIn.com - Hotel Reservatio").WebList("location").Select "Sydney"
5   Browser("AdactIn.com - Hotel Reservatio").Page("AdactIn.com - Hotel Reservatio").WebList("room_type").Select "Standard"
6   Browser("AdactIn.com - Hotel Reservatio").Page("AdactIn.com - Hotel Reservatio").WebList("hotels").Select "Hotel Creek"
7   Browser("AdactIn.com - Hotel Reservatio").Page("AdactIn.com - Hotel Reservatio").WebButton("Search").Click
8   sLocation = Browser("AdactIn.com - Hotel Reservatio").Page("AdactIn.com - Hotel Reservatio").WebEdit("location_0").GetROProperty("value")
9
10  If sLocation = "Sydney" Then
11      'Pass the script
12      Reporter.ReportEvent micPass, "Verify Location Field", "Location Field is correct"
13  Else
14      'Fail the script
15      Reporter.ReportEvent micFail, "Verify Location Field", "Location Field Value is incorrect"
16  End If
17
18  Browser("AdactIn.com - Hotel Reservatio").Page("AdactIn.com - Hotel Reservatio").WebRadioGroup("radiobutton_0").Select "0"
19  Browser("AdactIn.com - Hotel Reservatio").Page("AdactIn.com - Hotel Reservatio").WebButton("Continue").Click
20  Browser("AdactIn.com - Hotel Reservatio").Page("AdactIn.com - Hotel Reservatio").Link("Logout").Click
21  Browser("AdactIn.com - Hotel Reservatio").Page("AdactIn.com - Hotel Reservatio").Link("Click here to login again").Click
22
```

Figure 15-12– Editor View with script

9. Execute the script with Login page of the application visible and see the results. Collapse the results tree and you will see that the script passed.

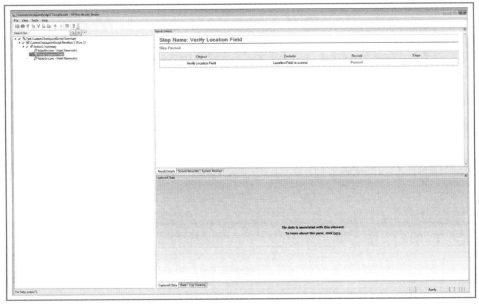

Figure 15-13– Test Results

Note: At expert level, we can directly type the Reporter Object and other statements in Editor View, we do not have to use step generator.

Exercise

1. Verify that [total price in Select Hotel page = Number of Rooms * Number of days* Price per night] using Custom Checkpoint.

2. Verify Total price of Hotel selected in Select a Hotel and Book a Hotel are same.

ଏଓ

16

Working with External Files

In many instances, automation tools need to interface with external files such as Text files (which can be configuration files) or with Excel files, which can store data.

Using its VBScript capability, UFT can be used to interact with many different types of external files like Text files, Excel, Word, PDF, Databases, and any other files which have an open object model reference available.

An important point to note is that most of these features are provided by VBScript as a language, and not UFT as a tool. UFT acts as an IDE (Integrated Development Environment) to execute the required VBScript code.

Example

While automating a student management portal application for one of our clients we found that they had multiple environments, which included development, integration, testing, and staging. Each one of them had separate URLs to access the application. They wanted us to execute our scripts on each of these environments. One option available to us was to hard-code the URL of the application in one of the script functions. Based on the environment we would need to change the URL. The other more sensible option was to create a text file (.txt) and add the URL in the file. Instead of modifying the script or function, we could now just get our UFT script to read from the external text file, and launch the URL based on the path mentioned in the file. This was a better option, as it did not involve any code changes.

In this chapter, we will discuss how to work with excel files and text files.

Key objectives:

- Working with File System Object and Text Files.
- Working with Excel Files.
- Importing Data from Excel File in UFT.

16.1 Working with Text Files

We have seen automation frameworks will usually use Text files to store configuration parameters.

To Read or Write to Text files, you use the **File System Object** in UFT script.

Read from Text File

Let us discuss the steps and code you need to **Read from a Text File.**

1. Create a **File System Object**

   Dim fso

   Set fso = CreateObject("Scripting.FileSystemObject")

The **FileSystemObject** (FSO) object model allows you to use the familiar *object.method* syntax with a rich set of properties, methods, and events to process folders and files.

2. Open a Text File using **OpenTextFile** method.

   Dim fso, ts

   var ForReading = 1;

   Set fso = CreateObject("Scripting. FileSystemObject")

   Set ts = fso.OpenTextFile("D:\test.txt", ForReading, True)

3. Use any of the following methods to read from the text file.

- Read – Read a specified number of characters from a file.
- ReadLine – Read an entire line (up to, but not including, the newline character).
- ReadAll – Read the entire contents of a text file.

For example, let us use **ReadLine**.

   Dim fso, ts

   var ForReading = 1;

   Set fso = CreateObject("Scripting. FileSystemObject")

   Set ts = fso.OpenTextFile("D:\test.txt", ForReading, True)

   Do Until ts.AtEndOfStream

   s = ts.ReadLine

   msgbox s

Loop

4. Close the File and objects using **Close** method and setting objects to **Nothing**.

   Dim fso, ts

   var ForReading = 1;

```
Set fso = CreateObject("Scripting. FileSystemObject")

Set ts = fso.OpenTextFile("D:\test.txt", ForReading, True)

        Do Until ts.AtEndOfStream

            s = ts.ReadLine

            msgbox s

Loop

ts.close

Set fso = Nothing

Set ts = Nothing
```

Note: AtEndofStream will help to read the file until it reaches its end.

Exercise

1. Create a Text file in D drive, test.txt
2. Add "Hello World First" text in the first line and "Hello World Second" in the second line. Save and close the file
3. Create a new UFT GUI Test Script and go to Editor View
4. Copy the above code in UFT Editor View
5. Verify the messages popped up.

Writing from Text File

Let us discuss the steps or code you need to **write to a text file**

1. Create a **File System Object**

   ```
   Dim fso

   Set fso = CreateObject("Scripting.FileSystemObject")
   ```

2. Open a Text File using **OpenTextFile** method

   ```
   Dim fso, ts

   var ForWriting = 2;

   Set fso = CreateObject("Scripting. FileSystemObject")

   Set ts = fso.OpenTextFile("D:\test.txt", ForWriting, True)
   ```

Alternatively use **CreatetTextFile** Method to create a text file

```
Dim fso, f1

Set fso = CreateObject("Scripting.FileSystemObject")

Set ts = fso.CreateTextFile("D:\test.txt", True)
```

3. Use any of the following methods to read from the Text file

- Write – Write data to an open Text file without a trailing newline character.
- WriteLine – Write data to an open Text file with a trailing newline character.
- WriteBlankLines – Write one or more blank lines to an open Text file.

For example, let us use WriteLine

```
Dim fso, tf

Set fso = CreateObject("Scripting.FileSystemObject")

Set ts = fso.CreateTextFile("D:\test.txt", True)

' Write a line with a newline character.

tsWriteLine("Testing 1, 2, 3.")

' Write three newline characters to the file.

ts.WriteBlankLines(5)

' Write a line.

ts.Write ("Hello World.")

ts.close

Set fso = Nothing

Sct ts – Nothing
```

Exercise

1. Create a new UFT GUI Test script and go to Editor View.
2. Copy the above code in UFT Editor View.
3. Verify that there is no txt file with name test.txt in the D: drive.
4. Execute the script.
5. After execution, verify that test file in D: drive contains relevant content written.

> **Note:** You can always search on Google and find a number of ways of reading and writing to a Text file. As mentioned, this is not a UFT feature-set but of the VBScript language which is being used within UFT.

16.2 Working with Excel Files

We can also use VBScript within UFT to read/write from Excel files. You need to perform the following key steps to work with Excel Sheet:

- Creating Excel Object
- Open WorkBook
- Get the Excel Sheet
- Write/Retrieve Data from Corresponding Sheet
- Closing the Excel WorkBook

Let us see how to work with Excel files

1. Create an **Excel Object**

    Set ExcelObj = CreateObject("Excel.Application")

The above line of code will help you create Excel object

2. Open Workbook

    ExcelObj.Workbooks.Open("D:\Test.xls")

3. Get the WorkSheet within the Workbook

    Set NewSheet = ExcelObj.Sheets.Item(1)

4. Read/Write data into Excel Sheet

    Read Data:

    MyVal = NewSheet.Cells(row,col)

Write Data:

    NewSheet.Cells(row,col) = "MyVal"

Note: Row stands for Row number and col. stands for Column number in Excel Sheet

5. Saving and Closing the Workbook

    ExcelObj.ActiveWorkbook.Save

    ExcelObj.Application.Quit

    Set ExcelObj = Nothing

So sample code to read from existing Excel Sheet will be:

```
Set ExcelObj = CreateObject("Excel.Application")

ExcelObj.Workbooks.Open "C:\File.xls"

Set NewSheet = ExcelObj.Sheets.Item(1)

'Retrieve data to Excel Sheet

MyVal = NewSheet.Cells(row,col)

ExcelObj.ActiveWorkbook.Save

ExcelObj.Application.Quit

Set ExcelObj = Nothing
```

Exercise

1. Create an Excel file in D drive, Test.xls.
2. Add "Hello World First" in first column and first row and "Hello World Second" in the second column first row. Save and close the file.
3. Create a new UFT GUI Test script and go to Editor View.
4. Copy the below code in UFT Editor View.

```
Set ExcelObj = CreateObject("Excel.Application")

ExcelObj.Workbooks.Open  "D:\Test.xls"

Set NewSheet = ExcelObj.Sheets.Item(1)

'Retrieve data to Excel Sheet

MyVal = NewSheet.Cells(1,1)

Msgbox MyVal

MyVal2 = NewSheet.Cells(1,2)

Msgbox MyVal2

ExcelObj.ActiveWorkbook.Save

ExcelObj.Application.Quit

Set ExcelObj = Nothing
```

5. Verify that messages pop-up with correct values.

Note: You can always search using Google and find a number of ways of reading and writing from Excel files. As previously mentioned, this is not a UFT but a VBScript feature-set that is being used within UFT.

16.3 Using UFT DataTable Object to read from External Files

Apart from using Excel Object to read and write to Excel Sheets, UFT also provides a utility object to work with external Excel files.

For example, if your application has a login page, and you need to enter username and password, you would want to store that username and password in an external Excel file so that it can be re-used by all other scripts which have to use login function.

We can use **Excel** object as mentioned in section above to read from Excel sheets and login to the application.

But UFT also provides an alternate way using the **DataTable** object. Data table represents the UFT design-time data table and its associated sheets and parameters.

Let us see the steps to read/write from Excel sheet using Data table object:

Test Scenario – Lets consider a simple login and logout scenario in our hotel reservation application and fetch username and password from an external data source.

1. Create a new GUI Test in UFT using **File → New → Test** and name it DataImportScript.

2. Making sure Login window of our Hotel Application is open, start recording and record below workflow.

   a. Login to the application by entering username and password.

   b. Click on logout link once logged in.

   c. Click on "Click Here to login again" to go back to login page.

Stop Recording (by clicking on **Stop Recording** button in Record toolbar) after recording the above workflow. You will notice the following script.

```
1  Browser("AdactIn.com - Hotel Reservatio").Page("AdactIn.com - Hotel Reservatio").WebEdit("username").Set "adactin123"
2  Browser("AdactIn.com - Hotel Reservatio").Page("AdactIn.com - Hotel Reservatio").WebEdit("password").SetSecure "511af1ac419e5b62da256061e4f79a56732df2216511ba827c77"
3  Browser("AdactIn.com - Hotel Reservatio").Page("AdactIn.com - Hotel Reservatio").WebButton("Login").Click
4  Browser("AdactIn.com - Hotel Reservatio").Page("AdactIn.com - Hotel Reservatio").Link("Logout").Click
5  Browser("AdactIn.com - Hotel Reservatio").Page("AdactIn.com - Hotel Reservatio").Link("Click here to login again").Click
```

Figure 16-1 – Editor View

The username and password here is hard-coded within the script. So let us try to use an external Excel Sheet and use data from that sheet.

3. Create an Excel Sheet and let us name it as Login.xls

4. Add 2 columns and name them UserName and Password and add the login data to the sheet. Use the encoded password in the password field from the Editor View.

> **Note**: Alternatively you can get password encoded string using Password Encoder utility in Start → All Programs → HP Software → HP Unified Functional Testing → Tools → Password Encoder.

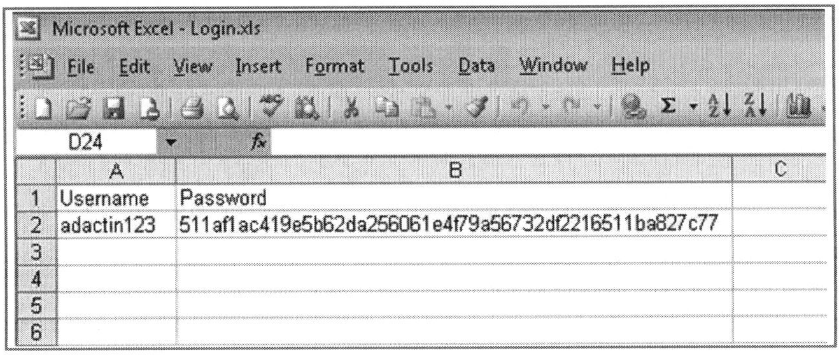

Figure 16-2 – Excel based datasheet

5. Go to Editor View in UFT GUI Test script and we will use ImportSheet Method to Import Data from Excel Sheet.

ImportSheet Method

This method imports a sheet from a specified file, to a specified sheet in the run time data table. Using this method we can import the data in our external excel file and get that data into the UFT scripts built-in datatable.

The column headings in the sheet you import must match the datatable parameter names in the action for which the sheet is being imported. Otherwise, your test or component may fail.

Syntax

DataTable.ImportSheet(*FileName, SheetSource, SheetDes*)

Argument	Type	Description
FileName	String	The full path of the Excel table from which you want to import a sheet.
SheetSource	Variant	The name or index of the sheet in the file that you want to import. Index values begin with 1.
SheetDest	Variant	The name or index of the sheet in the Data Table that you want to replace with the *SheetSource*. Index values begin with 1.

Example

The following example uses the **ImportSheet** method to import the first sheet of the *name.xls* table to the name sheet in the test's run time data table.

DataTable.ImportSheet "C:\name.xls", 1,"name"

Let us go to the Editor View of our script and type the following statement to import login data into our script.

DataTable.ImportSheet "D:\UFT\\Login.xls", 1, 1

Note: Please make sure to change the path based on, where you have stored the sheet. Your Editor View code will look like the following.

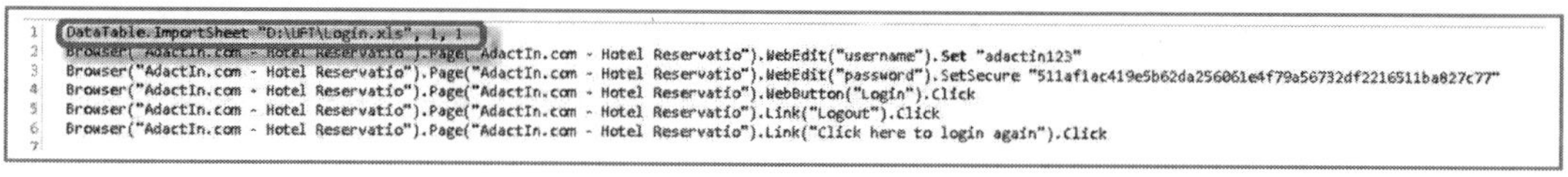

```
1  DataTable.ImportSheet "D:\UFT\Login.xls", 1, 1
2  Browser("AdactIn.com - Hotel Reservatio").Page("AdactIn.com - Hotel Reservatio").WebEdit("username").Set "adactin123"
3  Browser("AdactIn.com - Hotel Reservatio").Page("AdactIn.com - Hotel Reservatio").WebEdit("password").SetSecure "511af1ac419e5b62da256061e4f79a56732df2216511ba827c77"
4  Browser("AdactIn.com - Hotel Reservatio").Page("AdactIn.com - Hotel Reservatio").WebButton("Login").Click
5  Browser("AdactIn.com - Hotel Reservatio").Page("AdactIn.com - Hotel Reservatio").Link("Logout").Click
6  Browser("AdactIn.com - Hotel Reservatio").Page("AdactIn.com - Hotel Reservatio").Link("Click here to login again").Click
7
```

Figure 16-3 – ImportSheet step in Editor View

6. Now we need to get the value of username and password from the DataTable. So will use the Value method of Class DataTable to read data from DataTable.

Syntax

To read a value

DataTable.Value(ParameterID [, SheetID])

or

DataTable(ParameterID [, SheetID])

Argument	Type	Description
ParameterID	Variant	Identifies the parameter (column) of the value to be set/retrieved. Index values begin with 1.
SheetID	Variant	**Optional.** Identifies the sheet to be returned. The SheetID can be the sheet name, index or dtLocalSheet, or dtGlobalSheet.
		If no Sheet is specified, the first sheet in the run time DataTable is used (global sheet). Index values begin with 1.

Example

The following example uses the Value property, to get the value in the current row of the first parameter (column) in the sheet.

PA4 = DataTable.Value (1, 1)

Note: You could omit the word **Value** in the statements above, because Value is the default property for the DataTable object.

So let us go into the Editor View of our script and type below statement to import login data into our script-

sUsername = DataTable.Value ("Username", 1)

sPassword = DataTable.Value ("Password",1)

Our script will look like below

```
1  DataTable.ImportSheet "D:\UFT\Login.xls", 1, 1
2  sUsername = DataTable.Value ("Username",1)
3  sPassword = DataTable.Value ("Password",1)
4  Browser("AdactIn.com - Hotel Reservatio").Page("AdactIn.com - Hotel Reservatio").WebEdit("username").Set "adactin123"
5  Browser("AdactIn.com - Hotel Reservatio").Page("AdactIn.com - Hotel Reservatio").WebEdit("password").SetSecure "511af1ac419e5b62da256061e4f79a56732df2216511ba827c77"
6  Browser("AdactIn.com - Hotel Reservatio").Page("AdactIn.com - Hotel Reservatio").WebButton("Login").Click
7  Browser("AdactIn.com - Hotel Reservatio").Page("AdactIn.com - Hotel Reservatio").Link("Logout").Click
8  Browser("AdactIn.com - Hotel Reservatio").Page("AdactIn.com - Hotel Reservatio").Link("Click here to login again").Click
9
```

Figure 16-4 – Get value from DataTable

7. Replace the hardcoded value of username and password by using variable values from the Excel Sheet

```
1   DataTable.ImportSheet "D:\UFT\Login.xls", 1, 1
2   sUsername = DataTable.Value ("Username", 1)
3   sPassword = DataTable.Value ("Password",1)
4   Browser("AdactIn.com - Hotel Reservatio").Page("AdactIn.com - Hotel Reservatio").WebEdit("username").Set sUsername
5   Browser("AdactIn.com - Hotel Reservatio").Page("AdactIn.com - Hotel Reservatio").WebEdit("password").SetSecure sPassword
6   Browser("AdactIn.com - Hotel Reservatio").Page("AdactIn.com - Hotel Reservatio").WebButton("Login").Click
7   Browser("AdactIn.com - Hotel Reservatio").Page("AdactIn.com - Hotel Reservatio").Link("Logout").Click
8   Browser("AdactIn.com - Hotel Reservatio").Page("AdactIn.com - Hotel Reservatio").Link("Click here to login again").Click
9
10
```

Figure 16-5 – Replace parameter values

8. Save the script.

9. Close Login.xls sheet if already open.

10. Execute the script and confirm the script can be executed with correct username and password.

11. In the Test Results, select DataTable tab. You will find data from Login.xls in this sheet. This DataTable in results is called Run time DataTable.

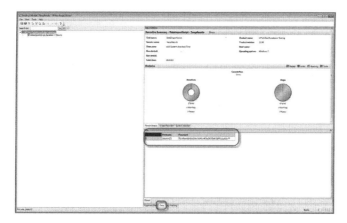

Figure 16-6 – Data Pane in Test Results

> **Note:** If you want to pick data from a specific row of DataTable, you can use method **DataTable.SetCurrentRow(RowNumber),** to set current row.

For example, consider that in your login.xls sheet, the first row contains admin user, second row contains member user, and third row contains guest user. Now as part of the test case, you need to login as a member user, how will you instruct your test to go to the second row? You can use the SetCurrentRow method to accomplish this.

In practical scenarios, we tend to use combination of ImportSheet, SetCurrentRow, and Value methods, while working with external sheets.

Exercise

1. Create a function for Search a Hotel, which has only one parameter "ID" which is the row of the Excel datasheet which stores the data and row number you want to use.

2. Create an Excel sheet search.xls which has parameters Location, Number of rooms, and Adults per Room.

3. Update Search.xls with 3 multiple rows of data, for each of field values of parameters (make sure data values do exist in the application).

4. Create a new script and use functions Login, Search Hotel, and Logout. Call Search Hotel with different parameters values (1 for row1 and 2 for row2 and 3 for row3 of data).

> **Hint:** Within the search function, you will need to use ImportSheet, SetCurrentRow, and Value methods.

> **Note:** Similar to Excel Object we can also use VBScript to read and write data into database using ADODB Connection Object. Please refer to online help to see sample programs to work with databases.

છ×

17

Debugging Scripts

Introduction

I believe one cannot be an expert in any tool if he or she does not know how to debug issues, or does not know how to troubleshoot problems encountered while using the tool.

Debugging is an integrated feature of any automation tool. Automation scripts do fail, and we should be able to pinpoint exactly where the issue is, so that it can be fixed.

HP UFT comes with some nifty debugging features, which should be used while isolating reasons for failure of scripts. We would want to have the ability to execute one step at a time, or pause at a particular step or being able to peek at values of variables at runtime. All these features can be found within UFT.

Example

At one of our telecom clients, they had around 150 automation scripts, and they were not currently executable after a new build was released to the test team. The core automation team had left after the release and nobody knew how to fix the scripts. The only way we could figure out what went wrong with the script and understand the application workflow was by using the debugging features of UFT. That proved invaluable to us in getting the scripts up and running again!

In this chapter we will learn how to debug UFT scripts.

Key objectives:

- Understand Step Into, Step Over and Step Out.
- Breakpoint.
- Run from Step.
- Watches and Variables in Debug Viewer.

17.1 Understand Step Into, Step Out and Step Over

UFT provides three useful features Step Into, Step Over and Step Out.

Step Into: Step Into runs only the current step in the active test or function library, which means that it only executes one step at a time. Once that step is executed, script will pause at the next step and wait for users input before executing the next step.

If the current step calls another Action or a Function, the called Action or Function is displayed in the UFT window, and the test or function library pauses at the first line of the called Action or Function.

Let us look at an example of using Step Into statement:

Note: Save any previously created script.

1. Open a new UFT GUI Test script using **File** → **New** → **Test** and name it DebugScript1.
2. Go to **View** → **Editor View.**
3. In Editor View tab enter type lines of code.

```
1    'AdactIn - Sample Debug Code
2
3    Dim a
4    Dim b
5    Dim c
6    a = 5
7    b =10
8    c = a+b
9    Msgbox c
```

Figure 17-1 - Editor View code

4. Select **Run** → **Step Into** or Press **F11.**

Figure 17-2 – Step Into menu option

5. Click **Run** on default Run Dialog box.

Figure 17-3 – Run Dialog box

6. Verify that Script starts execution and stops at step "a = 5".

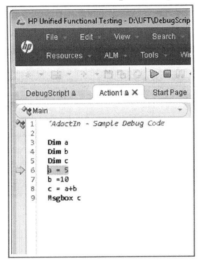

Figure 17-4 – Run Paused at Step

7. Press **F11** again or Select **Run** → **Step Into**. Verify that Script moves to next line, which contain "b=10".

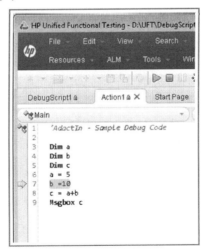

Figure 17-5 – Run Paused at Second Step

It is important to note that we are executing one line at a time, instead of the whole script executing from start to finish.

8. Keep pressing F11 again or Select Run → Step Into until complete script is executed.

Note that once all lines of script are executed, the script will finish execution automatically.

Step Out: After using Step Into to enter a function in a function library, you can use the Step Out command. Step Out continues the run to the end of the function, returns to the calling test or function library, and then pauses the run session at the next line (if one exists).

Step Over runs only the current step in the active test or function library.

Step Over: If the current step calls a user-defined function, the called function is executed in its entirety, but the called function script is not displayed in the UFT window. The run session then returns to the calling test or function library, and pauses at the next line (if one exists).

17.2 Breakpoints

Many times when debugging, we would want our script to pause at a certain step so that we can verify that all the steps that have been executed till that point work as expected.

Breakpoints "pause" the script execution before the step at which breakpoint has been applied. Do note that we "pause" the script and do not "Stop" the script, which means that if we press F5 or F11 again, script will continue its normal execution.

It is one of the most widely used debugging features in any development IDE (Integrated Development Environment) and UFT provides that to us through Editor View.

Let us see how to add a breakpoint in our script.

Note: Save any previously created script.

1. Create a new UFT GUI Test script from **File → New → Test** and name it DebugScript2.

2. Go to Editor View.

3. In Editor View type below lines of code.

```
1    'AdactIn - Sample Debug Code
2
3    Dim a
4    Dim b
5    Dim c
6    a = 5
7    b =10
8    c = a+b
9    Msgbox c
```

Figure 17-6 – Editor View

4. In the left pane next to where line numbers of steps is written, click on the line number before which you would want your script to pause. For instance, in our case, we want our script to pause before line "c = a+b" is executed.

You will see a "Red" dot coming next to the step, on which you want to have a breakpoint.

In the snapshot below we click on left margin next to number "8" and we get a Red dot next to line number.

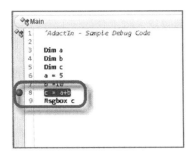

Figure 17-7 – Breakpoint Inserted

5. Go to **Run** → **Run** and Run the script. Verify script pause before execution of Line number 8.

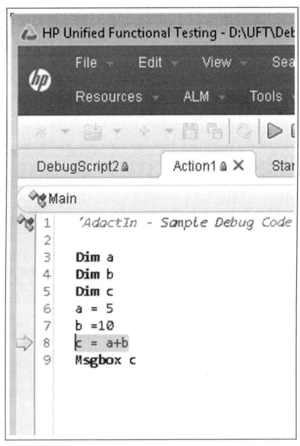

Figure 17-8 – Script Pause at Breakpoint

6. Press F11 to move to next step.

7. Press F11 again to get Msgbox prompt.

Figure 17-9 – Message box prompt

Note: As we see in the above example, Breakpoint pauses our script execution at a certain step and from there on we can execute one step at a time to isolate which step is causing our script to fail.

17.3 Run from Step

Occasionally, you will see that your scripts are pretty big and you do not want to execute the whole script. In such cases, you can start from some point mid-way in the script and continue your testing from there.

Example

For example:

Once while working on a manufacturing based application, we had a script which had 300 lines of code. The first 200 lines were data input lines. So ideally we had to verify results after 200th line. Since, we had already manually entered the data in the application we didn't want to execute the first 200 lines of code. So we used "Run from Step" function to execute script from the 201st step.

Let us see how to use Run from Step

Note: Save any previously created script.

1. Open a new UFT test using **File → New → Test** and name is DebugScript3.

2. Go to Editor View tab.

3. In Editor View type below lines of code.

```
1    'AdactIn - Sample Debug Code
2
3    Dim a
4    Dim b
5    Dim c
6    Dim d
7    Dim e
8    Dim f
9
10
11   a = 5
12   b =10
13   c = a+b
14   Msgbox c
15
16   d = 15
17   e = 20
18   f = d+e
19
20   Msgbox f
```

Figure 17-10 – Editor View

4. Now let us assume we want to verify test execution only from line 16, which reads "d = 15" and do not want to worry about lines 11, 12, 13 which calculate values for variable c.

   a. Enter your cursor at beginning of line 16 (which is "d=15").

   b. Right Click and Select **Run from Step.**

   c. Click **Run** on default **Run Dialog**.

✂ Cut	Ctrl+X	
📋 Copy	Ctrl+C	
📋 Paste	Ctrl+V	
✖ Delete		
Comment	Ctrl+M	
Uncomment	Ctrl+Shift+M	
Indent	Tab	
Outdent	Shift+Tab	
Insert Step	▶	
Action	▶	
➡ Go to Definition	Ctrl+Return	
🖑 Insert/Remove Breakpoint	F9	
Enable/Disable Breakpoint	Ctrl+F9	
▶ Run from Step...		
Debug from Step...		
Run to Step...		
➕ Add to Watch	Ctrl+T	
Select All	Ctrl+A	

Figure 17-11 – Run from Step menu option

5. Verify that scripts only execute starting from line 16 – Till end.

Figure 17-12 – Message box prompt

As you see, "Run from Step" option can considerably reduce the debugging effort.

17.4 Watches and Variables in Debug Mode

Apart from using Msgbox, which is a fairly good debugging option and widely used, we can use Debug Viewer to look at variable values at run time within the script.

The drawback with using Msgbox is that we have to manually insert it everywhere for every variable whose value we want to prompt. Once we have finished debugging, we would then need to remove the Msgbox commands from our script to clean up the script.

A better option will be to see variable values through the Debug Option.

Panes in Debug Menu

1. To see various panes in Debug menu, go to **View → Debug**.

Figure 17-12 – Debug Options

Breakpoint Pane - Displays the information about all breakpoints inserted into your action, scripted component, function library, or user code file and enables you to enable or disable any or all breakpoints in a run session.

Call Stack Pane - Displays information about the functions, methods, or context currently relevant to your run session.

Local Variables pane - Displays the current values and types of all variables in the current context of the document.

Console pane - Enables you to run VBScript commands in your paused run session.

Watch pane - Displays the current values and types of variables, and VBScript expressions that you add to the Watch pane.

2. Select the panes and confirm that you can see Debug panes in the bottom pane

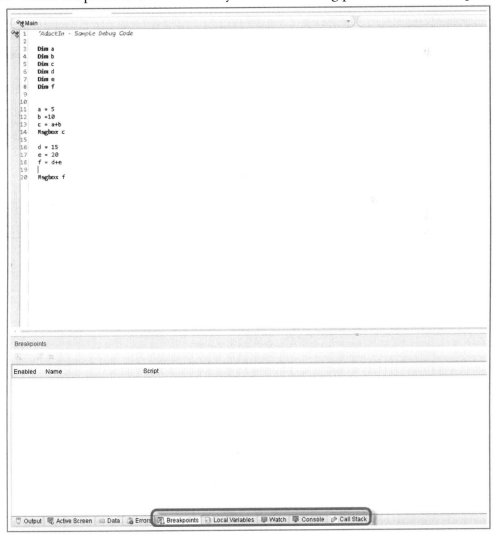

Figure 17-13 – Debug panes

Using Local Variables Tab

Local Variables Tab - While running your script in debug mode (Step into mode), if you want to see current value of any of the variables used in the script you can see those in Variables tab.

Watches Tab - This tab enables you to view the current values and types of selected variables, properties and VBScript expressions in your test.

Difference between Variables tab and Watches tab

1. While Variable tab only shows values for variables, the Watches tab shows values for both variables and expressions. For instance, Variables tab will only show values for variables a, b, c but Watches tab can show values for expression "a+b".

2. All variables and their corresponding values are shown automatically in variables tab, but you specifically need to add variables and expressions to Watch to see their values.

> Note: As a thumb rule, you will use Watches tab to see values of expressions or specific variable values, incase you have a long list of variable names.

Let us see how to use Variables tab and the Watches tab practically.

Note: Save any previously created script.

Note: Make sure Local Variables and Watch pane is open

1. Open a new UFT test using **File → New Test** and name the script as DebugScript4.

2. Go to **Editor View** tab.

3. In **Editor View** type below lines of code.

```
1   'AdactIn - Sample Debug Code
2
3   Dim a
4   Dim b
5   Dim c
6   Dim d
7   Dim e
8   Dim f
9
10
11  a = 5
12  b =10
13  c = a+b
14  Msgbox c
15
16  d = 15
17  e = 20
18  f = d+e
19
20  Msgbox f
```

Figure 17-14 – Editor View script

4. Select **Run** → **Step Into** or Press **F11**.

5. Click **Run** on default Run Dialog.

6. Press F11 so that line "a=5" is executed and cursor moves to next line "b=10". Select Variables tab (in Debug viewer) and see the value of variable a.

You will notice value of variable is 5. Value of other variables is still empty as they have not been assigned a value.

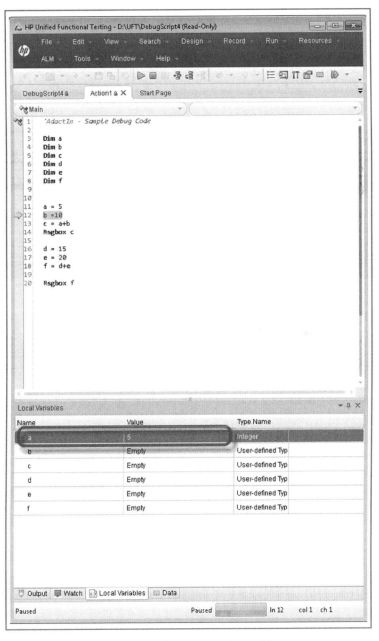

Figure 17-15– Values in Local variables pane

7. Select express "a+b" expression in line 12, right click and select "**Add to Watch**".

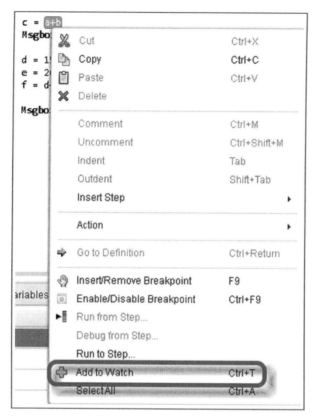

Figure 17-16– Selection of Add to Watch option

8. Go to Watches tab in Debug Viewer and check for result of "a+b" expression.

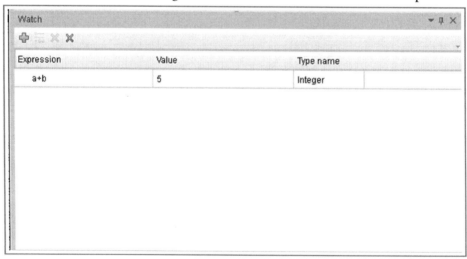

Figure 17-17– Add to Watch pane

Note: current "a+b" is 5 as b is still empty.

9. Go back and select the cursor in your script (which is on line "b=10") and press F11 again. Check for changes in Variables tab and Watches tab.

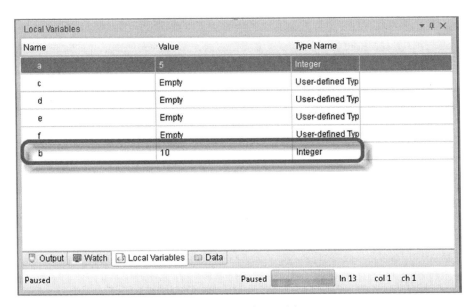

Figure 17-18– Local Variables pane

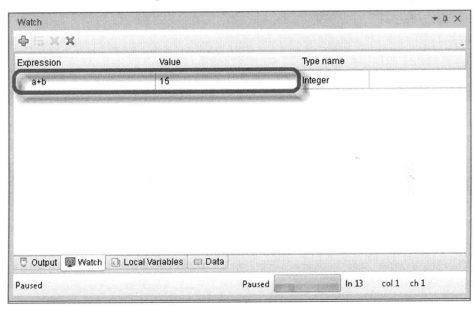

Figure 17-19–Watch pane

10. Press F11, until end of script and keep looking for the changes in values of variables c, d, e, f during the script execution.

Exercise

1. Open and execute any of your previously created scripts and use Step Into feature to execute the script step by step.

2. Also monitor the variables values set in Variables tab.

ℰℐℐ

18

Multiple Choice Questions Set-2

1. Syntax errors in UFT GUI Test script can be seen in

   A. Debug viewer

   B. Missing Resources tab

   C. Information tab

   D. Errors tab

2. Which menu option contains Check Syntax option?

   A. Tools

   B. Design

   C. Run

   D. Resources

3. Which operator do you use to concatenate two strings in VBScript?

   A. &

   B. &&

   C. concat

   D. +

4. The correct syntax of the conditional statement starting with Do is _____.

   A. Do while

   B. Do until

   C. Do next

   D. Both A. and B

5. You can modify an object stored in a shared object repository by

   A. Using the Object Repository Manager.

   B. Using the Object Repository window.

   C. Copying it to the local Object Repository and then modify its properties.

   D. You cannot modify properties of objects stored in Shared Object Repository.

6. Which data table method can retrieve data from an excel file?

    A. OpenSheet

    B. ExportSheet

    C. ImportSheet

    D. GetSheet

7. Panes that can be viewed from Debug Menu option are:

    A. Watch, Variables, Debug, Breakpoints and Call Stack

    B. Watch, Data, Command, Errors and Call Stack

    C. Watch, Variables, Console, Breakpoints and Call Stack

    D. View, Variables, Command, Data, and Errors

8. What is the purpose of the GetROProperty method?

    A. To retrieve a property value of a run time object

    B. To retrieve a property of a test object

    C. To retrieve a property value of a test object

    D. To retrieve a property of a Repository Object

9. Which object is used to read/write data from Text files

    A. TextFile object

    B. File system object

    C. File object

    D. OpenTextFile object

10. What is the extension of function library file in UFT?

    A. .mts

    B. .tsr

    C. .qfl

    D. .fl

Answers

Q1. Answer: D

Explanation – Syntax Errors in UFT can be seen in Errors pane. Click on Design → Check syntax and Errors pane opens up.

Note - This has changed between QTP 11.0 and UFT 11.5. In QTP 11.0 Syntax errors were displayed in Information tab and you could access it from Tools → Check Syntax.

Q2. Answer: B
Explanation – Check Syntax option is available in Design menu.

Q3. Answer: A
Explanation – & is used to concatenate two strings.

Q4. Answer: D
Explanation – Both do while and do until are correct.

Q5. Answer: A
Explanation – Object in shared repository can be modified in shared object repository.

Q6. Answer: C
Explanation – ImportSheet method is used to import data from excel sheet into UFT.

Q7. Answer: C
Explanation – Debug pane view option contains Watches, Variables, Call Stack, Console and Breakpoints.

Q8. Answer: A
Explanation – GetROProperty is used to retrieve property value of run time object. TestObject is object which is stored in the Object Repository while run time object is accessed during script execution.

Q9. Answer: B
Explanation – File system object is used to access, file, folders and text files.

Q10. Answer: C
Explanation – Extension of Function Library file is .qfl.

❧

19

Working with Dynamic Objects

In most real-life applications, we find objects whose properties change at runtime. For instance, a web browser will have a variable date/time stamp in the title or the window title will contain the id number of the latest order you have booked. These types of objects, whose properties change at run time are called dynamic objects.

Since we are using Object Repository and save the object properties statically in our object repository, the UFT script will fail since objects properties are being generated at run time.

In this chapter we will see how UFT can handle these dynamic objects.

Example

While testing a banking application, which had account number generated at runtime, hyperlinks to those newly generated account numbers were created. As part of the test case steps, we had to click on the newly created account number link, modify the account and add add-ons to the account. So how do we deal with such objects like account numbers which are dynamic and whose properties values are generated at run time?

We will learn how to work with objects whose properties change dynamically in this chapter.

Key objectives:

- Understand Dynamic Objects: Create a Test Scenario.
- Syntax for Descriptive Programming.
- Handling Dynamic Objects using descriptive programming.
- Regular Expression alternative to handling Dynamic Objects.

19.1 Understanding Dynamic Objects

Dynamic objects are objects whose property values change at run time. For example, there are some web based applications, whose browser title includes the date and time stamp indicating when the browser window was opened. The title property of the browser will always be dependent on current date and time. How do we handle such objects using UFT?

Let us take an example from our application:

Test Scenario – Cancel a booked order.

Pre-condition – Login window of hotel application is open.

1. Create a new test from **File → New → Test** and name the test as DynamicObjectScript.

2. Login (Use the username/password with which you have registered earlier).

3. Search for Hotel

    i.   Select a location, e.g., Sydney

    ii. Select number of rooms, e.g., 2

    iii. Select adults per room, e.g., 2

    iv. Click on Search button

4. Select a Hotel

    i.   Select one of the hotel Radio Button, e.g., select radio button next to Hotel Creek.

5. Book a Hotel

    i.   Enter First Name - Test

    ii.   Enter Last Name - Test

    iii. Enter Address - Test

    iv.   Enter 16-digit Credit Card number -1212121212121212

    v.   Enter Credit Card type – Mastercard

    vi.   Enter Expiry Month - October

    vii. Enter Expiry Year - 2015

    viii. Enter CVV number -111

    ix.   Click on Book Now

6. In the Booking confirmation page, get the new Order No. generated.

7. Click on Booked Itinerary page and go to row where you can see your booking order number.

8. Click on Cancel <Order Number> button and click OK on the Confirmation Prompt.

9. Click on Logout and then on link "Click here to login again".

10. Stop Recording (by clicking on Stop Recording button in Record toolbar) after recording the above workflow. The script shown below will be generated.

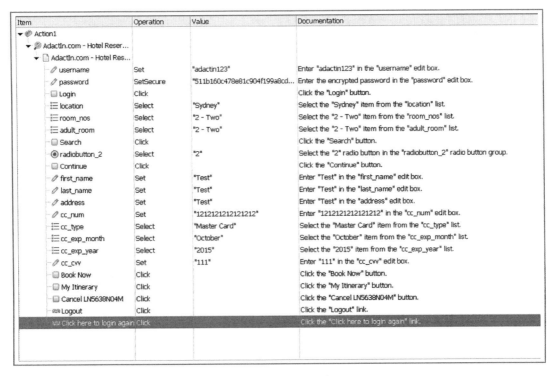

Item	Operation	Value	Documentation
▼ Action1			
▼ AdactIn.com - Hotel Reser...			
▼ AdactIn.com - Hotel Res...			
username	Set	"adactin123"	Enter "adactin123" in the "username" edit box.
password	SetSecure	"511b160c478e81c904f199a8cd...	Enter the encrypted password in the "password" edit box.
Login	Click		Click the "Login" button.
location	Select	"Sydney"	Select the "Sydney" item from the "location" list.
room_nos	Select	"2 - Two"	Select the "2 - Two" item from the "room_nos" list.
adult_room	Select	"2 - Two"	Select the "2 - Two" item from the "adult_room" list.
Search	Click		Click the "Search" button.
radiobutton_2	Select	"2"	Select the "2" radio button in the "radiobutton_2" radio button group.
Continue	Click		Click the "Continue" button.
first_name	Set	"Test"	Enter "Test" in the "first_name" edit box.
last_name	Set	"Test"	Enter "Test" in the "last_name" edit box.
address	Set	"Test"	Enter "Test" in the "address" edit box.
cc_num	Set	"1212121212121212"	Enter "1212121212121212" in the "cc_num" edit box.
cc_type	Select	"Master Card"	Select the "Master Card" item from the "cc_type" list.
cc_exp_month	Select	"October"	Select the "October" item from the "cc_exp_month" list.
cc_exp_year	Select	"2015"	Select the "2015" item from the "cc_exp_year" list.
cc_cvv	Set	"111"	Enter "111" in the "cc_cvv" edit box.
Book Now	Click		Click the "Book Now" button.
My Itinerary	Click		Click the "My Itinerary" button.
Cancel LN5638N04M	Click		Click the "Cancel LN5638N04M" button.
Logout	Click		Click the "Logout" link.
Click here to login again	Click		Click the "Click here to login again" link.

Figure 19-1 – Keyword View

11. Replay the script again and see if it can be played back. You will notice that the script will fail with the error shown below.

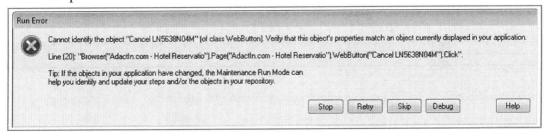

Figure 19-2 – Run Error

Any clue why we got this error?

Well, the reason for this error is that Button "Cancel LN5638N04M" no longer exists (in your case you will have a different Order Number). We created a different Order No. and Label name changed for the new order. Cancel <Order Number> is a dynamic object.

12. Click on the **Stop** button on above error message.

13. Go to **Resources** → **Object Repository** and expand the object repository and select Cancel <Order Number> Object.

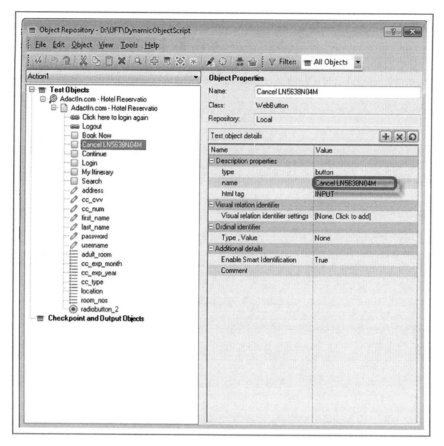

Figure 19-3 – Object Repository

You will notice that Property Name of the button changes dynamically, based on the order we need to cancel.

14. Close the repository and let us try to find a solution to the above problem.

19.2 Why and When to use Descriptive Programming

Below are some of the situations when descriptive programming can be considered useful:

1. The objects in the application are dynamic in nature and need special handling to identify the object. The best example would be of clicking a link which changes according to the user of the application, Ex. "Logout <username>".

2. Use descriptive programming when Object Repository is getting huge due to the number of objects being added. If the size of Object Repository is huge, then it decreases the performance of UFT, while recognizing an object.

3. 3. When you don't want to use Object Repository at all. The first question would be why you have chosen not to use Object Repository and what the alternative to it is? Consider the following scenario, which would help understand why not to use the Object Repository.

Scenario 1: Suppose we have a web application that has not yet been developed. Recording a script and adding the objects to repository would need the application to be developed and its user interface available. That would mean waiting for the application to be deployed, before we can start off writing UFT scripts. But if we know the description/object properties of the objects that will be developed, then we can still kick start with UFT script creation.

Scenario 2: Suppose an application has 3 navigation buttons on each and every page. Let the buttons be "Cancel", "Back," and "Next". Now, recording action on these buttons would add 3 objects per page in the repository. For a 10-page flow, this would mean 30 objects, which could have been represented just by using 3 objects. So instead of adding these 30 objects to the repository, we can just write 3 descriptions for the object and use it any page.

4. Modification to a test case is needed, but the Object Repository is read only or in shared mode, i.e., changes to shared object repository may affect other scripts as well.

5. When you want to take action on similar types of objects, i.e., suppose we have 20 textboxes on the page, and their names are in the form txt_1, txt_2, txt_3 and so on. Now, adding all 20 object in the object repository would not be a good automation approach.

19.3 Descriptive Programming Syntax

One of the possible solutions to deal with dynamic objects is to use descriptive programming.

There are a number of ways of using descriptive programming to define test objects like using name/value pairs, using description object or using child objects. Most common among them is using name/value pairs method.

Note: Using description objects or child objects is out of scope of this book. But more information on this can be found on UFT help guide.

You can describe an object directly in a statement by specifying property and value pairs, describing the object instead of specifying an object's name.

The general syntax is:

TestObject("PropertyName1: =PropertyValue1", "..." , "PropertyNameX:=PropertyValueX")

TestObject—the test object class could be WebEdit, WebRadioGroup, etc....

PropertyName: =PropertyValue—the test object property and its value.

Each property: =value pair should be separated by commas and quotation marks. Note that you can enter a variable name as the property value, if you want to find an object based on property values you retrieved during a run session.

19.4 Handling Dynamic Object using Descriptive Programming

Based on the example shown to us in the previous section, let us try to resolve the problem using descriptive programming.

Let us split the overall solution in 2 parts, the first part to get the order number and the second part to use the order number to create dynamic objects.

Part-1 – To get order number

1. We will use GetROProperty method to get order number value. So let us manually go to booking order confirmation page (search for a hotel, select a hotel and book a hotel).

2. First step is to add Order No. field into Object Repository. Make sure Order No. object is visible in the application.

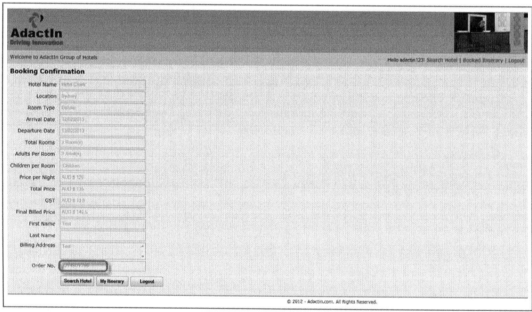

Figure 19-4 – Order No. object in application

3. So, Go to **Resources** → **Object Repository** and click on **Add objects** button and add Order Number object.

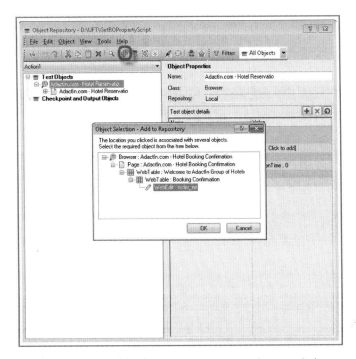

Figure 19-5– Add Object to repository selection dialog

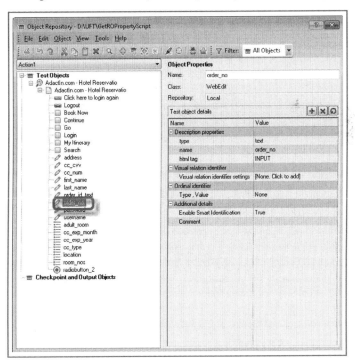

Figure 19-6– Object added to repository

4. **Close** Object Repository.

5. Now we need to know which property of the Order No. object will store order number information. So we use Object Spy and spy on Order No. field.

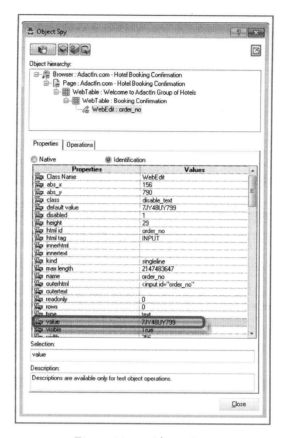

Figure 19-7– Object Spy

We see that "value" property of "order_no" Object saves order number information.

6. Let us go back to script and go to Editor View (View → Editor) and put our cursor after Book Now click step.

7. Add a Wait (8) statement since there is some delay in generation of order number.

8. We need to capture the Order No. from order number field after this step.

```
4.   Browser("AdactIn.com - Hotel Reservatio").Page("AdactIn.com - Hotel Reservatio").WebList("location").Select "Sydney"
5.   Browser("AdactIn.com - Hotel Reservatio").Page("AdactIn.com - Hotel Reservatio").WebList("room_nos").Select "2 - Two"
6.   Browser("AdactIn.com - Hotel Reservatio").Page("AdactIn.com - Hotel Reservatio").WebList("adult_room").Select "2 - Two"
7.   Browser("AdactIn.com - Hotel Reservatio").Page("AdactIn.com - Hotel Reservatio").WebButton("Search").Click
8.   Browser("AdactIn.com - Hotel Reservatio").Page("AdactIn.com - Hotel Reservatio").WebRadioGroup("radiobutton_2").Select "2"
9.   Browser("AdactIn.com - Hotel Reservatio").Page("AdactIn.com - Hotel Reservatio").WebButton("Continue").Click
10.  Browser("AdactIn.com - Hotel Reservatio").Page("AdactIn.com - Hotel Reservatio").WebEdit("first_name").Set "Test"
11.  Browser("AdactIn.com - Hotel Reservatio").Page("AdactIn.com - Hotel Reservatio").WebEdit("last_name").Set "Test"
12.  Browser("AdactIn.com - Hotel Reservatio").Page("AdactIn.com - Hotel Reservatio").WebEdit("address").Set "Test"
13.  Browser("AdactIn.com - Hotel Reservatio").Page("AdactIn.com - Hotel Reservatio").WebEdit("cc_num").Set "1212121212121212"
14.  Browser("AdactIn.com - Hotel Reservatio").Page("AdactIn.com - Hotel Reservatio").WebList("cc_type").Select "Master Card"
15.  Browser("AdactIn.com - Hotel Reservatio").Page("AdactIn.com - Hotel Reservatio").WebList("cc_exp_month").Select "October"
16.  Browser("AdactIn.com - Hotel Reservatio").Page("AdactIn.com - Hotel Reservatio").WebList("cc_exp_year").Select "2015"
17.  Browser("AdactIn.com - Hotel Reservatio").Page("AdactIn.com - Hotel Reservatio").WebEdit("cc_cvv").Set "111"
18.  Browser("AdactIn.com - Hotel Reservatio").Page("AdactIn.com - Hotel Reservatio").WebButton("Book Now").Click
19.  wait(8)
20.
21.  Browser("AdactIn.com - Hotel Reservatio").Page("AdactIn.com - Hotel Reservatio").WebButton("My Itinerary").Click
22.  Browser("AdactIn.com - Hotel Reservatio").Page("AdactIn.com - Hotel Reservatio").WebButton("Cancel LN5638N04N").Click
23.  Browser("AdactIn.com - Hotel Reservatio").Page("AdactIn.com - Hotel Reservatio").Link("Logout").Click
24.  Browser("AdactIn.com - Hotel Reservatio").Page("AdactIn.com - Hotel Reservatio").Link("Click here to login again").Click
```

Figure 19-8– Editor View

9. Use Step generator to create a step using GetROProperty to get property value of "value" property.

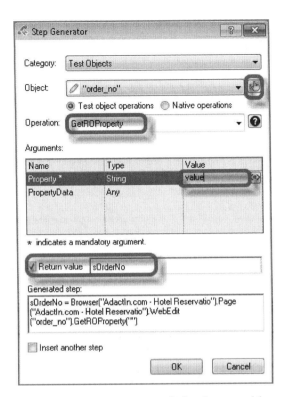

Figure 19-9– Step Generator dialog box to add step

10. You will see below line in the Editor View.

```
Browser("AdactIn.com - Hotel Reservatio").Page("AdactIn.com - Hotel Reservatio").WebButton("Book Now").Click
wait(8)
sOrderNo = Browser("AdactIn.com - Hotel Reservatio").Page("AdactIn.com - Hotel Reservatio").WebEdit("order_no").GetROProperty("value")
Browser("AdactIn.com - Hotel Reservatio").Page("AdactIn.com - Hotel Reservatio").WebButton("My Itinerary").Click
Browser("AdactIn.com - Hotel Reservatio").Page("AdactIn.com - Hotel Reservatio").WebButton("Cancel LN5638N04M").Click
Browser("AdactIn.com - Hotel Reservatio").Page("AdactIn.com - Hotel Reservatio").Link("Logout").Click
```

Figure 19-10– Editor View script

11. Now we will need to use Descriptive Programming for Object "Cancel HN360QMGJ5". As mentioned in previous section we will use name/value pair method of descriptive programming. So comment the already existing line in code, where we click on "Cancel HN360QMGJ5" button and copy it as a separate line manually.

```
21  Browser("AdactIn.com - Hotel Reservatio").Page("AdactIn.com - Hotel Reservatio").WebButton("My Itinerary").Click
22  'Browser("AdactIn.com - Hotel Reservatio").Page("AdactIn.com - Hotel Reservatio").WebButton("Cancel LN5638N04M").Click
23  Browser("AdactIn.com - Hotel Reservatio").Page("AdactIn.com - Hotel Reservatio").WebButton("Cancel LN5638N04M").Click
24  Browser("AdactIn.com - Hotel Reservatio").Dialog("Message from webpage").WinButton("OK").Click
```

Figure 19-11– Comment line

12. Use Descriptive Programming to replace Cancel button with description Programming syntax.

Browser("AdactIn.com - Hotel Reservatio").Page("AdactIn.com - Hotel Reservatio"). WebButton("value:=Cancel "&sOrderNo).Click

```
18  Browser("AdactIn.com - Hotel Reservatio").Page("AdactIn.com - Hotel Reservatio").WebButton("Book Now").Click
19  wait(8)
20  sOrderNo = Browser("AdactIn.com - Hotel Reservatio").Page("AdactIn.com - Hotel Reservatio").WebEdit("order_no").GetROProperty("value")
21  Browser("AdactIn.com - Hotel Reservatio").Page("AdactIn.com - Hotel Reservatio").WebButton("My Itinerary").Click
22  'Browser("AdactIn.com - Hotel Reservatio").Page("AdactIn.com - Hotel Reservatio").WebButton("Cancel H563BN04B").Click
23  Browser("AdactIn.com - Hotel Reservatio").Page("AdactIn.com - Hotel Reservatio").WebButton("value:=Cancel "&sOrderNo).Click
24  Browser("AdactIn.com - Hotel Reservatio").Dialog("Message from webpage").WinButton("OK").Click
25  Browser("AdactIn.com - Hotel Reservatio").Page("AdactIn.com - Hotel Reservatio").Link("Logout").Click
26  Browser("AdactIn.com - Hotel Reservatio").Page("AdactIn.com - Hotel Reservatio").Link("Click here to login again").Click
```

Figure 19-12– Descriptive Programming

Note: The important thing to note is that we are no longer storing Cancel button object in Object Repository but created our own definition through the code. Now, even if we delete this object from Object Repository, our script should execute fine.

13. Let us run the script now. Make sure your application is on login page.

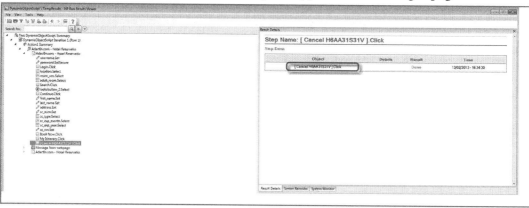

Figure 19-13– Test Results

You will notice that the object with the new order number was automatically created and generated.

19.5 Regular Expressions

Another way of handling dynamic values is using regular expressions.

A regular expression is a string that describes or matches a set of strings. It is often called a pattern, as it describes a set of strings.

Some of the most commonly used regular expression characters are listed below:-

Expression	Char	Description
Period	.	Matches any single character.
Asterisk	*	Matches zero to any number of occurrences of the preceding character.

Plus	+	Matches one to any number of occurrences of the preceding character.
Brackets	[A-Z][a-z]	Matches a range of characters.
	[0-9]	Matches a range of numbers.
	\w	Matches any alphanumeric character including underscore.
	\W	
		Matches any non-alphanumeric character.
Digit	\d	Matches any digit.
	\d{5}	Matches exactly four digits.
Combination of above expressions	.*	Combination of Period and Asterisk is the most commonly used regular expression to identify any possible string.

Note: A backslash (\) instructs UFT to treat the next character as a literal character, if it is otherwise a special character. The backslash (\) can also instruct UFT to recognize certain ordinary characters as special characters. For example, UFT recognizes \. as the special . character.

Example

To recognize the string shown below generically using regular expression

- "Adactin.com– Search Hotel"
- "Adactin.com – Book Hotel"
- "Adactin.com – Select Hotel"

We could use regular expression – "Adactin\.com- .* Hotel"

Backslash will get "." treated as literal character and .* will help recognize any strings Search, Book, or Select.

Note: Regular expression should be used when after generic recognition of an object UFT finds only one instance of the object. If UFT finds more than one object, which matches the string specified by UFT regular expression, we cannot use regular expression. In that case we would have to use descriptive programming. For example, in our above exercise to delete an order, if we use regular expression to identify the cancel order No. button (e.g., Cancel.*), it will recognize all the Cancel <Order No> buttons, not just the one which we have booked (assuming that our Itinerary screen will show multiple orders). So we cannot use regular expression in the above exercise as UFT, will not be able to identify unique object. The best option in the above scenario would be to use descriptive programming to perform an exact match.

We could use regular expressions in UFT for:

- Matching the property value of a dynamic object in Object Repository.

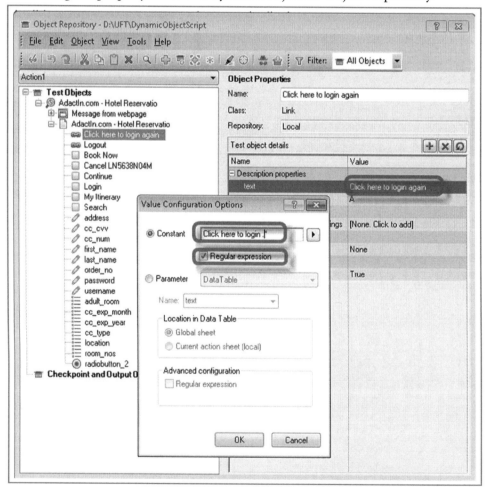

Figure 19-14– Regular Expression in Object Repository

Note: Click on Object Property Value to open **Value Configuration** pop-up, where regular expression can be set.

- Matching Checkpoint with varying values.

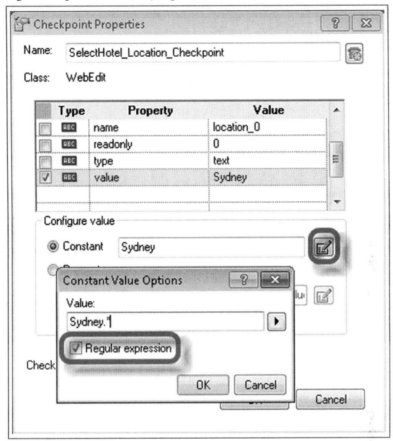

Figure 19-15– Regular Expression in Checkpoints

Exercise

1. Create a new script and perform just login and logout of the application using descriptive programming (name/values pairs) for the whole script, instead of using object repository.

℘

20

Recovery Scenario

When we execute our scripts, we will come across scenarios where we see unexpected application behaviour. For example, we might see an Automatic Update pop-up dialog in Windows while we are executing our scripts or if our application is web based, you might temporarily see "Page Not found" messages, due to problems with the application environment.

Example

In one of the investment banking applications we tested, whenever there was high user load on the application, we temporarily used to get "Page not found" message, or the application would become slow and keep loading for up to 2 mins. Our UFT scripts used to fail, since they did not find the required objects. Since we would run these scripts overnight, this presented an ongoing problem and we could only come to know about these issues with the application in the morning.

How would UFT scripts deal with these kinds of exceptional scenarios? Should the UFT script just fail with "Object Not Found" error? Can we make UFT scripts smart enough so that they automatically detect these exceptions and perform corrective actions?

UFT provides the "Recovery Scenario" feature to handle such exceptions.

In this chapter, we will define different types of exceptions that can be handled by UFT and discuss the corrective actions that can be taken to prevent the script from failing under exceptional scenarios.

Also it's important to note that recovery scenarios should be used to handle unexpected events and not expected events. For instance, an incorrect username or password scenario should not be handled using recovery scenario as you already know when and at which line of the script that problem would arise.

Recovery scenarios of UFT should be used when you do not know at which line of a script an unexpected event can happen.

For instance, a recovery scenario can handle a windows automatic updates pop-up by automatically clicking the default button in the message box programmatically. You cannot handle this pop-up directly in your script, since you cannot predict at what point you will get the pop-up. Therefore, for these types of events, a recovery scenario can be used.

Key objectives:

- Sample scenario which needs exception handling.
- Understand how to use the Recovery Scenario wizard.
- Execute a script with Recovery Scenario.
- Disable Recovery Scenario for script.

20.1 Need for Recovery Scenario

Need for Recovery Scenario

When running tests in unattended mode (e.g. nightly runs), if unexpected event occur, the test execution can be suspended until you perform the operation needed to recover from the unexpected event. So, you need recovery scenario to handle unexpected events, errors or application crashes during a run session, which can disrupt your run session and distort results.

Key Steps to configure Recovery Scenario

- Defining the trigger event that interrupts the run session.
- Specifying the recovery operation(s) required to continue.
- Choosing a post-recovery test run operation.
- Specifying a name and description for the recovery scenario.
- Specifying whether to associate the recovery scenario to the current test and/or to all new tests.

20.2 Create a Test Scenario

Let us first automate the scenario given below in the new script by recording.

Test Scenario – Record the below scenario on Hotel Application (assuming login window is available)

1. Create a new UFT GUI Test from **File** → **New** → **Test** and name it as RecoveryScenarioScript.
2. Start Recording.
3. Login (Use the username/password with which you have registered earlier).
4. Search for Hotel.
    i.   Select a location, e.g., Sydney
    ii. Select number of rooms, e.g., 2
    iii. Select adults per room, e.g., 2

iv. Click on Search button

5. Select a Hotel.

    v. Select one of the Hotel Radio buttons, e.g., select radio button next to Hotel Creek.

6. Book a Hotel.

    vi. Enter First Name - Test

    vii. Enter Last Name -Test

    viii. Enter Address -Test

    ix. Enter 16-digit Credit Card number -1212121212121212

    x. Enter Credit Card type – Mastercard

    xi. Enter Expiry Month - October

    xii. Enter Expiry Year - 2015

    xiii. Enter CVV number -111

    xiv. Click on Book Now

7. After you see Booking confirmation page, click on Logout and then on link "Click here to login again".

8. **Stop** recording. Once you have recorded this script you would see the script below.

Item	Operation	Value	Documentation
▾ Action1			
▾ Adactin.com - Hotel Reser...			
▾ Adactin.com - Hotel Res...			
username	Set	"adactin123"	Enter "adactin123" in the "username" edit box.
password	SetSecure	"511b3120668a41533d3bb2109...	Enter the encrypted password in the "password" edit box.
Login	Click		Click the "Login" button.
location	Select	"Sydney"	Select the "Sydney" item from the "location" list.
room_nos	Select	"2 - Two"	Select the "2 - Two" item from the "room_nos" list.
adult_room	Select	"2 - Two"	Select the "2 - Two" item from the "adult_room" list.
Search	Click		Click the "Search" button.
radiobutton_2	Select	"2"	Select the "2" radio button in the "radiobutton_2" radio button group.
Continue	Click		Click the "Continue" button.
first_name	Set	"Test"	Enter "Test" in the "first_name" edit box.
last_name	Set	"Test"	Enter "Test" in the "last_name" edit box.
address	Set	"Test"	Enter "Test" in the "address" edit box.
cc_num	Set	"1212121212121212"	Enter "1212121212121212" in the "cc_num" edit box.
cc_type	Select	"Master Card"	Select the "Master Card" item from the "cc_type" list.
cc_exp_month	Select	"October"	Select the "October" item from the "cc_exp_month" list.
cc_exp_year	Select	"2015"	Select the "2015" item from the "cc_exp_year" list.
cc_cvv	Set	"111"	Enter "111" in the "cc_cvv" edit box.
Book Now	Click		Click the "Book Now" button.
Logout	Click		Click the "Logout" link.
Click here to login again	Click		Click the "Click here to login again" link.

Figure 20-1 – Keyword View

9. Replay the script for successful playback.

10. Go to Editor View (**View → Editor**) and now modify the script to change expiry year to 2011.

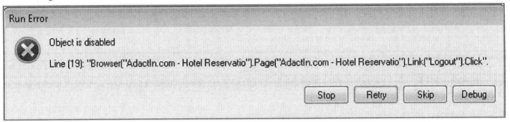

```
1   Browser("AdactIn.com - Hotel Reservatio").Page("AdactIn.com - Hotel Reservatio").WebEdit("username").Set "adactin123"
2   Browser("AdactIn.com - Hotel Reservatio").Page("AdactIn.com - Hotel Reservatio").WebEdit("password").SetSecure "511b3120668a41533d3bb2109e9115988b7722bc0e553f1e74b4"
3   Browser("AdactIn.com - Hotel Reservatio").Page("AdactIn.com - Hotel Reservatio").WebButton("Login").Click
4   Browser("AdactIn.com - Hotel Reservatio").Page("AdactIn.com - Hotel Reservatio").WebList("location").Select "Sydney"
5   Browser("AdactIn.com - Hotel Reservatio").Page("AdactIn.com - Hotel Reservatio").WebList("room_nos").Select "2 - Two"
6   Browser("AdactIn.com - Hotel Reservatio").Page("AdactIn.com - Hotel Reservatio").WebList("adult_room").Select "2 - Two"
7   Browser("AdactIn.com - Hotel Reservatio").Page("AdactIn.com - Hotel Reservatio").WebButton("Search").Click
8   Browser("AdactIn.com - Hotel Reservatio").Page("AdactIn.com - Hotel Reservatio").WebRadioGroup("radiobutton_2").Select "2"
9   Browser("AdactIn.com - Hotel Reservatio").Page("AdactIn.com - Hotel Reservatio").WebButton("Continue").Click
10  Browser("AdactIn.com - Hotel Reservatio").Page("AdactIn.com - Hotel Reservatio").WebEdit("first_name").Set "Test"
11  Browser("AdactIn.com - Hotel Reservatio").Page("AdactIn.com - Hotel Reservatio").WebEdit("last_name").Set "Test"
12  Browser("AdactIn.com - Hotel Reservatio").Page("AdactIn.com - Hotel Reservatio").WebEdit("address").Set "Test"
13  Browser("AdactIn.com - Hotel Reservatio").Page("AdactIn.com - Hotel Reservatio").WebEdit("cc_num").Set "1212121212121212"
14  Browser("AdactIn.com - Hotel Reservatio").Page("AdactIn.com - Hotel Reservatio").WebList("cc_type").Select "Master Card"
15  Browser("AdactIn.com - Hotel Reservatio").Page("AdactIn.com - Hotel Reservatio").WebList("cc_exp_month").Select "October"
16  Browser("AdactIn.com - Hotel Reservatio").Page("AdactIn.com - Hotel Reservatio").WebList("cc_exp_year").Select "2011"
17  Browser("AdactIn.com - Hotel Reservatio").Page("AdactIn.com - Hotel Reservatio").WebEdit("cc_cvv").Set "111"
18  Browser("AdactIn.com - Hotel Reservatio").Page("AdactIn.com - Hotel Reservatio").WebButton("Book Now").Click
19  Browser("AdactIn.com - Hotel Reservatio").Page("AdactIn.com - Hotel Reservatio").Link("Logout").Click
20  Browser("AdactIn.com - Hotel Reservatio").Page("AdactIn.com - Hotel Reservatio").Link("Click here to login again").Click
```

Figure 20-2 – Updated Editor View

11. Replay the script again and see if can successfully re-play back. You will notice that script will fail with the following error.

Run Error

Object is disabled

Line [19]: "Browser("AdactIn.com - Hotel Reservatio").Page("AdactIn.com - Hotel Reservatio").Link("Logout").Click".

Stop   Retry   Skip   Debug

Figure 20-3 – Run Error

12. Click on Stop button and stop the execution.

13. Go back to the application, and you will notice that there was a pop-up that the "Expiry date cannot be in past".

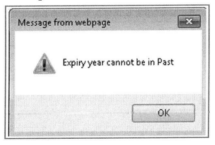

Figure 20-4– Application Pop-up

Note: Please note that this may not be ideal unexpected scenario because in our case, we know that the year is in the past. For sake of this example, to understand recovery scenario, let us assume that this is an unexpected pop-up thrown by the application.

20.3 How to use Recovery Scenario Wizard

Setting up Recovery Scenario Wizard is a four step process:

Let us now see how Recovery Scenario wizard can help us resolve this problem.

Note: Keep Expiry Year pop-up open. In case you have closed it; you can manually re-produce it by selecting 2011 as expiry year and clicking on Book Now button.

1. In UFT, go to **Resources → Recovery Scenario Manager**.

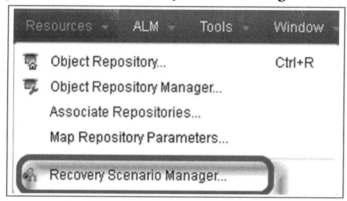

Figure 20-5– Recovery Scenario Manager menu option

2. You will see Recovery Scenario Manager window opens up. Click on **New Scenario** Icon.

Figure 20-6– Recovery Scenario Manager window

3. You will see Recovery Scenario Wizard opens up. Click on **Next** button.

Figure 20-7– Recovery Scenario Manager Wizard

4. You will see Select Trigger Event window.

This window defines the type of error that triggers Recovery Scenario. There are four possible types of trigger events.

Pop-up Window - UFT detects a pop-up window and identifies it according to the window title and textual content.

Objects state - UFT detects a specific test object state and identifies it according to its property values and the property values of all its ancestors. Note that an object is identified only by its property values, and not by its class.

Test Run Error - UFT detects a run error and identifies it by a failed return value from a method.

Application Crash - UFT detects an application crash and identifies it according to a pre-defined list of applications.

In our scenario, we saw this is a pop-up window that we need to handle. So we select **Pop-up window.**

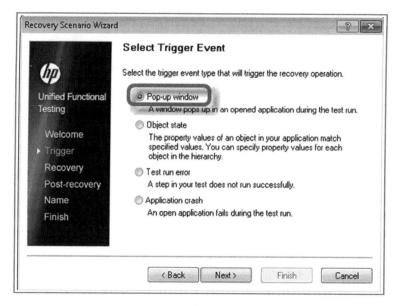

Figure 20-8– Select Trigger Event

5. Click **Next**.

6. You will see **Specify pop-up Window Conditions** window.

This window helps Recovery Scenario to find out which pop-up window is an unexpected window.

Note: Make sure pop-up window for which you want to generate Recovery Scenario is open, otherwise manually open the pop-up.

Click on the **Hand** icon and point your cursor on the "OK" button of "Expiry date is in the past" window.

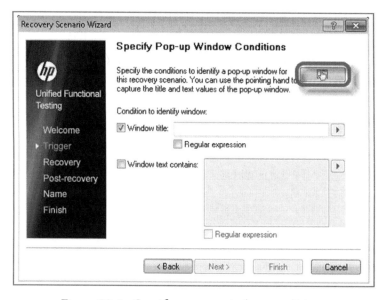

Figure 20-9– Specify pop-up window conditions

7. You will notice that Specify Pop-up Window Conditions window is automatically populated with pop-up window details.

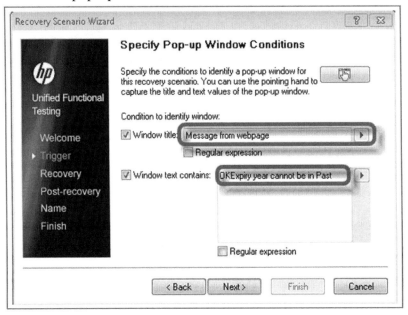

Figure 20-10– Pop-up window details

8. Click **Next** button.

9. Click **Next** in Recovery Operation screen.

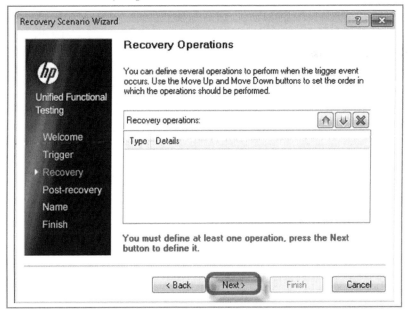

Figure 20-11– Recovery Operations dialog

10. You will see Recovery Operations page. This page enables you to specify the operations UFT performs after it detects the trigger event.

Keyboard or mouse operation - UFT simulates a click on a button in a window or a press of a keyboard key.

Close application process - UFT closes specified processes.

Function call - UFT calls a VBScript function.

Restart Microsoft Windows - UFT restarts Microsoft Windows.

In our case we want to perform mouse operation by clicking on OK button so we select **Keyboard or mouse Operation** option.

Figure 20-12– Recovery Operation selection

11. Click **Next**.

12. In the next Recovery Operation – Click Button or Press Key screen, select **Click Default button/Press ENTER key.**

Note: You could choose to click on a specific label by using Hand icon and select the button you want to click in the pop-up window. Alternatively you could also Press key or key combinations using the Press key or key combination option and enter combinations like ALT+F1, etc.

Figure 20-13– Keyboard or mouse operation selection

13. Click **Next**. Uncheck the checkbox **Add another recovery operation.**

"Add another recovery operation" checkbox is used if any particular recovery scenario needs multiple recovery operations. For e.g., Click on Ok button and Close the application process.

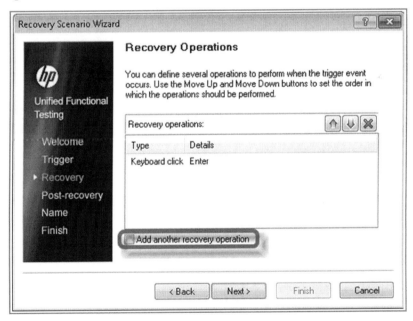

Figure 20-14– Recovery Operations summary

14. In the next Post-recovery Test Results Options window, select "**Repeat current step and continue option**.

This window enables you to define post-recovery test run options, which specify how to continue the run session after UFT has identified the event and performed all of the specified recovery operations.

For instance, in our scenario, once the recovery scenario clicks on "OK" in the pop-up, we notice that the expiry year defaults to the 2012 year and we will need to click on "Book Now" button again.

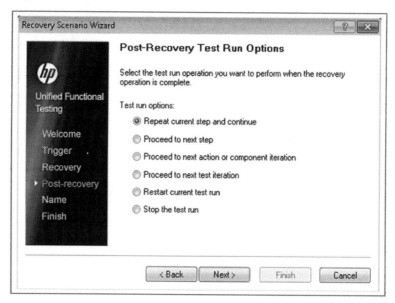

Figure 20-15– Post Recovery Test Run Options

15. Click on **Next** button.

16. Give the Scenario a **Scenario Name** and Click **Next** again.

Figure 20-16– Name and Description

17. Click Checkbox **Add scenario to current test** and Click **Finish.**

Checking "Add Scenario to current test" checkbox would associate the recovery scenario with the current script.

We could also check checkbox "Add scenario to default test settings" which would by default make the current recovery scenario link to any new script created in UFT.

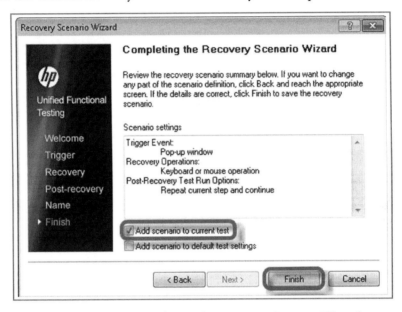

Figure 20-17– Completing the Recovery Scenario Wizard

18. Click on Close button of Recovery Scenario Manager.

Figure 20-18– Recovery Scenario Manager

19. Save the Recovery Scenario to Local scripts folder. It will be saved with .qrs file extension.

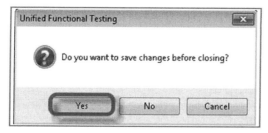

Figure 20-19– Save recovery scenario

20.4 Execute the Script with Recovery Scenario

Let us now execute our script and check if the Recovery Scenario wizard handles the pop-up:

1. Logout of the application and get the application back to Login page.

2. Save the script.

3. With expiry year set to be 2011, let us run the script by clicking on **Run** button.

4. Notice that pop-up is handled by the script this time.

5. Verify the results. You will notice that a warning message appears in the results and shows that recovery scenario was invoked.

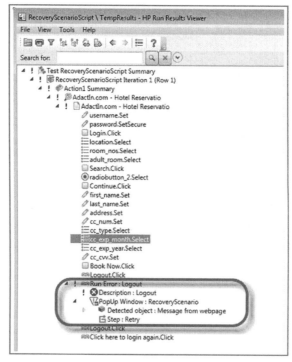

Figure 20-20– Test results

6. Close the Test results window after verification.

20.5 Disabling Recovery Scenario for a Script

In case you have already associated a recovery scenario to a script and would like to disable or delete it, we can do it from **File** → **Setting**

1. Open UFT interface with RecoveryScenarioScript.
2. Go to **File** → **Settings** → **Recovery** to open Recovery window.

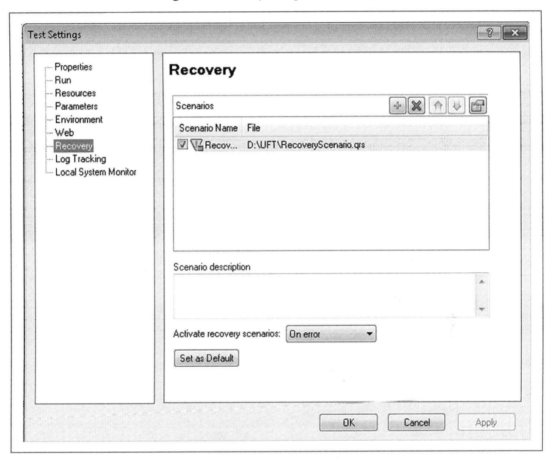

Figure 20-21– Recovery Test Settings

3. To disable the Recovery Scenario, uncheck the checkbox next to Recovery scenario .qrs file and press **Apply** button. You can later enable it by checking it.
4. To delete the Recovery Scenario, click on **Delete** icon.
5. To view properties of Recovery Scenario, click on **Edit** icon.

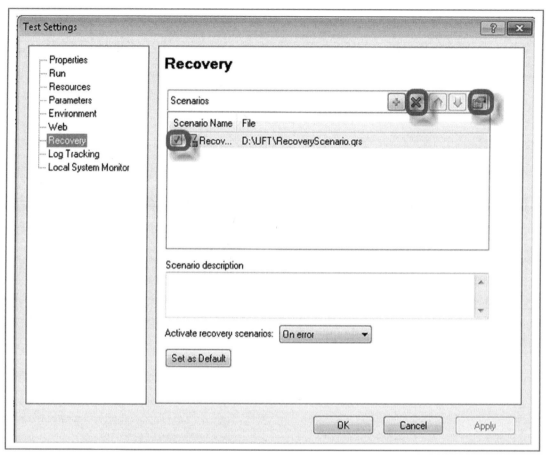

Figure 20-22– Edit, Delete, Disable Recovery Scenario

6. Click **OK** to close the dialog box.

Exercise

1. Create a new recovery scenario for "Test Run error" **Trigger Event,** and select "Any Error" in type of test run error.

2. In Recovery Option select **Function call,** and create a new function in your external function library file, which will close the browser and call that function in recovery operation.

3. Select Post recovery operation, **Stop the test run.**

4. Save the Recovery operation.

5. Open any existing script and change any of the object properties deliberately to induce "Test Run error".

6. Execute the script and check if Recovery operation is invoked.

಼

21

Batch Execution

A batch run means executing all the scripts in a suite at the same time, unattended.

There are multiple ways to achieve this:-

- First way is to use Test Batch Runner tool of UFT. This tool comes with UFT and is available in Start → All Programs.
- Second way is to use Test Management tools like Quality Center/ALM to execute scripts in a batch.
- Third way is to create a Master UFT script which will execute calls to other UFT scripts as "Call to existing Action" option. Refer to our *Actions* chapter on how to call existing actions.
- Fourth way is to use some custom utilities like MultiTestManager, which can run UFT scripts as a batch. You can search more on these utilities on the internet.
- Fifth way it is create a driver script in VBScript and use UFT object model (UFT Application object) to call UFT scripts one at a time.

In this chapter, we will see how to use Test Batch Runner tool to run UFT scripts in a batch.

We will see how to use HP Quality Center/ALM to execute scripts in a batch in a later chapter.

21.1 Adding Tests to Batch Runner

Let us see how to add tests to Test Batch Runner in UFT

1. Go to **Start → All Programs → HP Software → HP Unified Functional Testing → Tools → Test Batch Runner**.

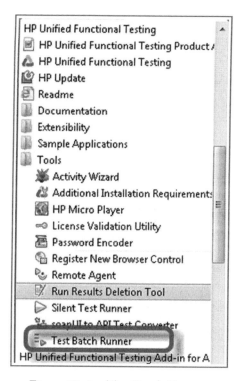

Figure 21-1 – Test Batch Runner

2. In the Test Batch Runner go to **Tests** → **Add**.

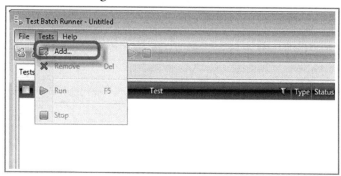

Figure 21-2 – Add Tests

3. Select the tests you want to execute from the file system location, where the tests are stored.

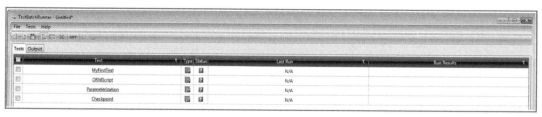

Figure 21-3 – Batch Runner View after Tests are added

4. Select the tests which you want to execute in the current run by selecting corresponding check-boxes.

Figure 21-4 – Select tests

5. Save the Batch Run File as BatchExecution.mtb by clicking on **Save** button.

Figure 21-5 – Save Batch Runner

6. Go to **Test → Run** to run the tests or Click on **Run** Icon.

Figure 21-6 – Run tests

Note: You can also add .mtb file in Windows Scheduler for automation execution at scheduled time.

Exercise

1. Add all your working scripts to Batch runner and run them as a suite.

☙

22

Integration with Quality Center

HP Quality Center/Application Lifecycle Management (QC/ALM) is a test management tool, which acts as a central repository for testing artifacts and helps to manage the testing process right from project releases to defect tracking. QC/ALM provides an intuitive and efficient method for scheduling and running tests, collecting results, analyzing the results, and managing test versions. It also features a system for tracking defects, enabling you to monitor defects closely from initial detection until resolution.

UFT integrates pretty well with QC/ALM. We can use QC/ALM as a repository for storing UFT scripts and also for batch execution of scripts and storing test results.

Example

We have used the combination of QC/ALM with UFT at number of our client installations. Most recently, we had set up an automation framework for a client having a learning management system. We created an automation framework for them, stored all our UFT scripts in QC/ALM and executed the scripts from QC/ALM. This made the knowledge transfer to the client team very straight forward and intuitive as they knew that all their scripts and test results are within QC/ALM. All they needed to do was to click a button to execute the UFT scripts from QC/ALM.

As part of this chapter we will cover how we can store UFT scripts in QC/ALM and how to execute automation scripts from QC/ALM.

Key objectives:

- UFT – QC/ALM integration setup.
- Saving UFT script in QC/ALM from UFT.
- Launching UFT script from QC/ALM.
- UFT script execution from QC/ALM.

22.1 UFT – QC/ALM Integration Setup

In order to execute UFT scripts from QC/ALM on a particular test machine, we need the following components set up on the machine.

1. We should be able to access QC/ALM client on that machine (assuming that you already have QC/ALM server installed).

2. We need to have UFT installed on that machine.

3. We need to install UFT add-ins for QC/ALM on that machine. Although there is backward compatibility of UFT with older versions of QC/ALM, it is advisable to install and integrate UFT and QC/ALM of same versions. You will find UFT add-in for QC/ALM in the UFT installation itself.

    a. You will find the add-ins once you start UFT Setup file.

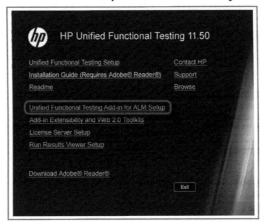

Figure 22-1 – UFT Add-in for ALM Setup

Note: Make sure you have admin rights to install this add-in on your machine.

4. Once you install this add-ins, launch UFT.

5. Go to **Tool → Options → GUI Testing → Test Runs**. Make sure that checkbox "**Allow other HP products to run tests and components**" is checked. Close the dialog box after selection.

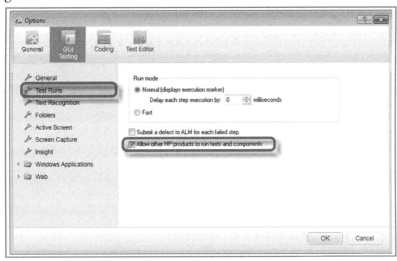

Figure 22-2 – Allow other HP products to run tests and components

22.2 Saving UFT GUI Test Script in QC/ALM from UFT

You can save UFT GUI Test script in a QC/ALM project.

Pre-conditions:

- You should have the QC/ALM project in which you want to set up QC/ALM.

- You should have username/password and appropriate rights to created new tests in QC/ALM.

- Integration Setup requirements in previous section are completed

1. Launch UFT.

2. **File → Open** the script that you want to save in QC/ALM. Let's say that in our case we open MyFirstTest (the first script we created).

3. Select **ALM → ALM connection.**

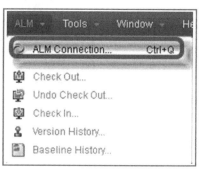

Figure 22-3 – ALM Connection

4. You will see **HP ALM Connection** dialog box.

5. Enter the server name in the **Server URL, User name** and **Password** and Click on **Connect** button.

Figure 22-4 – Connect to Server

6. Select **Domain** and **Project** in which we want to store UFT GUI Test script and click on **Login** Button.

Figure 22-5 – Connect to server

7. Click on **Close** button once connected to project.

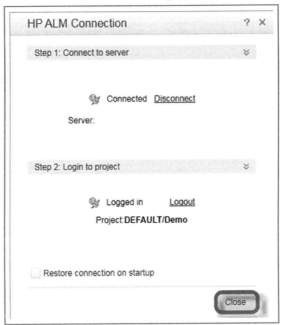

Figure 22-6 – Close HP ALM Connection Dialog

8. With UFT GUI Test script open go to **File → MyFirstTest Save As** In the Save Test dialog Select **ALM Test Plan** tab.

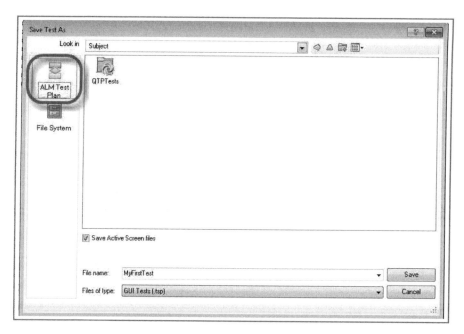

Figure 22-7 – Save Test Dialog

9. Save the script in any folder in Test Plan. In case there is no folder; we can create a new folder by clicking on New folder icon in Test Plan tab in ALM. For example, Subject\QTPTests.

10. Select QTPTests folder and Click on **Save** Button.

Figure 22-8 – Save UFT GUI Test Script

11. If you login to QC/ALM project and go to **Test Plan** tab you will notice that your tests are saved in QC/ALM.

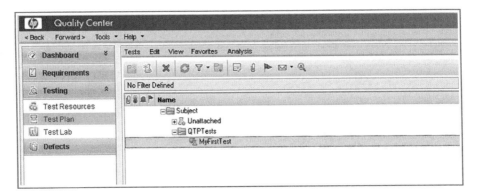

Figure 22-9 – UFT GUI Test Script in QC/ALM

12. Click on **Test Script** tab to see the UFT GUI Test script.

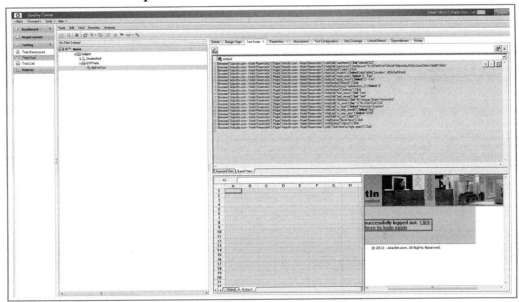

Figure 22-10– Test Script view in QC/ALM

You will see UFT Expert and Keyword View in the Test Script tab.

22.3 Launching UFT GUI Test Script from QC/ALM

You can create a new UFT GUI Test script from within QC/ALM and open that in UFT and edit.

1. Login to your QC/ALM project.

2. Go to your **Test Plan** tab.

3. Select the folder under which you want to create your new UFT GUI Test script.

4. Click on **New Test** and in the New Test Dialog select **QuickTest_Test** as Test type and Type **TestName** 'MyQCSampleTest'.

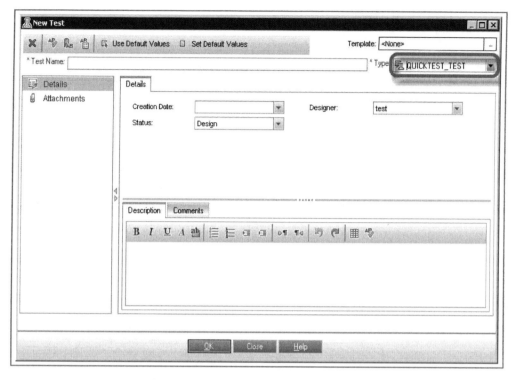

Figure 22-11– New Test in QC/ALM

5. Click **OK**. Notice that an empty UFT test is created.

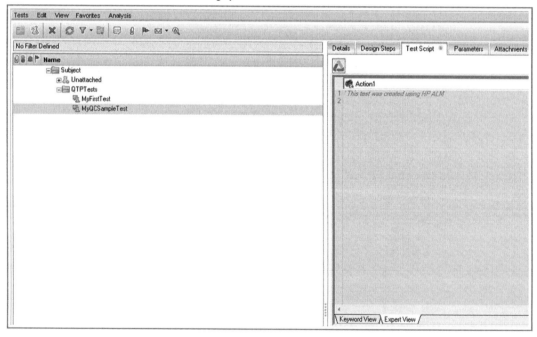

Figure 22-12– Test Script view of new UFT Test

6. In order to edit this test and add steps to this test, click on **UFT icon** at the top left corner in the Test Script tab.

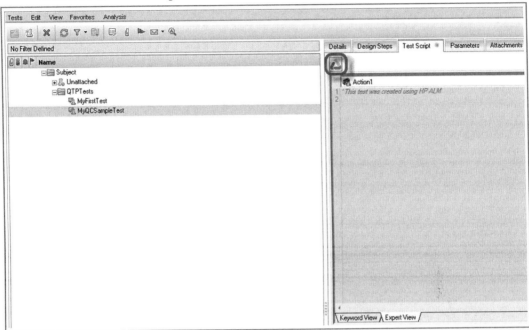

Figure 22-13– UFT Launch icon

7. This will launch UFT, and now you can edit the test and add more steps in UFT. This UFT session is automatically connected to QC/ALM Project.

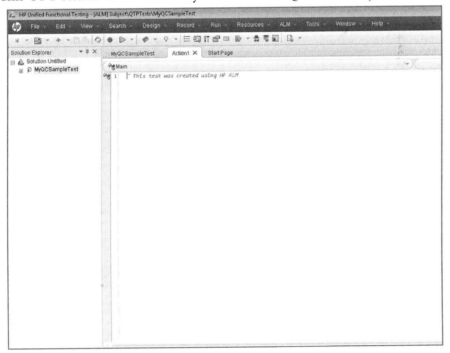

Figure 22-14– QC/ALM script opened in UFT

8. Once editing is complete, Press **File → Save** and test will be updated in QC/ALM.

22.4 Executing UFT GUI Test Script from QC/ALM

Now let us see how to execute a UFT GUI Test script from QC/ALM

1. Go to **Test Lab** Tab of QC/ALM and select the **Test Set** in which you want to execute UFT GUI Test script.

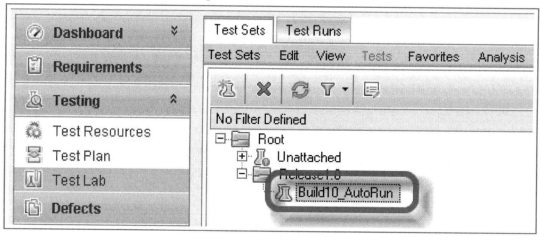

Figure 22-15– Test-Set in QC/ALM

2. Select **Execution Grid** tab of the Test Set and Select "**Select Tests**" button.

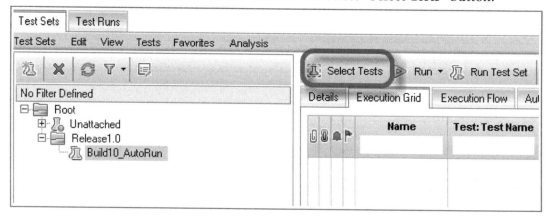

Figure 22-16– Select Test in Execution Grid of QC/ALM

3. This will open **Test Plan** tree view. From that view, select the UFT GUI Test scripts which you would like to execute as part of this run and drag them on to Execution Grid or press the **Green arrow** button. In our case, select MyFirstTest.

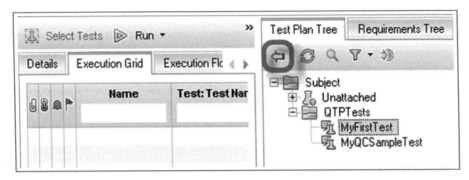

Figure 22-17– Add Test to Execution Grid

4. You see MyFirstTest test added to the Execution Grid.

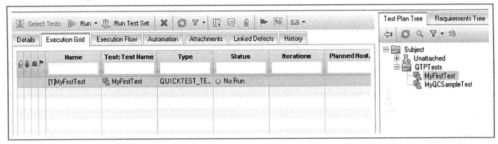

Figure 22-18– Test added to Execution Grid in QC/ALM

5. Make sure your login page of the application is open as this is what the test expects.

6. Click on **Run** button at top of the Execution Grid. You would see Automatic Runner dialog box pops-up.

7. In Automatic Runner Dialog box select **Run All Tests Locally** Checkbox. Click on **Run All** button. Selecting Run all Tests Locally option, configures UFT tests to be executed locally on the host machine.

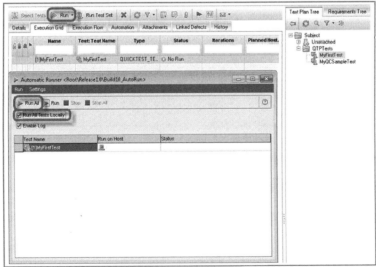

Figure 22-19– Run UFT Tests in QC/ALM

8. Notice that Test will be executed and you get the test result status back in Automatic Runner dialog box

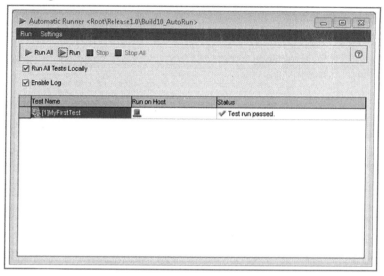

Figure 22-20– Automatic Runner

9. Close the dialog box by clicking on **Cross** icon. You will notice that result Passed/ Failed will be updated in Execution Grid too.

Let us see the Test Results now.

10. If you double click on the **Run** it will open Test Run Instance dialog.

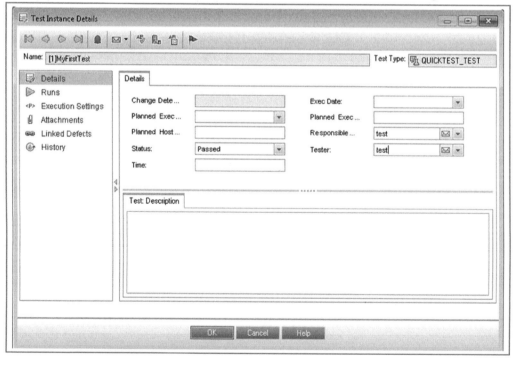

Figure 22-21– Test Instance Details

11. Select the **Runs** Tab and click on **Launch Report**.

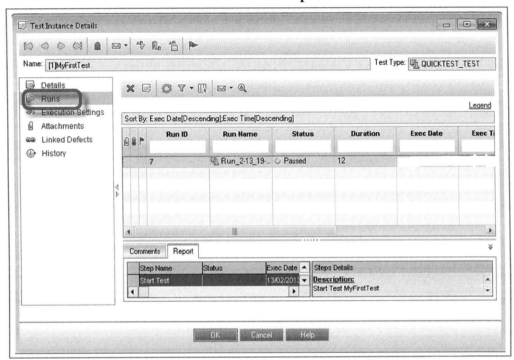

Figure 22-22– Test Run Details

> **Note:** All the test results are stored in QC/ALM, and can be referenced at a later stage. So QC/ALM acts as a repository of UFT scripts, helps to execute UFT scripts and then stores test results as well.

Exercise

Assuming you have QC/ALM setup available, complete the following exercises:

1. Save all the scripts created till now within QC/ALM's Test Plan tab.

2. Create a new Test Set for execution within QC/ALM and execute all the scripts as a batch.

3. Verify the test results for each the scripts.

ϾϿ

23

Automation Frameworks

Being a part of the software testing domain, we would have heard the term 'Automation Frameworks' time and again. Again, it is a very common question one encounters at interviews too. In this chapter we will try to understand the answers to three basic questions:

- Why do we need a framework? What are the advantages of frameworks?
- What exactly is automation framework? What are the components of the framework?
- How to implement frameworks? What are the different types of frameworks?

23.1 Why do we need Automation Frameworks

1. Maintainability

One of the key reasons behind creating an automation framework is to reduce the cost of script maintenance. If there is any change in the functionality of the application, then we need to get our scripts fixed and working utilising the least amount of time and effort.

Ideally, there should not be too much need to update the scripts, in case the application changes. Most of the fixes should be handled at the framework level itself.

2. Productivity

If I ask you how many manual test cases we can automate in a day that might be a difficult question to answer. But the important thing to ask is whether we can increase our productivity by automating more test cases per day?

Yes, we can. If we have an effective framework, we can increase the productivity many fold. In one of my previous projects, we increased the productivity from 3-4 test cases a day to 10-12 test cases a day, mainly through effective framework implementation.

3. Learning curve

If you have a new person joining your team, you would like to reduce the effort in training the person, and have him/her up and running on the framework as soon as possible.

Creating an effective framework helps reduces the learning curve.

As a best practice, I always advise my clients to keep the framework as simple as possible.

4. Make result analysis easier

Once the test cases are automated, a lot of time is spent by the testing team on analysing the results. Sometimes they are not detailed enough, which might make it hard to pinpoint the error. Most often it is not script failure but environment or data issues that turns out to be the source of problems. A better reporting format in the framework will cut down on result analysis time considerably.

23.2 What Exactly is an Automation Framework

Frameworks are a set of guidelines which define how we will structure the various components in an automation environment. These components include object repository, test data, functions, reports and batch execution script.

When the development team begins development, it creates a high level design of the application. Similarly, we, as an automation team, need to create an automation framework to define how different automation components will interact with each other. We can also call it high level design for automation components.

So what are components of the frameworks? Let us see below:

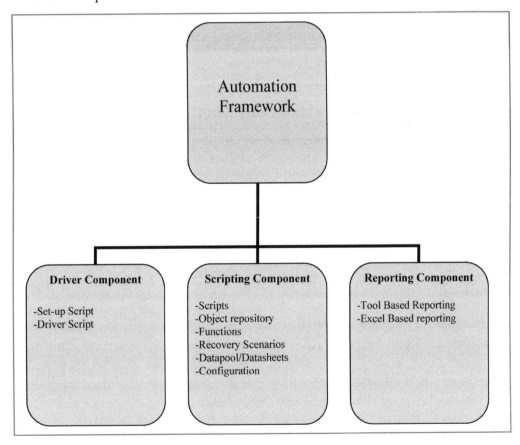

Figure 23-1 – Automation Framework Components

At a high level, Automation Framework can be divided into three components:

- **Driver Component** – How will you execute the script as a batch? What setup will you need before you start execution?
- **Scripting Component** – How will you structure all key components of your automation framework?
- **Reporting-** How will you get your results?

Together, all these components make up an **Automation Framework.**

So, let us understand what exactly is stored within these components.

- **Setup Script** – This script defines what setup you need before you can start script execution.

Example

In one of our projects, we had to install the new desktop thick client application, before we could kick-off the automation test execution. So we created a setup script which downloads the latest thick client and installs it on the test machines to setup the environment.

- **Driver Script** – Most of the time we need to run our scripts overnight. So we need a driver script which can run scripts as a suite (one after another).

We discussed in previous chapters that we could use Batch Runner as the driver program or we could use Quality Center/ALM as batch program for UFT. But if you have different automation tools, you might need to select a different batch program.

- **Scripts** – These are the actual automation programs, which execute just like manual test cases.
- **Object Repository** – A common place where all object properties and information is stored.
- **Functions** – Modular programs which can be re-used across scripts.
- **Configuration File** – Configuration file is the file in which we can set up application URL and other variable parameters in our application.
- **Recovery Scenario** – Exception handling scenarios in our application.
- **Data Pool** – Test data that will drive our scripts.
- **Tool Based Reporting** – Most of the automation tools will have their own reporting format. For instance, UFT results can be viewed in UFT results viewer. It is also important to think about where to store these results for future reference and the ease of drilling down to the results you are looking for.

HP Quality Center/ALM as a test management tool provides a good result storage solution for HP UFT.

- **Excel Based Reports** – Not all tools have corresponding test management tools to store results. Quite often and as part of a framework, the automation team has to develop their own excel drivers (at times database driven) to store results in Excel Sheets, for easy viewing and analysis.

23.3 Types of Frameworks

This brings us to the next important question of how to implement frameworks and what the different types of frameworks are.

Automation developers have different reasons for following a particular framework and every framework has its own advantages and disadvantages.

At a high level, we can divide frameworks into the following categories

- Level 1- Record- Replay
- Level 2- Data Driven Framework
- Level 3- Test Modularity Framework
- Level 4 - Hybrid Framework
- Level 5 - Keyword Driven Framework

I would call Level 1 as the lowest level of framework and Level 5 as the highest.

Let's understand more on each of the different levels.

Level 1 - Record-Replay

This is not really a framework, but helps as a starting point to an introduction to frameworks.

- This framework provide the ability to capture/record the user actions and later to playback them.
- Also called as Capture/Replay approach.
- Enhance the recorded script with verification points, where some property or data is verified against an existing baseline.
- Also note that as part of this framework, we use a shared object repository across all the scripts.

Advantages

- Fastest way to generate scripts.
- Automation expertise not required.

Disadvantages

- Little re-use of scripts.
- Test data is hard coded into the script.

- New scripts always take same time to automate as previously automated scripts.
- Maintenance is a nightmare.

One of the key issues with this framework is that if the application workflow changes or if the test data changes, we need to go into each script and modify the script.

For instance, if you have 500 automation scripts for your application and username or password changes for your login page, you would need to go into each of the scripts and fix them, which can be a nightmare.

This leads us to our next level of framework, which resolves this issue.

Level 2 – Data Driven Framework

In this framework, while test case logic resides in test scripts, the test data is separated and kept outside the test scripts. Test data is read from the external files (Excel files, Text files, CSV files, and database) and loaded into the variables inside the test script. Variables are used both for storing input values and verification values. Test scripts themselves are prepared using record replay approach.

Since the data is stored outside the script, if as in our previous example the username or password changes, we would need to change just one datasheet and all our 500 scripts will be fit for execution. So we saved on huge maintenance effort using this framework.

Also we can use the same script to run for multiple sets of data defined in external datasheets helping us achieve more return on investment on effort spent on automation.

Advantages

- Test data can be changed at one central place and there is no need to modify the scripts.
- Changes to the Test data do not affect the Test scripts.
- Test cases can be executed with multiple sets of data.

Disadvantages

- If functional workflow of the application changes, it will be a maintenance nightmare.
- No re-use of code.

One of the key issues with the above framework is that if the workflow of the application changes, you would need to go back and fix all the scripts again.

For instance, assuming you have 500 scripts, and in each script you login to the application. Due to a new business requirement, apart from just username and password, your application now also requires your business unit name to be entered before login. This represents a change in application. Even though your data resides outside the script, you still need to go into each of the scripts and add extra lines of code to enter the business unit name. This approach is still a nightmare!

Let us look at the next level of frameworks which helps to handle this issue.

Level 3– Test Modularity Framework

As part of this framework we divide the application-under-test into libraries (Functions or Action based). These library files are then directly invoked from the test case script. This framework embodies the principle of abstraction.

In this framework, we can re-use a lot of the existing code, which helps to improve productivity.

Considering our earlier example where our login workflow has changed. We will be able to handle that issue using this framework more simplistically, as we would have created login as a separate function. This login function will be invoked from all our scripts. So we just need to add a step in the login function to enter value in business unit field and all our scripts should be fine.

So, as we would have understood, I would consider modular and data driven frameworks work differently, one utilizes a modular approach and the other focused around data.

Advantages

- Higher level of code re-use is achieved in Structured Scripting compared to "Record & Playback".
- Automation scripts are less costly to develop due to higher code re-uses.
- Easier Script Maintenance.

Disadvantages

- Technical expertise is necessary to write Scripts using Test Library Framework.
- More time is needed to plan and prepare test scripts.
- Test Data is hard coded within the scripts.

Level 4– Hybrid Framework

In the previous section, we saw the advantages with data driven framework and test modularity framework. Should we not get benefits of both the data driven and modular approach?

This is exactly what we do in a hybrid framework. We keep data outside our scripts and create modular functions.

Advantages

- Higher level of code re-uses.
- Test Data is at central location and can be changed on demand.
- Higher productivity and more scripts can be automated as we build the libraries.

- Easier script maintenance.

Disadvantages

- Technical expertise is necessary to write scripts and understanding of existing functions could take time.

- More time is needed to plan and prepare test scripts.

- Can be used by expert automation testers only.

> **Note: Hybrid frameworks constitute** 80-90% of the frameworks, which are highly successful.

Level 5– Keyword Driven Framework

Hybrid framework has a lot of advantages, but the disadvantage is that it gets too technical. Inherently testers are not programmers and so automation gets limited to automation testers only and cannot be done by functional testers or business analysts.

Keyword driven framework makes it easier for functional testers and business analysts to be involved in automation. Let us see how.

The keyword driven or table driven framework requires the development of data tables (usually Excel Sheets) and keywords, **independent of the test automation tool** used to execute them. Tests can be designed with or without the application.

For example, instead of recording a script to login into the application, if we had an Excel Sheet to store username and password and re-use, wouldn't that be easy enough for functional testers? See table below.

Object	Action	TestData
Object Repository	**(KEYWORD)**	
WebEdit(UserName)	Set	adactin123
WebEdit(Password)	Set	Xxxxx
WebButton(Login)	Click	
Browser(Adactin.com)	Verify	Loads

But how will the script actually run?

Embedded within the back-end, there will be an intermediate component, which will translate this Excel Sheet at run time and create an automation script on the fly.

The key point to remember about this framework is that the intermediate component to translate high level excel sheet statements written by non programmers and create scripts automatically is the complex part and can take time. Usually we would need expert programmers to write the intermediate component.

Advantages

- Provides high code re-usability.
- Test tool independent.
- Independent of Application Under Test (AUT), same function works for other applications (with some limitations).
- Tests can be designed with or without AUT (Application under Test).

Disadvantages

- Initial investment being pretty high, the benefits of this can only be realized if the application is considerably bigger, and the test scripts are to be maintained for a few years.
- Debugging of this kind of framework can be very hard.
- Test data is hard-coded within every Excel based test script, which leads to data issues.
- A high level of automation expertise is required to create the keyword driven framework.

Even though keyword driven framework might look like the coolest thing to work on, I have seen a lot of keyword driven frameworks fail due to their disadvantages. Most commonly, I have seen that keyword driven frameworks end up being so complicated, that it is hard for anyone to debug and isolate the problem in case the script fails.

HP Business Process Test is one of the successful keyword driven frameworks, which comes bundled with HP Quality Center/HP ALM (though you need to purchase a separate licence for it.).

Personally, I prefer implementing the hybrid framework since it is simple to debug and handover to functional teams. Some of the keyword driven frameworks we encountered or developed were too hard for client teams to understand and they ended up not using the framework.

~

24

Multiple Choice Questions Set-3

1. Which recovery option is best for a pop-up message that states "Network Drive is not accessible"?

   A. Close application process

   B. Function call

   C. Restart Microsoft Windows

   D. Keyboard or mouse operation

2. After execution of UFT GUI Test from QC/ALM, test results are stored within QC/ALM?

   A. Yes

   B. No

3. What is the file extension of Recovery Scenarios file?

   A. .rsf

   B. .qrs

   C. .qrf

   D. .rfq

4. In a Batch Test process, the test list is saved in file format as

   A. *.mtb

   B. *.mts

   C. *.mbt

   D. *.mtr

5. Which method is used for sending information to the test results?

   A. Reporter.log()

   B. Reporter.reportevent()

   C. Reporter.msgbox()

   D. Reporter.report()

6. UFT GUI Test is stored in which tab of Quality Center?

    A. Test Plan

    B. Test Lab

    C. Test Resources

    D. Requirement

7. Can you edit UFT GUI Test in QC/ALM without opening UFT?

    A. Yes

    B. No

8. Business Process Test (BPT) is an example of which type of framework?

    A. Hybrid Framework

    B. Keyword Driven Framework

    C. Data Driven Framework

    D. Test Modularity Framework

9. Which character is used to treat dot as a literal character while using regular expression?

    A. *

    B. $

    C. \

    D. /

10. Which of the following represents correct syntax for descriptive programming?

    A. WebButton("name:Cancel").Click

    B. WebButton("name=Cancel").Click

    C. WebButton("name:=Cancel").Click

    D. WebButton("name&Cancel").Click

Answers

Q1. Answer: D
Explanation – Keyboard of mouse operation is the best recovery option since it is a pop-up window

Q2. Answer: A
Explanation – Yes, UFT test results are stored in QC/ALM after execution from QC/ALM.

Q3. Answer: B
Explanation – Extension of recovery scenarios files is .qrs

Q4. Answer: A
Explanation – Extension of file when you save Batch Test file is .mtb

Q5. Answer: B
Explanation – Reporter.ReportEvent method is used to log results.

Q6. Answer: A
Explanation – UFT GUI Test is stored in Test Plan tab of QC/ALM

Q7. Answer: B
Explanation – No, you cannot edit UFT GUI Test in QC/ALM without actually opening UFT. You need to have UFT on that machine to edit the test.

Q8. Answer: B
Explanation – HP BPT is a type of keyword driven framework.

Q9. Answer: C
Explanation – Backslash is used as an escape character in regular expression.

Q10. Answer: C
Explanation – Correct syntax is WebButton("name:=Cancel").Click which has ":="

ɘ⅃

25

What's New with UFT 11.5

This chapter lists the new features in UFT 11.5 which did not exist in previous versions of QuickTest. This section is divided into General UFT enhancements which are generic to UFT and new GUI Test features. New API testing based features are out of scope of this book and not included in this chapter.

25.1 General UFT – New Features

One Composite Unified Tool for Application Testing

Unified Functional Testing (UFT) helps to test both the applications (GUI) layer and the business (API/Web Services) layer of your application, all in one product.

UFT includes all of its predecessors' (QuickTest and Service Test) capabilities along with new features.

If you use HP ALM (Application Lifecycle Management), then you can also create and run business process tests, from within UFT in addition to creating and editing individual GUI and API business components.

New IDE

The new IDE now has enhanced editor and coding capabilities:

- Improved statement completion.
- Customized and built-in code snippets.
- Class and function browsers.
- Go To dialog box.

MDI: Edit multiple Testing Documents Simultaneously

In UFT, you can open and work with multiple documents stored in the same solution, including GUI or API tests, individual actions, business components, function libraries, and code files.

As you navigate from one document to another in the UFT document pane, relevant panes update to display the relevant data, and the Solution Explorer synchronizes to show you the currently active.

This is a great enhancement from previous versions of QTP, where users could not open multiple tests at the same time.

Error pane

The Errors pane displays a list of errors generated when opening, working with, saving, or running tests, components, function libraries, and user code files.

The Errors pane reports the following types of errors:

- Code syntax errors
- Missing resources (GUI testing only)
- Missing references (API testing only)
- Missing property values (API testing only)

Code syntax errors in previous versions of QTP were shown in Information pane, which is now removed. Also missing resources pane has been removed and replaced with composite error pane.

Automatically export test results

You can instruct UFT to automatically export run results in HTML or PDF format after every run session. Select **Tools > Options > General** tab **> Run Sessions** to set your preferences for the export.

In previous versions of QTP, the user had to manually export the results to HTML or pdf format.

Select Licence Types From Within the Add-in Manager Dialog box

If your concurrent licence server has more than one valid licence type installed, you can select the licence you want to use in the Add-in Manager dialog box. You have the option to choose a different licence each time you open UFT (By default, your selection from the previous session is used).

25.2 GUI Testing – New Features

Insight- Image-based Object Identification

Along with object properties based recognition, UFT also introduces new image-based identification (Insight), using which UFT recognizes user interface controls instead of object properties. This enables UFT to perform basic steps such as clicking, dragging, and dropping controls in applications that could not previously be tested. You can even use insight to test applications that run remotely on non-Windows operating systems.

This feature will be pretty helpful in scenarios where application controls are custom built (using non-standard development languages) and could not be recognized in **Default** recording mode. These controls can now be automated using Insight image based recording.

File Content Checkpoints

The new file content checkpoint compares the textual content of a file that is generated during a run session with the textual content of a source file. This enables you to verify that the generated file in the application contains the expected results. For example, you may want to verify that a PDF file generated during a run session displays the local corporate address at the top of every page. You can perform a checkpoint on text in one line, multiple lines, or the entire document, as needed.

This feature is quite important and will be very helpful when testing reporting features in applications.

Support for MSAA-Based (Microsoft Office and Plug-in) Controls

UFT can identify windowless objects that were developed using the MSAA (Microsoft Active Accessibility) API. For example, the controls within the Microsoft Office ribbons are identified as independent objects. UFT recognizes these controls just like any other standard Windows objects.

Generate Automated GUI Tests from Sprinter Exploratory Tests

With Sprinter, HP's manual testing solution, you can perform exploratory tests using an enhanced set of capture and annotation tools.

You can now export the captured user actions, test objects, and comments, to an XML file and then import this file into UFT. UFT converts the imported file to a GUI test with a local object repository. Each step in the newly created test represents an operation that the user performed during the sprinter exploratory test.

New GUI Testing Support for Qt and Adobe Flex Applications

UFT now includes support for testing Flex and Qt GUI applications.

More Ways to Check the Images in Your Application

The enhanced bitmap checkpoint now enables you to specify multiple areas to compare or ignore within the bitmap that you are checking. It also supports checking whether a specific image appears anywhere within the run time bitmap. This image can be a segment of the bitmap that UFT captures when you create the checkpoint, or a bitmap file that you load from an external file.

Record Toolbar

The Record Toolbar now combines all the controls needed to record your application in an accessible movable nonintrusive toolbar. It provides the ability to control the recording session by starting, stopping, or pausing the recording, as well as selecting the mode in which UFT records the steps performed on the application. You can also add actions, checkpoints, and output values from the toolbar while recording, enabling you to record an entire test containing multiple actions in one recording session.

🙜

26

Best Practices in Automation

This section defines some of the best practices in automation

26.1 Best Practices in Automation

Best Practices While Maintaining Shared Object Repository

The following steps should be followed by the automation tester, for creating shared object repositories for test automation scripts in UFT.

In UFT, each test has its own set of objects associated with it. These objects can be either:

Local = stored within the test à action. Use local objects for objects specific to the test script.

OR

Global (Shared) = stored as an external file (.tsr) & then called amongst different tests.

The points below are to be followed for Global Object Repositories in UFT:

- All application test objects should be stored in Global Object Repository.
- No object should be stored in Local Object Repository.
- Naming of Object Repository should follow naming conventions as pre-defined in your organization's naming conventions document. If no naming conventions document exists, it is highly recommended creating one before start of test automation.
- Global Object Repository should not have objects that are identified by dynamic properties.
- Inform the automation test reviewer for any modifications done to existing Global Object Repositories, including the specific details about the name of the object that was added/updated.

Best Practice While Creating New Automation Scripts

The following steps should be followed by the automation tester for the creation of new test automation scripts:

1. After a newly created test automation script is completed, the automation tester needs to execute (run) the complete script independently from the beginning to the

end, check for all verification points within the script, and also to ensure there are no script failures within the newly created test automation scripts.

2. If there are more manual test cases to be automated for the same functional area of the AUT, the automation test developer can then continue creating new scripts.

OR

3. Inform the automation test reviewer of the successful completion of the test automation script along with script details, such as the script's name and the project name under which it is stored.

Best Practices While Reviewing Scripts Created by the Automation Developer

The following steps should be followed by the automation test reviewer for reviewing of test automation scripts created/modified by the automation test developer.

1. Open the latest version of script that needs to be reviewed to the local machine.

2. Open the automation script and ensure the following:

- Automation framework is correct.

- Appropriate error handling is in place.

- Object repository (global/local) does not contain objects that have dynamic properties in them.

If any discrepancies found in the above, inform the automation test developer to fix the script accordingly.

3. Once step 2 is verified, run the test automation script as is and analyse the test results.

- Ensure no errors are reported in the log.

If any error is reported in the log, inform the automation test developer to fix the script.

4. Once step 3 is verified, inform the Functional Tester of the test automation script along with the details of the script, such as the script name and the project name under which it is stored. This is to inform the functional test team that the test cases it had given to the automation team for automation have been automated.

ひ

27

Sample Naming and Coding Conventions

27.1 Sample Naming Conventions

Following a standardized naming and coding conventions ensures that the automation components including names of tests, functions, objects and variables are consistent throughout our framework. This reflects good coding practice and assists in code maintenance later on.

1. Automation components naming convention – As a sample you can follow these naming conventions for automation components which will be used during automation.

Subtype	Syntax	Example
Test	**[Product]_[TestType]_[Test Name]**	*HA_BP_FindHotel*
Library	**[Product]_[FunctionType]_[Library Name]**	*HA_GBF_Hotelbooking.qfl*
Data Table	[Product]_ [DataTableType]_[Table Name]	HA_DE_FindHotel.xls
Object Repository	[Product]_[Repository Name]	HA_SharedOr.tsr
Objects	[Object Type]_[Object Description]	Btn_Submit

Syntax Description

- **Product/Project [Product]**
    - **HA** Hotel Application
- **Function Types   [FunctionType]**
    - **GBF**: Global Business Function
    - **LBF**: Local Business Function
    - **VF**: Verification Function
    - **UF**: Utility Function
    - **RF**:   Recovery Function

- **Test Types**   [**TestType**]
  - **BP**: Business Process Script
  - **TC**: Test Case Script
  - **UT**: Utility Script
  - **UI**: User Interface Script
- **Data Table Types**   [**DataTableType**]
  - **DE**:   Data Entry Data table
  - **DL**:   Data Loop Data Table
- **Objects**
  - **Btn**:   WebButton
  - **Ed**:   WebEdit
  - **Tbl**:   WebTable
  - **Cb**:   WebCombobox
  - **Lnk**:   WebLink
- **Extensions:**
  - Library: **qfl**
  - Datatable: **xls**
  - Shared Repository: **tsr**
  - Recovery Scenaio: **qrs**
2. Descriptive names

Names should use mixed case and should be as complete as necessary to describe its purpose or related function points. In addition, test names could be followed by the test case ID, to indicate the related test case.

27.2 Coding Conventions

1. VBScript Coding Conventions

Variable Naming Convention

For purposes of readability and consistency, use the prefixes listed in the following table, along with descriptive names for variables in your VBScript code.

Subtype	Prefix	Example
Boolean	Bln	blnFound
Integer	Int	intQuantity
Object	Obj	objCurrent

String	Str	strFirstName
Variant	Var	varData

Descriptive Variable and Procedure Names

The body of a variable or procedure name should use mixed case and should be as complete as necessary to describe its purpose. In addition, procedure names should begin with a verb, such as InitNameArray or CloseDialog.

For frequently used or long terms, standard abbreviations are recommended to help keep name length reasonable. In general, variable names greater than 32 characters can be difficult to read.

When using abbreviations, make sure they are consistent throughout the entire script. For example, randomly switching between Cnt and Count within a script or set of scripts may lead to confusion.

2. Code Commenting Conventions for functions

Heading	Mandatory	Comment Contents
Function	Mandatory	Name of the function and the description.
Inputs	Mandatory	List of variables passed into the function as the parameters.
Outputs	Mandatory	List of variables as the output of the function.
Returns	Mandatory	List of variables returned by the function.
Usage	Optional	Information about specifically how the function is implemented, and how that might affect its usage in a script.
See Also	Optional	Linking to any related topic – similar / opposite functions, type definitions.

Example:

```
'****************************************************************
```

' Function: JustATest

'

'   An example function for demonstrating comment format.

'

' Inputs:

'

'   x – An integer governing something.

'   y – A string used for something else.

'

```
' OutPuts:
'
'        z – An integer value for something.
'
' Returns:
'
'        An integer error code (0 for success).
'
' History:
'
'        QA1   Create   2.1E   2013-02-06
'        QA2   Update   2.1I   2013-02-09
'
' Usage / Implementation Notes:
'
'        Passing x = 0 may cause a divide by zero error, so avoid that.
'        The value in 'y' will be overwritten.
'
' See Also:
'
'        <JustAnotherTest>
'********************************************************************
Function JustATest(x As Integer, y As String)
' lines of code
End Function
```

಄

28

Common UFT Issues and FAQs

28.1 UFT Issues and FAQs

In order to keep this book simple and concise, there were quite a few topics we could not cover in detail. Keeping the larger audience of this book in mind, we have addressed a few of these topics and questions in this section.

What are the different ways to synchronize your scripts?

Many a time, your application performance will vary and this will need your UFT script's execution speed to be appropriately manipulated.

In one of the applications that we tested, it took more than 60 seconds for an application form to save and confirm that save was successful. How does UFT support these situations?

There are four ways to handle synchronization in UFT:

- Use Global Synchronization Timeout
- Use Static Wait Statements
- Use Dynamic Synchronization Point
- Use .Exist property

Global Synchronization Timeout

If you go to **File → Settings → Run** you will notice there is an Object Synchronization Timeout defined with default value of 20 seconds.

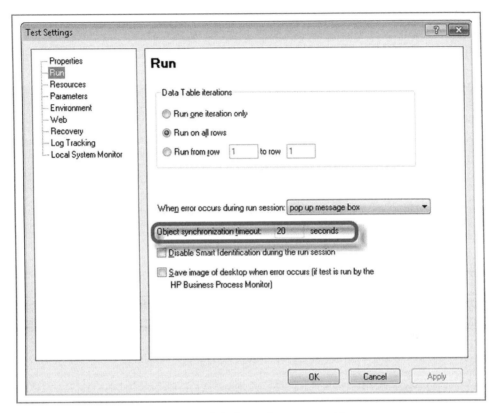

Figure 28-1 – Global Synchronization Timeout

This means that if UFT is not able to find an object or action on application (e.g. saving a form) is still being processed, it will wait for 20 seconds for the application to respond. If the application does not respond even after the default time, UFT will flag a run time error. Also, it's important to note that if the application responds before 20 seconds, UFT automatically moves on to the next step and does not wait the whole 20 seconds.

Ideally, it is not advisable to increase this time beyond 20 seconds, as this will slow down the scripts when there are genuine application issues.

Static Wait Statements

The simplest and easiest way to handle synchronization will be to use static wait statements in scripts. If you know that the application can take up to 60 seconds to respond, you can enter a wait statement in the editor view script (after the step where you want UFT to wait) which will **'pause'** the script for 60 seconds. See below statement.

wait(60)

The disadvantage of using static wait statements is that script will **wait for the entire 60 seconds,** even though the application might respond quicker in most instances.

Automation testers should be careful while adding wait statements, as this increases the overall test execution time of the automation suite.

Dynamic synchronization points

UFT provides another feature, synchronization points, which can be inserted by navigating to **Design → Synchronization Point**. Synchronization points can be inserted only in the recording mode.

The key idea behind inserting synchronization point is to get UFT to wait until a particular object achieves its expected property value. For instance, if a user clicks on the save button, we can wait until the edit button is enabled on the screen, which will be a cue that "save" has completed successfully.

UFT will 'pause' the test until the object property achieves the specified value or until the specific timeout amount has been exceeded. UFT uses one of the object's properties as the waiting criteria. For example, 'title property for window, 'label' property for buttons, etc.

Steps to insert synchronization point:

- Make sure the application object on which you want to insert synchronization point is visible.
- Place your cursor in UFT script at the step at which you want to insert synchronization point.
- Start Recording.
- Go to Design → **Synchronization Point** and click on **Synchronization point.**
- Place the Hand icon on the object on which you want to insert Synchronization point.
- In **Add Synchronization Point** dialog select the **Property Name,** which will show a change and give a visual cue to the user that the previous background operation has finished (for example, enable or disable button can be verified by inspecting the property enabled).
- Enter the expected property value for the above property selected. For example, for enabled property expected value can be true once background operation has finished).
- Provide timeout value – maximum time UFT is going to wait for property value to appear.
- Press OK on **Add Synchronization Point** dialog.
- Stop Recording.

You will see the method defined below

object.**WaitProperty** (*PropertyName, PropertyValue,* [*TimeOut*])

Object - A test object of type ActiveX.

Property Name - The name of the property whose value is checked.

PropertyValue - The value to be achieved before continuing to the next step.

TimeOut - Optional, the time is specified, in milliseconds, after which UFT continues to the next step if the specified value is not achieved. If no value is specified, UFT uses the time set in the object synchronization timeout option in the run pane of the test settings dialog box.

Browser("AdactIn.com - Hotel Reservatio").Page("AdactIn.com - Hotel Reservatio"). WebEdit("order_no").WaitProperty "disabled", 1, 10000

> **Note:** Use synchronization point when object property changes a value, which signifies an operation has been completed.

Exist Property

This property is a global property and is common for all objects.

You can use exist property to check if the operation has been completed. This works on the assumption that new objects will appear or old objects will not appear in the application, after the operation is completed.

For example, to synchronize login operation in our script, we can use exist property.

For example, the statement below will make the script wait for up to 60 seconds, until user is logged in.

```
Browser("Adactin.com - Hotel Reservatio").Page("Adactin.com - Hotel Reservatio").WebEdit("username").Set "adactin123"
Browser("Adactin.com - Hotel Reservatio").Page("Adactin.com - Hotel Reservatio").WebEdit("password").SetSecure "503de0c4581f45290e11b042f5117b92edbc08ab083b36a97ed0"
Browser("Adactin.com - Hotel Reservatio").Page("Adactin.com - Hotel Reservatio").WebButton("Login").Click

If Browser("Adactin.com - Hotel Reservatio").Page("Adactin.com - Search Hotel").Link("Logout").Exist(60) Then

    Reporter.ReportEvent micdone, "Login Step", "User Logged in Successfully"
    'More Steps in the script

Else

    Reporter.ReportEvent micFail, "Login Step", "User Unable to Login"
    ExitAction
End If
```

Figure 28-2 – Exist statement

> **Note:** By default, if the **Exist** property does not find an object, it will wait for 20 seconds (which is the global synchronization timeout). If you want to wait for more than 20 seconds, you need to define your **timeout** value.

For example:

Browser("AdactIn.com - Hotel Reservatio").Page("AdactIn.com - Search Hotel").Link("Logout"). Exist(60)

In above statement, if the object appears before 60 seconds, the script will move on to next step and will not wait for complete **timeout** duration.

What are the different types of recording levels in UFT?

There are four types of recording levels -- Default (or Context Sensitive Recording), Analog Recording, Low Level recording and Insight Recording.

You can switch between recording modes from Record Toolbar

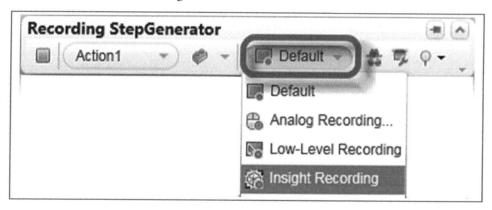

Figure 28-3 – Record Toolbar – Recording Levels

Default Recording

- Default recording mode.
- Identify objects on application using object properties.
- Records operations performed on objects.

Example: Recording where we enter username and password in login page.

Analog Recording

- Records exact mouse and key board operations.
- Records every move of the mouse.
- Used while recording operations that cannot be recorded at object level.
- Cannot edit steps within UFT.

Example: Recording when we are testing applications, which needs mouse movement like providing digital signatures.

Sample editor view code:

Desktop.RunAnalog "Track1"

Window ("Microsoft Internet Explorer").RunAnalog "Track2"

Low Level Recording

- Record on any object, irrespective of whether UFT identifies those objects.
- Records all run time objects as Window or WinObject.

- Records keyboard input. Mouse clicks are recorded based on mouse coordinates.
- Use when:
1. Objects are not recognized by UFT or
2. Exact object co-ordinates are important in the test.

Example: Use when there are certain custom objects in your application, which are not recognised by default by UFT.

Sample Editor View code:

Window("Microsoft Internet Explorer"). WinObject("Internet Explorer_Server"). Click 10,200

Window("Microsoft Internet Explorer"). WinObject("Internet Explorer_Server"). Type "UFT"

<u>Insight Recording</u>

This mode enables you to record on any control (object) displayed on your screen, irrespective of whether UFT recognizes the object's technology, and is able to retrieve its properties or activate its methods.

In this mode, UFT recognizes controls based on their appearance, and not their native properties. This can be useful to test controls from an environment that UFT does not support or even from a remote computer running a non-Windows operating system.

You can switch to Insight recording midway through a recording session. After you record the necessary steps using Insight recording, you can return to normal recording mode for the remainder of your recording session.

Sample of the Editor View insight recording code:

Figure 28-4 – Insight recording Editor View code

Corresponding object repository for insight recording:

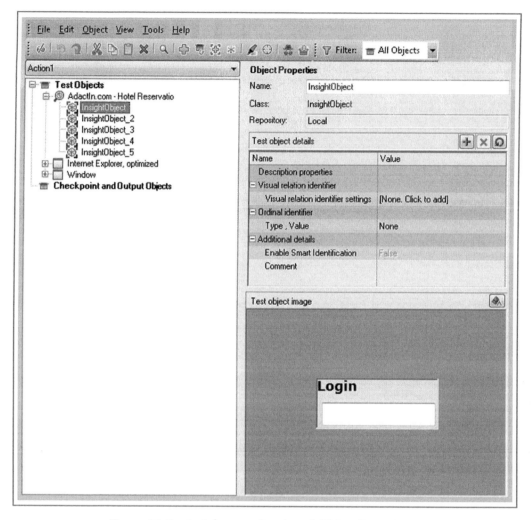

Figure 28-5 – Insight recording based Object Repository

How can you force VBScript or UFT to declare variables?

By default, VBScript does not require us to declare variables (unlike C, C++ and many other languages). But as a good coding practice, it is always advisable to declare variables before we use them in our script.

We can use **Option Explicit** statement to force VBScript to declare variables.

When you use the Option Explicit statement, you must explicitly declare all variables before using them in script. If you attempt to use an undeclared variable name, an error occurs.

For example,

Option Explicit ' Force explicit variable declaration.

Dim b ' Declare variable.

a = "UFT"   ' Undeclared variable generates error.

b = "Training"   ' Declared variable does not generate error.

How to use With statement in UFT script?

The **With** statement allows you to perform a series of statements on a specified object without requalifying the hierarchy of the object, which means do not need to repeat the object's parent object statements for each and every step.

For example,

With Browser("AdactIn.com - Hotel Reservatio").Page("AdactIn.com - Hotel Reservatio")

> *.WebEdit("username").Set "adactin123"*

> *.WebEdit("password").SetSecure "4ffe76b5bf81a5c0168c57c97e46"*

> *.WebButton("Login").Click*

End With

In the above example we do not need to repeat object statement *Browser("AdactIn.com - Hotel Reservatio").Page("AdactIn.com - Hotel Reservatio")* for every step.

Note: You can nest With statements by placing one With block within another. However, because members of the outer With blocks are masked within the inner With blocks, you must provide a fully qualified object reference in an inner With block to any member of an object in an outer With block.

Why and how to use relative path in Unified Functional Testing

As a good development practice, we should never hard-code paths in our script. For instance if you need to access your function library file, we should not use absolute paths like "D:\UFT\FunctionLibary\HotelApp.qfl". The key reason for that being that if you need to run the same script on another machine which does not have D: drive, it would be a huge maintenance effort to change the path in the scripts every now and then.

The best solution is to keep the relative path in the script like "HotelApp.qfl", instead of specifying the complete absolute path.

You can define search path by going to **Tools → Options → GUI Testing → Folders.**

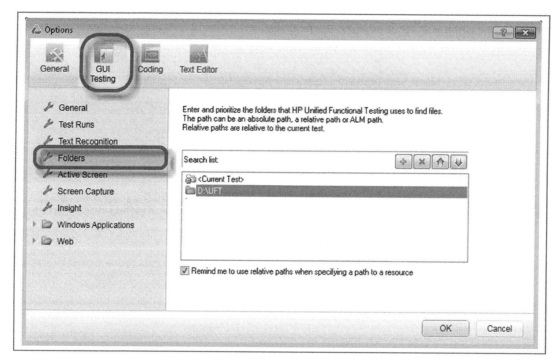

Figure 28-6 – Folders options

After defining search path in Folder options, you can refer to files using relative paths (e.g. 'HotelApp.qfl') instead of absolute path (e.g. D:\UFT\FunctionLibary\HotelApp.qfl). Other files for which you should include relative path include shared object repository, recovery scenario, external data files and external configuration files.

How does UFT know which properties to store in Object Repository to uniquely identify the object?

In one of our previous exercises, we considered an example of identifying a car and concluded that we can recognize a car by three properties, namely color, make, and registration number. Based on that analogy, we learnt that UFT recognizes objects by storing properties in the object repository, which helps to uniquely identify the object.

A commonly asked question is how does UFT know which properties will help it uniquely identify the object? Objects can be of varied types like button, edit field or combo box. Now from our previous car analogy about looking for our parked car, how do we know that the color, make, and registration number will help us uniquely identify the car?

The answer is that this information is already pre-defined and saved in UFT. UFT knows how to identify an object based on its class and the properties that will help to uniquely identify the object. If these mandatory property values are not sufficient to uniquely identify an object, UFT can add some assistive properties and/or an ordinal identifier to create a unique description.

This information is stored in the Object Identification tab.

1. Go to **Tools → Object Identification…** and Open Object identification dialog.

2. Select any of the environment categories. In our case let us select **Web.**

3. Select **WebButton** Class.

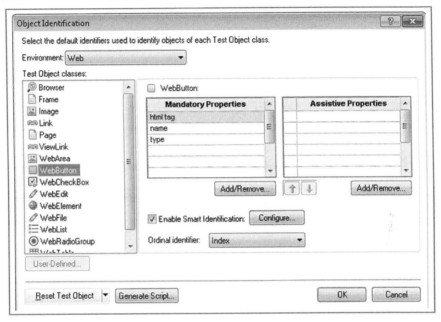

Figure 28-7 – Object Identification

Mandatory properties are properties for a specific test object class that UFT always learns.

Assistive properties are properties that UFT learns only if the mandatory properties that UFT learns for a particular object in your application are not sufficient to create a unique description. If several assistive properties are defined for an object class, then UFT learns one assistive property at a time and stops as soon as it creates a unique description for the object. If UFT does learn assistive properties, those properties are added to the test object description.

In addition to learning the mandatory and assistive properties specified in the Object Identification dialog box (**Tools > Object Identification**), UFT can also learn ordinal identifiers for each test object. The **ordinal identifier** assigns the object a numerical value that indicates its order relative to other objects with an otherwise identical description (objects that have the same values for all properties specified in the mandatory and assistive property lists). This ordered value enables UFT to create a unique description when the mandatory and assistive properties are not sufficient to do so.

Because the assigned ordinal property value is a relative value and is accurate only in relation to the other objects displayed when UFT learns an object, changes in the layout or composition of your application page or screen could cause this value to change, even though the object itself has not changed in any way. For this reason, UFT learns a value for the ordinal identifier only when it cannot create a unique description using all available mandatory and assistive properties.

What is Smart Identification and when is it used in scripts?

Typically, if even one of the on-screen object property does not match the recorded object property, the test will fail.

In smart identification, UFT does not give an error if the property values do not match, but uses **Base filter** and **Optional Filter** properties to uniquely identify an object. Within Optional Filter properties, if a property value does not match, script proceeds to compare the next property until it finds one unique object in the application. Smart identification for an object can be enabled/checked in Object Identification dialog box.

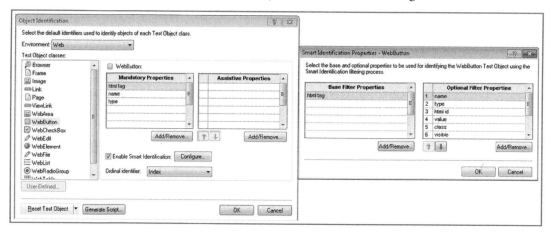

Figure 28-8 – Smart Identification

What is the difference between the Functions and Actions and which one should be used?

Actions are specific to UFT, while the functions are generic and a feature of VB scripting. Actions can have an object repository associated with it while functions can't. A function is just lines of code with some/none input parameters and a single return value while an action can have more than one input/output parameters. But it is important to note that Functions use the object repository of the script, and do not have their own object repository.

So next question is should we use Actions or Functions?

I personally prefer to use Functions with UFT scripts (with shared object repository). The reason for that is Functions are flexible and lightweight and can be modified using Function library file. If I need to modify multiple Functions, I can open one library file and modify all the required Functions. But to modify Actions, I need to modify every Action separately (assuming all external actions are stored as separate a script).

If you are keeping your scripts version-controlled in a tool like CVS or any other version controlling tool, checking out and checking-in Actions would mean check-in/check-out of multiple files and more overhead.

I have seen quite a few scenarios where testers started automation using reusable Actions and later moved to using Functions.

How do we check if a particular object exists on screen or not?

In many common scenarios we would need to verify if a particular object exists or not. For example, how can we confirm that our login to an application was successful? We can confirm that by checking if the logout link exists on the webpage once user is logged in.

To confirm existence of objects, we use Exist property. This property is a global property and is common for all the objects.

For example, the Exist statement in the example below will confirm if login is possible or not.

```
Browser("Adactln.com - Hotel Reservatio").Page("Adactln.com - Hotel Reservatio").WebEdit("username").Set "adactln123"
Browser("Adactln.com - Hotel Reservatio").Page("Adactln.com - Hotel Reservatio").WebEdit("password").SetSecure "503de0c4581f45290e11b042f5117b92edbc08eb083b36a97ed0"
Browser("Adactln.com - Hotel Reservatio").Page("Adactln.com - Hotel Reservatio").WebButton("Login").Click

If Browser("Adactln.com - Hotel Reservatio").Page("Adactln.com - Search Hotel").Link("Logout").Exist Then

    Reporter.ReportEvent micPass, "Login Step", "User Logged in Successfully"
    Browser("Adactln.com - Hotel Reservatio").Page("Adactln.com - Search Hotel").Link("Logout").Click
    Browser("Adactln.com - Hotel Reservatio").Page("Adactln.com - Logout").Link("Click here to login again").Click

Else

    Reporter.ReportEvent micFail, "Login Step", "User Unable to Login"

End If
```

Figure 28-9– Object Existence in Editor View

Note: By default, if Exist property does not find an object, it will wait for 20 seconds (which is global synchronization timeout). If you would not like UFT to wait for entire duration, you can use the statement given below in which case UFT will wait only for 5 seconds.

Browser("AdactIn.com - Hotel Reservatio").Page("AdactIn.com - Search Hotel").Link("Logout"). Exist(5)

What is the use of Transactions in UFT?

Measuring transaction time is a performance testing feature. Using transactions, you can measure how long it takes to run a section of your test and this can be achieved by defining **transactions**. A transaction represents the process in your application that you are interested in measuring. Transactions that are added in UFT can be used in integration with tools like HP LoadRunner or Performance to measure performance of specific transactions.

You define transactions within your test by enclosing the appropriate sections of the test with **startTransaction** and **endTransaction** statements. For example, you can define a transaction that measures how long it takes to save the booking order.

StartTransaction step signals the beginning of the time measurement. The time measurement continues until the **EndTransaction** step is reached. The test results for the EndTransaction step include the transaction name, end status and total duration.

How to check if checkpoint is passed or failed?

Use below code to check if checkpoint passes or fails.

chk_PassFail = Browser(...).Page(...).WebEdit(...).Check (Checkpoint("Check1"))
if chk_PassFail then
MsgBox "Checkpoint passed"
else MsgBox "Checkpoint failed"
end if

What is an environment variable and how do we use environment variables in UFT?

It is a variable which can be used across reusable actions and is not limited to one reusable action.

There are two types of environment variables:

- User-defined
- Built-in

You can retrieve the value of any environment variable. But you can set the value of only *user-defined* environment variables.

To set the value of a user-defined environment variable:
Environment (VariableName) = NewValue

To retrieve the value of a loaded environment variable:
CurrValue = Environment (VariableName)

Example

The following example creates a new internal user-defined variable named MyVariable with a value of 10, and then retrieves the variable value and stores it in the MyValue variable.

*Environment.Value("**MyVariable**")=10*
*MyValue=Environment.Value("**MyVariable**")*

Environment Variables can be found under **File → Settings → Environment**. You can create new user-defined variables or load them from external files.

How to check if parameter exists in DataTable or not?

The best way would be to use the code shown below:

On error resume next
val=DataTable("ParamName",dtGlobalSheet)
if err.number<> 0 then
'Parameter does not exist
else
'Parameter exists
end if

What are Virtual Objects?

Your application may contain objects that behave like standard objects but are not recognized by UFT. You can define these objects as virtual objects and map them to standard classes, such as a button or a checkbox. UFT emulates the user's action on the virtual object during the run session. In the test results, the virtual object is displayed as though it is a standard classFor example, suppose you want to record a test on a Java application containing a custom object divided into four parts, which behaves like a button when the user clicks any of the parts. When you record a test, the application matches the coordinates of the click on the button and opens the corresponding destination window.

To enable UFT to click at the required coordinates during a run session, you can define a virtual object for an area of the custom object, which includes its coordinates, and map it to the button class. When you run a test, UFT clicks the custom object in the area defined as a virtual object so that the correct destination window appears.

You can manage and create virtual objects from **Tools → Virtual Objects → Virtual Object Manager**.

You are unable to run UFT from QC/ALM?

Check that you have selected "Allow other mercury products to run tests and components" from

Tools → Options → GUI Testing → Test Runs Tab.

Does Unified Functional Testing support Macintosh operating systems?

No, UFT is not supported by the Macintosh OS.

Which environments does UFT support?

UFT supports functional testing of all major enterprise environments, including Windows, Web, .NET, Java/J2EE, SAP, Siebel, Qt, Oracle, PeopleSoft, Visual Basic, ActiveX, mainframe terminal emulators, and Web services.

How do we "Turn Off" UFT results after running a Script?

Go to **Tools > Options > General → Run Sessions** Tab and Deselect **View results when run session ends**.

This suppresses only the results window, but a log will be created and can be accessed if required from **View → Last Run Results** menu

How to open an application using VBScript in UFT Editor View?

Use SystemUtil object to open and close applications and processes during a run session.

A SystemUtil.Run statement is automatically added to your test when you run an application from the Windows Start menu or the Run dialog box while recording a test. If it is not added, you can add it manually and specify the path of the .exe file to be executed as an argument. Given below is a very common example of opening Internet Explorer.

Example:

SystemUtil.Run "C:\Program Files\Internet Explorer\iexplore.exe","www.google.com","C:\ Documents and Settings\Administrator","open"

How do we handle run time errors or exceptions in UFT?

There are two ways how run time errors can be handled. We can create a recovery scenario and link it to every script or we can use *On Error Resume next* statement.

On Error Resume Next causes execution to continue to the statement immediately following the statement that caused the run time error, or with the statement immediately following the most recent call out of the procedure containing the "On Error Resume Next" statement. This allows execution to continue despite a run time error.

28.2 Common Automation Interview Questions

I have been on the interview panels for many IT consulting companies and IT departments of non-IT companies. In my personal experience, questions are mainly focussed around relevant experience, real life scenarios and approach towards problem solving, which helps the interviewer judge the depth of automation experience a candidate possesses.

These are few of the questions I recommend that one needs to be prepared for:

- Can you explain the automation framework you have developed using QTP/UFT in your recent project?

Answer - Refer to our automation frameworks chapters to answer this question

- What are the key challenges you face during automation?

Answer - Some of the key challenges are

* Automation environment unavailability.
* Application is unstable.
* Features and workflows being changed frequently leading to maintenance issues.

* Test Data is changed frequently and needed regular modification and maintenance.

* Objects and their properties are changed frequently.

* Unreal expectations from the project manager or test manager, if they expect automation to happen at the click of a button.

* Automation tool's support to automate all features of an application.

* Managing test results for test execution on every build for future reference.

- How comfortable are you with scripting and programming (VBScript or VB)?

- If you have to choose between using Shared Object Repository and Local Object Repository, what will you choose and why?

Answer – Shared Repository, since if the objects/UI in the application change, there will be one central place where object properties can be modified saving huge maintenance overhead of making changes in all scripts. On the other hand using local object repository would mean redundant objects across scripts. Also it will be maintenance overhead to change object properties individually in all the scripts in case of object/UI changes.

- Any scenarios in your previous projects where you had worked on maintenance of scripts? What were the challenges encountered?

- How did you decide on your selection candidates (i.e., test cases to be automated) for automation in your previous projects?

Answer – Key criteria include

* Acceptance test cases.

* High priority business requirements.

* Test cases which need to be executed multiple times with different sets of data.

* Test environment preparation scenarios.

* Test cases which are complex and take a lot of time for automation.

* End-to-end business processes.

* Based on defects found earlier in the application.

- So what automation process will you follow, if you would need to automate the application from the ground up?

Answer – Refer to *Planning for Automation* chapter to answer this question.

- Will you use Actions or Functions in your automation framework?

Answer – Refer to *FAQs* section in this chapter above for the answer to this question.

- How many test cases can you automate in one day?

Answer – Now this really depends on how big the test case is, the type of application you are working with, and the automation framework you are using. At a very high level, if you start without any automation framework on a web based application and a test case with 10 steps each; you can automate up to 3-4 test cases a day. But as mentioned, it can vary a lot based on different factors and your expertise in the tool.

- How do you integrate UFT script with QC/ALM?

Answer – Refer to our *integration with QC/ALM* chapter to answer this.

- How do you manage relative paths in UFT?

Answer – Save Search Paths under Tools → Option → GUI Testing → Folders

- What are the best practices you follow while doing automation?

Answer – Refer to *Best Practices for Automation* chapter to answer this question.

- How do you handle dynamic objects in UFT? Or
- Have you used Descriptive Programming in UFT? Or
- How have you used Regular Expressions in UFT?

Answer – Refer to *Working with Dynamic Objects* chapter to answer this question.

- How do you get properties of objects from your application, using UFT?

Answer – Use GetROProperty method or use Output value feature of UFT.

- How can you report a custom message (Pass, Fail or Information message) from UFT script to be viewed in UFT test results after script execution?

Answer – Use Reporter.ReportEvent Method.

∾

29

Sample Test Cases for Automation

TEST CASE ID	OBJECTIVE	STEPS	TEST DATA	EXPECTED RESULTS
TC-101	To verify valid login details	1. Launch hotel reservation application using URL as in test data. 2. Login to the application using username and password as in test data.	URL:http://adactin.com/HotelApp/index.php User:{test username} Password:{test password}	User should login to the application.
TC-102	To verify whether the check-out date field accepts a later date than check-in date.	1. Launch hotel reservation application using URL as in test data. 2. Login to the application using username and password as in test data. 3. Select location as in test data. 4. Select hotel as in test data. 5. Select room type as in test data. 6. Select no-of-rooms as in test data. 7. Enter check-in-date later than the check-out-date field as in test data. 8. Verify that system gives an error saying 'check-in-date should not be later than check-out-date'.	URL: http://adactin.com/HotelApp/index.php User:{test username} Password:{test password} Location: Sydney Hotel: Hotel creek Room type: standard No-of-rooms:1 Check-in-date: today + 7 date Check-out date: today+5 date	System should report an error message.

TC -103	To check if error is reported if check-out date field is in the past	1. Launch hotel reservation application using URL as in test data. 2. Login to the application using username and password as in test data. 3. Select location as in test data. 4. Select hotel as in test data. 5. Select room type as in test data. 6. Select no-of-rooms as in test data. 7. Enter check-out-date as in test data. 8. Verify that application throws error message.	URL: http://adactin.com/HotelApp/index.php User:{test username} Password:{test password} Location: Sydney Hotel: Hotel Creek Room type: standard No-of-rooms:1 Check-in-date: today's -5 date Check-out-date: today's -3 date	System should report an error message 'Enter Valid dates'.
TC-104	To verify whether locations in Select Hotel page are displayed according to the location selected in Search Hotel	1. Launch hotel reservation application using URL as in test data. 2. Login to the application using username and password as in test data. 3. Select location as in test data. 4. Select hotel as in test data. 5. Select room type as in test data. 6. Select no-of-rooms as in test data. 7. Enter check-out-date as in test data. 8. Select No-of-adults as in test data. 9. Select No-of-children as in test data.	URL: http://adactin.com/HotelApp/index.php User:{test username} Password:{test password} Location: Sydney Hotel: Hotel Creek Room type: standard No-of-rooms: 1 Check-in-date: today's date Check-out-date: today+1 date No-of-adults: 1 No-of-children: 0	Location displayed in Select Hotel should be the same as location selected in search hotel form.

		10. Click on Search button. 11. Verify that hotel displayed is the same as selected in search Hotel form.		
TC-105	To verify whether Check-in date and Check-out date are being displayed in Select Hotel page according to the dates selected in search Hotel.	1. Launch hotel reservation application using URL as in test data. 2. Login to the application using username and password as in test data. 3. Select location as in test data. 4. Select hotel as in test data. 5. Select room type as in test data. 6. Select no-of-rooms as in test data. 7. Enter check-out-date as in test data. 8. Select No-of-adults as in test data. 9. Select No-of-children as in test data. 10. Click on Search button. 11. Verify that check-in-date and check-out-dates are the same as selected in search hotel form.	URL: http://adactin.com/HotelApp/index.php User:{test username} Password:{test password} Location: Sydney Hotel: Hotel Creek Room type: standard No-of-rooms:1 Check-in-date: today's date Check-out date: today+1 date No-of-adults: 1 No-of-children: 0	Check-in date and check-out date should be displayed according to the data entered in search hotel form.
TC-106	To verify whether no. of rooms entry in Select Hotel page is same as the number of rooms selected in search hotel page	1. Launch hotel reservation application using URL as in test data. 2. Login to the application using username and password as in test data.	URL: http://adactin.com/HotelApp/index.php User:{test username} Password:{test password}	No-of-rooms should be displayed and match with number of rooms in search hotel page

| | | 3. Select location as in test data.
4. Select hotel as in test data.
5. Select room type as in test data.
6. Select no-of-rooms as in test data.
7. Enter check-out-date as in test data.
8. Select No-of-adults as in test data.
9. Select No-of-children as in test data.
10. Click on Search button.
11. Verify that no-of-rooms is reflected according to the number of rooms selected in search hotel page. | Location: Sydney
Hotel: Hotel Creek
Room type: standard
No-of-rooms: 3
Check-in-date: today's date
Check-out date: today+1 date
No-of-adults: 1
No-of-children: 0 | |
| TC-107 | To verify whether Room Type in Select Hotel page is same as Room type selected in search hotel page | 1. Launch hotel reservation application using URL as in test data.
2. Login to the application using username and password as in test data.
3. Select location as in test data.
4. Select hotel as in test data.
5. Select room type as in test data.
6. Select no-of-rooms as in test data.
7. Enter check-out-date as in test data.
8. Select No-of-adults as in test data.
9. Select No-of-children as in test data. | URL: http://adactin.com/HotelApp/index.php
User:{test username}
Password:{test password}
Location: Sydney
Hotel: hotel Creek
Room type: Deluxe
No-of-rooms:1
Check-in-date: today's date
Check-out-date: today+1 date
No-of-adults: 1
No-of-children: 0 | Room type displayed should be the same as selected in search hotel page |

		10. Click on Search button. 11. Verify that room type reflected is the same as selected in search hotel page.		
TC-108	To verify whether the total price (excl.GST) is calculated as "price per night * no. of nights* no of rooms".	1. Launch hotel reservation application using URL as in test data. 2. Login to the application using username and password as in test data. 3. Select location as in test data. 4. Select hotel as in test data. 5. Select room type as in test data. 6. Select no-of-rooms as in test data. 7. Enter check-out-date as in test data. 8. Select No-of-adults as in test data. 9. Select No-of-children as in test data. 10. Click on Search button. 11. Select the hotel and click on Continue button 12. Verify that total-price(excl.GST) is being calculated as (price-per-night*no-of-rooms*no-of-days)	URL: http://adactin.com/HotelApp/index.php User:{test username} Password:{test password} Location: Sydney Hotel: Hotel Creek Room type: standard No-of-rooms:2 Check-in-date: today's date Check-out-date: today+1 date No-of-adults: 1 No-of-children: 0	Total price =2*1*125=250$
TC-109	To verify when pressed, logout button logs out from the application.	1. Launch hotel reservation application using URL as in test data.	URL: http://adactin.com/HotelApp/index.php	User should logout from the application.

| | | 2. Login to the application using username and password as in test data.

3. Select location as in test data.

4. Select hotel as in test data.

5. Select room type as in test data.

6. Select no-of-rooms as in test data.

7. Enter check-out-date as in test data.

8. Select No-of-adults as in test data.

9. Select No-of-children as in test data.

10. Click on Search button.

11. Select the hotel and click on continue button.

12. Enter the details and click on Book Now.

13. Check the details, click on logout and verify we have been logged out of the application. | User:{test username}

Password:{test password}

Location: Sydney

Hotel: Hotel Creek

Room type: standard

No-of-rooms:2

Check-in-date: today's date

Check-out-date: today+1 date

No-of-adults: 1

No-of-children: 0 | |
| TC-110 | To check correct total price is being calculated as "price per night*no of days*no of rooms in Book a hotel page | 1. Launch hotel reservation application using URL as in test data.

2. Login to the application using username and password as in test data.

3. Select location as in test data.

4. Select hotel as in test data. | URL: http://adactin.com/HotelApp/index.php

User:{test username}

Password:{test password}

Location: Melbourne

Hotel: Hotel Creek

Room type: standard | Total-price should be calculated as (price-per-night*no-of-rooms*no-of-days

Total Price= 125*2*1 = 250$

In book a hotel page |

		5. Select room type as in test data. 6. Select no-of-rooms as in test data. 7. Enter check-out-date as in test data. 8. Select No-of-adults as in test data. 9. Select No-of-children as in test data. 10. Click on Search button. 11. Select the hotel and click on Continue button 12. Verify that total-price is being calculated as (price-per-night*no-of-rooms*no-of-days + 10% GST")	No-of-rooms:2 Check-in-date: today's date Check-out-date: today+1 date No-of-adults: 1 No-of-children: 0	
TC-111	To check Hotel name, Location, room type, Total Day, price per night are same in Booking confirmation page as they were selected in previous screen	1. Launch hotel reservation application using URL as in test data. 2. Login to the application using username and password as in test data. 3. Select location as in test data. 4. Select Hotel as in test data. 5. Select room type as in test data. 6. Select no-of-rooms as in test data. 7. Enter check-out-date as in test data. 8. Select No-of-adults as in test data. 9. Select No-of-children as in test data. 10. Click on Search button.	URL: http:// adactin.com/ HotelApp/index. php User:{test username} Password:{test password} Location: Sydney Hotel: Hotel Creek Room type: standard No-of-rooms:2 Check-in-date: today's date Check-out-date: today+1 date No-of-adults: 1 No-of-children: 0	Data should be same as selected in previous screen

		11. Select the hotel and click on Continue button 12. Verify that total-price is being calculated as (price-per- night*no-of-rooms*no-of-days		
TC-112	To check correct Final billed price is Total Price + 10% Total price in Book a Hotel page	1. Launch hotel reservation application using URL as in test data. 2. Login to the application using username and password as in test data. 3. Select location as in test data. Select Hotel as in test data. 4. Select room type as in test data. 5. Select no-of-rooms as in test data. 6. Enter check-out-date as in test data. 7. Select No-of-adults as in test data. 8. Select No-of-children as in test data. 9. Click on Search button. 10. Select the hotel and click on Continue button 11. Verify that total-price is being calculated as (price-per-night*no-of-rooms*no-of-days)	URL: http://adactin.com/HotelApp/index.php User:{test username} Password:{test password} Location: Sydney Hotel: Hotel Creek Room type: standard No-of-rooms:2 Check-in-date: today's date Check-out-date: today+1 date No-of-adults: 1 No-of-children: 0	Final billed Price=125+12.5=137.5 in Book a Hotel page
TC-113	To verify whether the data displayed is same as the selected data in Book hotel page	1. Launch hotel reservation application using URL as in test data.	URL: http://adactin.com/HotelApp/index.php	Hotel: hotel Creek Room type: Standard No-of-rooms:2 Check-in-date: 27/07/2012

| | | 2. Login to the application using username and password as in test data.
3. Select location as in test data.
4. Select Hotel as in test data.
5. Select room type as in test data.
6. Select No-of-rooms as in test data.
7. Enter check-out-date as in test data.
8. Select No-of-adults as in test data.
9. Select No-of-children as in test data.
10. Click on Search button.
11. Select the hotel and click on Continue button
12. Verify that total-price is being calculated as (price-per-night*no-of-rooms*no-of-days) | User:{test username}
Password:{test password}
Location: Sydney
Hotel: Hotel Creek
Room type: standard
No-of-rooms:2
Check-in-date: today's date
Check-out-date: today+1 date
No-of-adults: 1
No-of-children: 0 | Check-out-date: 28/07/2012
No-of-adults: 1
No-of-children: 0 |
| TC-114 | Verify Order number is generated in booking confirmation page | 1. Launch hotel reservation application using URL as in test data.
2. Login to the application using username and password as in test data.
3. Select location as in test data.
4. Select hotel as in test data.
5. Select room type as in test data.
6. Select no-of-rooms as in test data. | URL: http://adactin.com/HotelApp/index.php
User:{test username}
Password:{test password}
Location: Sydney
Hotel: Hotel Creek
Room type: standard
No-of-rooms: 2
Check-in-date: today's date | ORDER no should be generated |

		7. Enter check-out-date as in test data. 8. Select No-of-adults as in test data. 9. Select No-of-children as in test data. 10. Click on Search button. 11. Select the hotel and click on Continue button 12. Verify that total-price is being calculated as (price-per-night*no-of-rooms*no-of-days)	Check-out-date: today+1 date No-of-adults: 1 No-of-children: 0	
TC-115	To verify whether the booked itinerary details are not editable.	1. Launch hotel reservation application using URL as in test data. 2. Login to the application using username and password as in test data. 3. Select location as in test data. 4. Select Hotel as in test data. 5. Select room type as in test data. 6. Select no-of-rooms as in test data. 7. Enter check-out-date as in test data. 8. Select No-of-adults as in test data. 9. Select No-of-children as in test data. 10. Click on Search button. 11. Select the hotel and click on Continue button	http://adactin.com/HotelApp/index.php User:{test username} Password:{test password} Location: Adelaide Hotel: Hotel Cornice Room type: standard No-of-rooms:2 Check-in-date: today's date Check-out-date: today+1 date No-of-adults: 1 No-of-children: 0	Details once accepted should not be editable

		12. Fill the form and click on Book Now button. 13. Click on My Itinerary button 14. Verify that the details are not editable		
TC-116	To check whether the booked itinerary reflects the correct information in line with the booking.	1. Launch hotel reservation application using URL as in test data. 2. Login to the application using username and password as in test data. 3. Select location as in test data. 4. Select hotel as in test data. 5. Select room type as in test data. 6. Select no-of-rooms as in test data. 7. Enter check-out-date as in test data. 8. Select No-of-adults as in test data. 9. Select No-of-children as in test data. 10. Click on Search button. 11. Select the hotel and click on Continue button 12. Fill the form and click on Book Now button. 13. Click on My Itinerary button 14. Verify that the details are reflected correctly as per the booking	http://adactin.com/HotelApp/index.php User:{test username} Password:{test password} Location: Sydney Hotel: Hotel Creek Room type: standard No-of-rooms:2 Check-in-date: today's date Checkoutdate: today+1 date No-of-adults:1 No-of-children: 0	Itinerary should reflect the correct information in line with the booking.

TC-117	To check whether "search order id" query is working and displaying the relevant details.	1. Launch hotel reservation application using URL as in test data. 2. Login to the application using username and password as in test data. 3. Click on booked itinerary button. 4. Enter the order id. 5. Verify that the relevant details are displayed	http://adactin.com/HotelApp/index.php User:{test username} Password:{test password} Order id :pick existing order id	Search Order ID query should display the relevant details for Order ID
TC-118	Verify that all the details of newly generated order number in booked itinerary page are correct and match with data during booking.	1. Launch hotel reservation application using URL as in test data. 2. Login to the application using username and password as in test data. 3. Book an order as in previous test cases 4. Click on booked itinerary button 5. Search for Order number 6. Verify all the details of order number are correct as entered during saving order	http://adactin.com/HotelApp/index.php User:{test username} Password:{test password} Location: Sydney Hotel: Hotel Creek Room type: standard No-of-rooms:2 Check-in-date: today's date Check-out-date: today+1 date No-of-adults: 1 No-of-children: 0	All the details in booked itinerary page should be same as those entered during booking
TC-119	To verify that the order gets cancelled after click on Cancel order number link	1. Launch hotel reservation application using URL as in test data. 2. Login to the application using username and password as in test data.		

		3. Book the Hotel as in previous test cases. Keep a note of order number generated 4. Click on Booked Itinerary 5. Search for order number booked 6. Click on Cancel <Order Number> 7. Click Yes on pop-up which asks where to cancel order or not 8. Verify that order number is cancelled and now longer exists in Booked Itinerary page	http://adactin. com/HotelApp/ index.php User:{test username} Password:{test password}	Order number should not longer be present in booked itinerary page after cancellation
TC-120	To Verify Title of every Page reflects what the page objective is. For example Title of Search Hotel page should have "Search Hotel"	1. Launch hotel reservation application using URL as in test data. 2. Login to the application using username and password as in test data. 3. Verify that title of each page is the same as the page objective 4. Click on Search hotel option and verify whether application directs to search hotel form 5. Click on booked itinerary button and verify that application directs to booked itinerary form	http://adactin. com/HotelApp/ index.php User:{test username} Password:{test password}	Title of each page should reflect its objective and the buttons should redirect as specified, to the relevant page.